CROSSING
THE LINE

'Safe to say very few have had a life like
Willie Anderson, who unspools its twists
and turns in a tale expertly laid out
by Brendan Fanning. A powerful,
uplifting story'

Independent.ie

'When he decided to do a book it would be
done right. Searingly honest'

Irish News

'One of the very best rugby books I've
read. Impactful, insightful, funny,
authentic – a great story worth telling'

Murray Kinsella

CROSSING THE LINE

The Flag, the Haka and Facing My Life

WILLIE ANDERSON

With Brendan Fanning

Reach Sport

To Heather, and our children
Jonathan, Thomas and Chloe.

And to Glen McLernon, who will
always be loved and never forgotten.

Reach Sport

www.reachsport.com

First published in Great Britain and Ireland in 2021 by
Reach Sport, a Reach PLC business,
5 St Paul's Square, Liverpool, L3 9SJ.

www.reachsport.com
@Reach_Sport

Reach Sport is a part of Reach PLC.
One Canada Square, Canary Wharf, London, E15 5AP.

Paperback ISBN: 9781914197475
Hardback ISBN: 9781914197154
eBook ISBN: 9781914197161

Photographic acknowledgements:
Willie Anderson personal collection, Inpho, Sportsfile, Mirrorpix.
Every effort has been made to trace the copyright.
Any oversight will be rectified in future editions.

Written with Brendan Fanning.
Design and production by Reach Sport.
Edited by Chris Brereton.
With thanks to Gill Hess Ltd.

Printed and bound by CPI Group (UK) Ltd,
Croydon, CR0 4YY.

Contents

Acknowledgements

THE IDEA OF WRITING A BOOK CROSSED MY mind a few times over the years but I never set aside the time to give it serious thought. I'm not 100 per cent sure why: maybe I thought nobody would be interested; maybe it was the fear of putting myself out there with the risk of being judged. The suggestion from Brendan forced me to sit down and think. I knew and respected him even though he didn't always write complimentary things about me!

The last bit didn't bother me in the slightest. If he could get my voice across with sincerity and a bit of humour then I was game. This has been an incredible journey, retracing my steps through childhood to where I am now. There weren't many straight roads travelled.

Along the way I have rekindled friendships and I'm deeply grateful to all who have contributed. Special mention to my wife Heather, and our children Jonathan, Thomas and Chloe for their love and support. They were always there through the trials and tribulations – and Thomas for his extra legal advice.

To my brother Ollie and sister Heather I thank them for their continuous honesty and frankness in helping to describe our life on the farm. I was lucky Mum and Dad sent me to

Omagh Academy, and blessed to have come across Dick Hinds and Jackie Reid, men who believed in me and gave Ollie and me a love of sport.

In Stranmillis I came under the wing of Jimmy Davidson, the greatest mentor in my life. He helped put me on the road to Ulster and beyond. Playing for my province and my country was a huge honour for me and I'm indebted to the men I played with, as I am to all my colleagues in Ulster Rugby, Irish Rugby and in particular the Ulster Academy at the tail end of my career.

A special mention to the many players I've had the privilege of coaching over the years: you have been an inspiration and source of energy that has sustained me during my coaching career.

To Davy Irwin, Frank Wilson and John Palmer, I owe you for your bravery and support in Argentina, and likewise to Jimmy McCoy who truly was a friend when I needed one. Thanks also to Carlos Guarna for keeping me sane when I was isolated and alone in Buenos Aires – he could so easily have walked away. To Stephen Aboud, a true friend over the last 35 years. He is a rugby genius who has challenged me every step of the way. To Davy Haslett for selflessly guiding me in my coaching career, and Patsy Forbes for giving me a job when I was badly stuck. To Matt Williams for giving me a chance to coach professionally with Leinster and Scotland, and to Mike Rodgers for opening the door to Sullivan Upper, I am so grateful.

Northern Ireland was a dangerous place to grow up. It was only when I sat down to write this did I appreciate the number of friends and acquaintances who lost their lives in the Troubles. Robert Glover, a good friend, was one of the victims – to his

ACKNOWLEDGEMENTS

wife Rhonda and daughters Lynn, Jan and Pamela, I thank you for allowing me to recount Robert's story.

I've been lucky in my life to have friends who didn't melt away like snow on the ditch. Dr Ben Glancy and his wife Marie, and their children Claire, Michael, Caoimhe and Labhaoise are a second family to me. Brian and Helen Wilson, Alan and Jenny Burns, Rev Terry Scott and Alison, Alan and Doreen McLean – you have all enriched my life with your company and support.

The passionate folks at Dungannon Rugby Club, where I learned so much from Stewart McKinney, have stood by me without question down the years. That's where I saw the power and effects of good coaching. Thanks also to Chris Campbell and Charlie Simpson in The Rainey for trusting me and inviting me in to coach.

This book isn't part of a pension plan. I wanted something down on paper that in years to come my grandkids could read and think: OK, he wasn't perfect, but he had spirit and compassion and was a good friend to have.

In Brendan Fanning I've made a good friend on what we call The Project. He has been my challenger, my confessor, and my guide, and without him I never could have brought this story to life.

And it would never have seen the light of day without Heather. She kept me on point and reined me in when I needed it. She has been doing that since I met her in Stranmillis all those years ago. She is, and will always be, my compass and my rock.

Willie Anderson, August 2021

WILLIE ANDERSON

WHEN I GOT THE EMAIL FROM ULSTER RUGBY about Willie's retirement in June 2020 I texted him pretty much straight away. Basically the message said if he hadn't made a book plan he should give it some thought. And I'd be keen. I've had a few punts from publishers over the years to ghost write players' stories and never had any problem knocking them back. This was different. If Willie was prepared to tell his life story, warts and all, it would be worth listening to – and I'm glad he agreed.

Given the span of time we relied on a host of characters to fill in some gaps. We contacted over a hundred people in putting this story together, some of them many times. All of them helped in some way.

A lot of calls went to Allan Buchanan in Dungannon Rugby Club, who was a fountain of knowledge on the club, and Barney McGonigle was a wonderful source on everything to do with Ulster and its rugby folk.

Typically I'd rattle a cage from Willie's past and he would end up re-engaging with folks he hadn't seen in years. It made for an eventful and interesting journey and I am indebted to all who took part.

Chris Brereton at Reach Sport has been down the ghosting road himself a few times so he understood this project straight away. Thank you to Paul Dove at Reach for sending Chris in my direction.

Covid-19 was a complicator. Thanks to Carlos Guarna in Buenos Aires, Claire Glancy in London and Big Ciaran Donaghy in Belfast for archive legwork.

Closer to home my *Sunday Independent* friend Tommy Conlon was the perfect sounding board on the script, as were

ACKNOWLEDGEMENTS

Trent and Fliss who gave up hours to patiently keep me in between the white lines. They are rock solid.

Speaking of lines, Willie only crossed ones I pushed him over. Genuinely he is an inspirational man with a huge heart and a tiny ego. He is supported by a loving family and I'm richer for the experience of meeting and becoming good friends with them: Heather, Jonathan, Thomas, Chloe and their mad dogs, as well as Willie's siblings, Heather and Ollie. And, of course, the big man himself. I hope his story helps people who get knocked back to keep on keeping on.

Brendan Fanning, August 2021

Foreword
by Gerald Seymour

A COUPLE OF YEARS BACK, I WANDERED UP THE
lane to my 'local' on a Friday night. It's a bit of an Irish pub, and
our landlord and landlady are from the north and the south of
the island. The bar that night was packed. Space was rammed
with huge young men wearing 'Ulster Rugby Under 20' on their
tracksuit tops. A big man sat rather bowed in a corner and was
seriously contemplating the filled pint in front of him. I asked
quietly, "Is that by any remote chance Mr Anderson?" Massive
arms snaked out and I was greeted with an incredible bearhug
and we both collapsed laughing.

I didn't know he was over, he didn't know where I lived. That
was the start of a brilliant weekend of rugby nostalgia. He was
in our village with the Ulster Academy for a tournament at a
local school. I reflected that it was so typical of a huge figure in

international sport, a legend in the game throughout Ireland, that he was away from home and running his eye over youthful playing talent, among youngsters and putting something considerable back into the game he loved and that had served him well.

Word spread in the bar among the English drinkers that among them was Willie Anderson, captain and coach in his time of his country's team.

I heard, "Isn't that the guy on a rugby tour nicked up a pole in Buenos Aires when pinching the Argie flag?"

And, "That's the guy who wouldn't take any intimidation from the All Blacks on their Haka thing, it's him."

Our regulars had identified the same man, and his character, that I had grown to like hugely, to respect greatly, many decades before.

Why I admired him: a sense of integrity rules his life.

There is a jut in that chiselled chin that seems to say, 'Tell them we're coming and Hell's coming with us' (apologies to Hollywood). Not a man to take a backward step, a captain that his team would want to follow, a leader.

And then, there is Willie's trademark: when the moment was ripe, usually but not always, there will be in those penetrating eyes of his a gleam of pure mischief.

The All Blacks will confirm it and all those Junta generals, heavy with their medals.

I rate him, above all else, as a buccaneer.

He's a man of those times before the boredom of much of today's rugby took hold. I think he managed without clipboard coaching, with few of those endless video inquests, with a contempt – more than anything else – for the robots playing with neither flair nor initiative. Chief of Willie Anderson's demands would have been 'passion'.

Whether as a player or his time as a coach, his players brimmed over with the pleasure of wearing the shirt of his side.

I need a moment of indulgence. I have to contradict myself. I am reminded of the *one* occasion when I did see Willie take that backward step, from a bar. When a degree of apprehension, even anxiety, slipped to his face. The mischief was gone, banished. The location of this moment was the public drinking area of the Bath Rugby clubhouse. London Irish, who at that time he coached, had suffered a grievous hammering on the field. That was speedily put behind them and he and the team were keeping the Guinness flowing. The Bath players, under the new professional regime, were not permitted contamination and were in a sealed off area no doubt eating nutrient food and sipping soft drinks... only Jeremy Guscott broke ranks to join the Irish.

Well into a cheerful session, someone looked at their wristwatch. That someone registered the time. The backward step was taken, for a hell of a good reason; Heather Anderson was coming to London for the weekend, would be boarding her flight at about that moment. The team were due to collect her at Heathrow, a hundred miles from Bath, and the flight time was 45 minutes. Panic was in the air, glasses were abandoned, the London Irish charabanc coughed into life and then screamed out into Great Pulteney Street to start a Grand Prix run to the airport.

I believe Heather is the rock in his life, the foundation on which this glorious and generous character is set and I like to think that the M4 that evening was littered with smoking police cars, that the bus pulled into the terminal, probably parking illegally, as Mrs Anderson came through the Arrivals door.

Willie's story is a grand story, one well worth telling. It deals with *craic* and laughter, with tragedies and courage, all the lessons that life throws up to trip us over and the happiness of good times. Something worth recalling – during his playing days, Ireland was in the stranglehold of a brutal conflict. Lines were clearly drawn, except in the world of rugby. Willie was part of that brotherhood of players, from north and south, who determined that historic and much-loved fixtures would continue. It is hugely to their credit that the stresses did not fracture the national team and the club sides.

I reckon I speak for many when I express my pride at being regarded as Willie Anderson's friend, and we are privileged.

Gerald Seymour, August 2021

Introduction: The Catwalk

IT'S LESS THAN A 10 MINUTE WALK ON A LOVELY autumn evening from Russell Square tube station to Yeomanry House on Handel Street in London. Heather and I are in good time. No need to rush. We are on our way to the showing of JW Anderson's Spring and Summer collection at London Fashion Week. Fashion shows were never the topic of conversation around the family table when I was growing up on the farm in Sixmilecross. And up until a few years ago they weren't discussed too much around the table in the Loup, near Magherafelt, where we live now. That has changed.

Jonathan William Anderson is our eldest son.

I'm not going to lie: we're feeling nervous, but fairly important, tonight. There's a lot of glitz and glamour around this event. Heather looks stunning in a JW dress in blue stripe, with JW logo bag. As an XXL it's harder for me to look the part, but I'm in a blazer and a nice shirt, and jeans. Jonny actually said I looked well.

The entrance is via a side street, stuffed with people. We are whisked past the press and the paparazzi and inside to another world. This is where the beautiful people hang out!

With banks of lighting illuminating the catwalk it's intensely hot. The actual show is a 17-minute whirl of action where everything has to run like clockwork. No dropped passes; no miscues; everyone needs to be on their game. Then it's over. This happens four times a year, so the intensity around each one is massive.

The backstage is loud and upbeat. Anna Wintour is there, wearing her trademark sunglasses. The long-time editor of Vogue, she is one of the most influential people in the fashion world. The notion of a show starting until she arrives and gets settled is not even entertained.

I actually met her at Jonathan's show in Paris. Security was massive simply because it was in the UNESCO building, but she came backstage and I dandered over to say hello. There were a few people who froze at the sight of this hairy-arsed farmer's son from Sixmilecross about to engage a legend of the fashion world.

"Hiya, I'm Jonathan's dad – nice to meet you!"

She was a bit startled all right. So was Jonathan who saw his career passing before his eyes. For safety sake I gave her a diluted version of my normal handshake. I have hands like shovels. That's exactly how I used them on the farm.

The pressure around a show is intense. For one of Jonathan's early shows he was looking for a wee boost and decided holy water would do the trick. There wasn't a lot of that around the house. Never mind: our great friends Ben and Marie Glancy rode to the rescue – and not for the first time. Marie got her mum Rita on the case and delivered enough holy water to float a small pleasure cruiser. Heather delivered a bottle before the show and was on hand when the models were getting dressed.

"Jonny will I sprinkle a bit on each model or how do you want to do this?" she asked.

"It's already sorted Mum," he says. "It's in the steam irons so we can spread it!"

We have three adult children: Jonathan is the eldest, then Thomas, then Chloe. And a few dogs. When Thomas was getting married, himself and his fiancée Pamela put a huge effort into getting the right venue for their wedding. They settled on the G in Galway, down the road from the Sportsground, where Thomas had played two seasons as a pro with Connacht. It was fabulous. He was a fine rugby player who won a Grand Slam in 2007 with the Ireland Under 20 side and got a place in the Ulster Academy. Between Ulster and Connacht he had eight seasons as a pro. It can't have been easy for him being my son, but he never presented it like that. I was immensely proud of the way he represented himself on the rugby field.

I remember going in to watch him on a warm August night in Ravenhill, an early season friendly for Ulster against Queensland Reds, in 2008. He was just graduating from the Academy into the senior squad and needed to make an impression.

He started at blindside flanker and gave the sort of performance that said this fella is here to stay. Then injury blighted his career. I didn't have to hound him into getting his law degree before he committed everything to rugby. He did that off his own bat. He was ready for what rugby players now call the 'afterlife' when it arrived.

Naturally enough there was a big rugby presence at Thomas's wedding, but first Heather and myself went down for a weekend to road-test the place. It was an arty, plush hotel and we got the royal treatment. At dinner the first night we got chatting to another couple and, as you do, you end up talking about your kids while trying not to bore people to death. The coincidence was we had something in common: a gay son.

"If you don't mind me asking, how did you cope when you found out he was gay?" the man asked Heather about Jonathan. There was a pause as she put down her knife and fork, and considered her answer.

"If memory serves me right we told him we loved him whether he was gay, straight or somewhere in between," Heather said. I'm not sure if that's the answer he was looking for.

Keep it simple man: tell him you love him; rinse and repeat.

I had consciously started doing that with our three kids after a horrific accident many years earlier where I knocked down and killed a neighbour's wee lad near our home. I struggled to deal with the guilt of that, a freak moment where we were both in the wrong place at the wrong time. It reinforced for me that none of us knows what's around the corner. So live in the moment, and never let a day pass without telling your loved ones that's exactly what they are: loved.

To be honest the gay thing with Jonny didn't knock a feather out of us. We did far more worrying about him being able to achieve all he wanted to achieve. He had a savage hunger to reach his goals, and dyslexia was like a fence that kept popping up every few steps. Chloe had the same battle. I'm afraid that might have been a gift from me. Thomas on the other hand breezed through schoolwork without breaking sweat. I was never diagnosed with dyslexia because it wasn't on anyone's radar in school in the 1960s and '70s, but I struggled with the written word. I'd read things back and see I'd left out bits I was sure I'd put in. I don't think I'd fit the standard symptoms but there are a few bits missing in my jigsaw. Jonny was full-on though.

As a child he was nuts about plants and animals. Then, encouraged by Heather, he gave full expression to his love of drama. When we'd have our friends Brian and Helen Wilson over he'd pressgang their three kids into a wee production along with Thomas and Chloe. An hour later the curtain would be pulled back and we'd have a full-on drama with children, animals and a set adorned with plants. There was a strong businessman in there as well.

If he could have gotten away with passing the hat around I'd say he'd have tried it.

Nowadays Jonny is pursuing his dream of being the best designer on the planet. Thomas, his operations director, is helping him at every turn. It helps that Thomas has a law degree; that he has a head for business and that he's always looking out for his big brother in a very competitive world. Sometimes I wonder if our third child had been a boy what position he'd be on the JW Anderson team. When Heather was in hospital having Chloe the nurse was sure we'd be getting a boy.

"What about the heart rate?" she said to Heather. "It's wild low. You're going to have another wee boy."

Sure enough, a blue name tag was produced. A few hours

later Chloe emerged with hair like mine: a black lump stuck on the top of her head, and a squashed nose like she'd already been in a ruck. She grew from daddy's wee girl into a beautiful young woman who never ceases to amaze me with her talent and tenacity. Like Jonathan she had to find a way to learn when dyslexia kept getting in the way.

At one stage it looked like she was going to do PE, like me, because she was a fine athlete, representing Ulster at netball and squash. When she moved from Magherafelt High School to The Rainey she picked up a hockey stick for the first time, and looked like a natural at that too. That change of schools was to prepare for A Levels, not available in the High School. I was inspired by the way she dealt with the hardship of a learning difficulty, the extra hours required to get to grips with stuff. When Chloe settled on a pharmacy degree as her target I knew she'd hit it dead centre. Now she works in that industry in London.

Over Christmas 2020 I got a bout of depression brought on a by a few events piling up. The pandemic was one of them. Thank God Chloe was around. She got stuck with us over the first lockdown and then came back for more over Christmas. When you're an adult spending that amount of time with your parents – quality time I hope – it gives you a great perspective. She always understood me. Being the youngest she was there after the boys had moved on, and she knew what buttons to push to help me function. Over that Christmas period she spent days and nights on end, talking and listening and being a rock of sense. I don't think Chloe got that from me. I was never a great man for the straight and narrow.

1

The Flag, Part I

Monday 4th August, 1980

Dear Heather

I hope this card finds you well. We're now in a place called Cordoba (Wed 6th Aug). I play tonight after having been sub for the first game. Since we got here I've never been so well treated. We have eaten and drunk like kings and we train every day. The rest of the fellas on tour are magnificent and I've never laughed as much. I'm glad to be playing tonight as it makes the tour. The weather is like late spring/ early summer but it gets cold at night. The first game, which we won 21–0, was played in a torrential thunderstorm. Tomorrow we go to Buenos Aires where we stay for 10 days and play three games. I will fly to Canada then. On Sat this week we will be going to see World XV v the Pumas. I think of you a lot and miss you and I'm looking forward to seeing you again. Have a great holiday in Greece.

All my love

Willie xxx

I didn't know a lot about the Penguins before they invited me to go on tour with them to Argentina. What did they want with a raw cub like me? I'd made my debut for Ulster the year before and was going well. Basically, they were a touring club, run by a fella called Tony Mason who was a rugby nut. The idea was they would head off somewhere nice for a few weeks with a decent squad of representative players, take on a few local teams, and promote the whole idea of rugby. Where do I sign?

It wasn't a freebie but it wasn't full whack either. Maybe £200/300 for my place. I worked on the farm that summer and begged and borrowed to get the rest together. This was exactly what had attracted me to the game in the first place: going off to foreign lands with a bunch of guys, playing rugby and having monumental craic. Heaven.

Even better, this was going to be a double barrelled affair. Stranmillis were heading to Canada on their own tour, but were short of bodies. Would I be able to hook up with them after the Penguins? Eh, yes I would. So the plan was to play a few games in Argentina and then fly to Canada to join up there and help out the Kings Scholars, as the Stran team was known, in their last couple of games.

What could possibly go wrong?

I already knew a good few of the guys on board the Penguins trip. We could almost put out an all-Irish team, with 12 of us in the squad of 25. Naturally enough it was the Ulster lads I knew best: Frank Wilson, Davy Irwin and Ronnie Hakin. All of them were international players by then. Frank and Ronnie's Test careers were short enough and in the rear-view mirror. But Davy's Irish career was just taking off. He had toured Australia with Ireland the previous summer, and then made his debut in the Five Nations a few months before we headed off. He looked like he would be wearing an Ireland jersey for years to come. Davy was a few years younger than me but we were mates with Ulster. On a personal level we had a connection. He was at Queen's studying medicine. He was marked out for big things.

All three were fellas you'd be happy to go anywhere with. Ronnie, like me, was a second row. He had toured New Zealand with Ireland in '76. He's a remarkable man who could sleep on command. Stewart McKinney was rooming with him on that trip and tells the story of the day of the Test match in Wellington, the highlight of the tour. There was a meeting scheduled for 1pm. It would take about a minute to go from their room to the meeting room. At 12.54 Ronnie says: "I'm going for a sleep." McKinney is gobsmacked. Ronnie sits into a chair and goes out like a light. Three minutes later he wakes up.

"Are we right?"

They go to the meeting.

Ronnie was such an athlete but you needed a cattle prod to get him out the gate.

So I'm sitting in Aldergrove with Davy Irwin and we're about to board the flight for London and beyond to South America. "So here we are about to head to Argentina," he says. "Wherever exactly in South America that may be."

I got on immediately with the other lads as well. The Leinster hooker Johnny Cantrell was made for touring life. Myself, Jack Moran, a loose head prop from Blackrock, and Gary Coakley, a full back from UCD: we called ourselves the bats. We would come out at night. They were great craic, lads you'd be laughing with only minutes after meeting them.

Argentina was a fascist state at the time. The military had

taken over in March 1976 when I was just turned 21. In the same month in Northern Ireland 11 people were either shot dead or blown up in five separate terrorist attacks. I wasn't following events in Argentina too closely.

It could have been one big hippy commune over there for all I knew. The Penguins say their touring policy is to give a detailed briefing on the destination and what to expect there. I'm not saying it didn't happen, but if it did it sailed clean over my head. None of the lads I've spoken to since can remember it either. Off we went.

The rugby was downright dangerous. Fine, I could cope with that happily enough. When you signed on for rugby in the 1970s and '80s you knew what you were getting. It was physically engaging all the time; violent a lot of the time; filthy some of the time. When you walked into the showers afterwards you wanted some sort of stripes. Literally. For a forward to have his back looking like a blank canvas was not really what you were after.

The first match was in Cordoba and the brutality started early. I remember one of the lads having his shoulder dislocated after some fella just jumped on him when he was exposed. There was loads of off-the-ball stuff. But the second game, in Paraná, was worse again. Fellas were getting wiped out left, right and centre and when we got ahead on the scoreboard their supporters started firing coins at us. Unbelievable stuff.

So we got stuck into them. That was the way I was. Rugby when I was growing up was always a fight, a confrontation. That's what Irish rugby is built on. With two wins from two games we were heading back to Buenos Aires and the mood was buoyant.

WILLIE ANDERSON

Banco Nación v The Penguins, Sunday 10ᵗʰ August, 1980

Banco Nación were not just a leading club in Argentina, they were stuffed with Pumas. Top of the heap was outhalf and captain Hugo Porta. Everyone was up for this. There was a good crowd, another fast and furious game, and we were delighted to win it.

The food after the game was incredible – as many steaks as you wanted. I remember being upstairs at the function and it was a fine set-up. I got talking to Porta. He seemed like a grand guy. Rugby wasn't the working man's game in Argentina and there was a well-to-do feel about that club. It was funny: on the field they'd take the eye out of your head but afterwards they were very concerned with etiquette and good behaviour.

After the function we headed back to the hotel for a while and then out on the town. It wasn't as lively as we'd hoped – like home, Sunday night wasn't the biggest night out. But there were a couple of places we stopped into. I brought the pipes, the calling card that nearly always worked. At one place I was told to shut up because there was a funeral parlour across the road. Everyone else loved us. As it goes, the group gets broken up as we go along. But the general vibe was that we would meet back at the hotel.

So I end up with Frank Wilson and another lad we'll call Mr A. We're heading back to the hotel when we pass this official looking building with yet another Argentine flag on it. It was the office of the Secretary of Information of Argentina, an important building. We don't twig this. The previous year I'd been in Canada with Stran and got this big, beautiful Canada flag with that lovely maple leaf on it. Walk into my room in college and it was the first thing you'd see hanging on the wall.

So this looked like the perfect companion: Canadian red on one wall, and Argentine sky blue with the sun god at its centre, to go on the other wall.

I got Mr A to come across the road with me, and tossed him up on my shoulders to get the flag which was out of my reach. There was a bit of fiddling around but we got the job done, and continued back to the hotel. There wasn't a mad dash to get away from the scene of the crime.

Other lads were arriving and we went up to Davy Irwin's room for a few beers. I'd say there was about 10 of us, having a few drinks and a laugh, rounding the night off. I'll admit I was showing off the flag. It's more than your average emblem. At one stage our attention was caught by the sound of sirens outside as a few police cars sped through the street.

"Willie, they're coming for you!"

We all laughed. A few minutes later the liaison man, Carlos Guarna, was at the door. He looked like he'd just been given bad news. Carlos was a member of the Banco Nación club who we had played that afternoon. He is a lovely, helpful man who I would get to know much better than planned over the weeks and months that followed. When he had got back to our hotel the receptionist called him over and said there was a serious problem, that one of the players had arrived back with the national flag under his jacket. That would be me.

So Carlos is asking questions.

'Relax Carlos it's only a flag – they're all over town for fuck's sake!'

He looked ill. 'This is no good,' he said. 'You don't understand. This is no good.'

That's when the mood in the room started to turn for the

worse. Next thing there were five or six policemen on the scene, heavily armed and wearing those long, dark blue coats.

They're fairly agitated. They want the flag back. 'No hay problema amigos'. And they want the culprits as well. That was tricky. It was entirely my idea to take the flag but Mr A, who helped me, was reversing at speed. He said his job would disappear if he was caught up in a criminal action. Fair enough. I wasn't thinking that far ahead. The police want the names of those involved. I already have my hands up.

By then we'd discovered a bit more about Argentina and how the military dealt with things. No one thinks it's a great idea to go down to the police station on my own so a couple of lads volunteer to give me some moral support: Davy Irwin and Frank Wilson. Observe the sons of Ulster, marching towards the Somme. There was a feeling of looking out for each other, of Ulstermen sticking together in a 'lads we'll sort this out and see ye later for a beer' sort of thing.

Carlos tells everyone in the room to get their passports. They take mine and Frank's and Davy's and the next one in the queue is John Palmer from Bath. He hadn't been with us at all. I think he had been with John Horton and Tony Swift and got back to the hotel before us. He only came down to the room when he heard what sounded like the makings of a party and went to investigate. He stayed for a beer. Ginger McLoughlin volunteered to come as well. They looked at his passport. They now had four blue ones and a green one. They weren't interested in green. The significance of that didn't really dawn on me at the time. A blue passport from the United Kingdom of Great Britain and Northern Ireland, with the crown front and centre, fitted the description.

They marched the four of us downstairs, with Ginger following close behind saying he'd follow on. We're out the door and into the squad cars. Sirens on again, lights flashing and off we go.

Policia de la Ciudad, No 1 Suipacha 1156

We're hustled in the door and it's like going into the land time forgot. Everything is in slow motion. Straight away they split us up. They put us in handcuffs at this point. I've never been in handcuffs before and it's a thoroughly demoralising experience. I'm on a bench in one part of the station with a policeman beside me all the time. Davy is on a chair in a corridor around the corner. I don't know where Frank and John are. I'm thinking over and over in my head that none of these lads would be going through this if it wasn't for me. Then the interrogation starts.

I was bracing myself for some physical abuse. But it's not fingernail-pulling stuff, just the same questions over and over. They have it in their heads that four people were involved and two people took the flag down. In order to keep Mr A out of it I think we make a bit of a balls of getting the right story across. They're not impressed. So it drags on and on for hours. I'm a big man and I like my food but I'm torn between nervous tension and needing to eat something. Then they bring us together and into this room where there's a long window down one side. It's a relief to see the others.

'You OK?'

'Yeah, you…?'

At one stage Davy says: "I think we've missed training lads. I need some sleep. San Isidro on Wednesday. We'll need to be out of here soon enough."

We're all wondering what comes next in the room with the long window. On the other side of the glass there is a bunch of people, mostly old women. I've no idea why they are there and what they're about.

Then the police tell us to strip. Bollock naked. It is humiliating, which I suppose is the object of the exercise. God knows what the old women made of it. There is a medical examination of some sort. Then it's back out for another wait, split up again. At some point they take our fingerprints.

I've got a feeling of nausea that's taken hold of me now. I'm a strong, athletic man with an outgoing personality and a willingness to have a go at any sort of craic. I don't feel any of those things now. Just the nausea. I want to stand up and say enough is enough but I feel diminished. That's a word I would never associate with myself. As a young fella I was no world class scholar in school, and I knew my limitations. But I was well able to get by. And once the door of the classroom opened and I was outside with concrete or grass under my feet I was a force to be reckoned with. Not now. I'm way out of my depth here. The tide is going out and I've no idea where it's going to take us. And it's 'us' we're talking about. My actions have made it 'us' instead of 'me'.

It was early hours Monday morning when they brought us in and it's very hard to keep a track of time. Where are the Penguins? Where is the Emperor, waddling in to tell them it's a stupid prank gone wrong and now we need to move on? The Emperor was making plans to fly home, along with most of the rest of the squad.

It was sometime the next day I think when a man from the Consulate came to see us. Dudley Ankerson was second secretary to the British ambassador in Buenos Aires. Like Carlos, I'd get to know him well. Dudley and the Embassy staff were magnificent. But they painted a scary picture that day.

"You don't appreciate the gravity of this situation," he said, slowly. "This is very, very serious to these people. There are a few generals in the Junta who would happily see you executed. Others want you doing 10 years hard labour in the south of Argentina. We have to be careful and hope they'll see sense."

I was struggling to process exactly what he was saying. He didn't sound like the third option was the favourite. I think we're into Wednesday now and it's still going on. Suddenly there's action. We each have a policeman guarding us and suddenly they're on their feet, wiping the dandruff off their shoulders and straightening their ties and sorting themselves out. I'm expecting the Police Commissioner to come through the door.

Then we're on the move. It's like an alarm has gone off and it's all hands on deck. The volume goes up as they hustle us down the stairs and out a side door into the alleyway. It's the first bit of daylight we've seen since Sunday, and it takes a few seconds to adjust. Then there is a huge roar coming from the main street where there are loads of camera crews and photographers and reporters. The police march us into the middle of it and into four squad cars, each of us in a back seat with a policeman on either side. It takes a few minutes to sort us out and it's like a feeding frenzy for the media. They're literally sticking cameras in the window, snapping away.

In time we would get to see some of the pictures. Frank made the cover of *Gente*, a popular glossy, gossip magazine in Argentina. The pictures would be carried far and wide. When we were coming on tour Frank's wife, Pauline, headed back over to Exeter with their wee girl to spend a few weeks with her dad, Ken. So we're just settling into our new regime when Ken is reading the *Daily Express* and sees the story. "Dear, did you know your husband is in prison in Argentina?"

When the press pack have had their fill we're away to see the Judge. Dudley Ankerson has organised legal representation for us, a man called Ricardo Molinas. His English is non-existent but we're told he knows his stuff. There is a translator on hand, and we have Carlos as well whose English is not bad. On the way in we see some familiar faces: teammates Johnny Cantrell and Ronnie Hakin, and Derek Wyatt who was managing the tour for the Penguins. They were in the corridor, kind of nodding and winking in support.

We had been charged with Disrespecting a National Symbol. We tell our story to the judge, trying to get the message across that it wasn't the picture the press were painting. There was no 'desecration' of the flag. We hadn't rolled it up and played football with it in the foyer of the hotel. We – well I – had no idea that it was taken as an insult to the nation. The judge kicked for touch and we were remanded in custody.

The courthouse would remind you a bit of City Hall in Belfast. When the hearing was over we were taken downstairs below ground level to the cells, and split up again. There was just about enough light down there to read the scratchings and marks left by previous prisoners. The walls are covered in messages. It's not even a bed along the side wall, more of a cement ledge a few feet off the ground.

There was a lump of shite in the corner of the cell.

I perch myself on the edge, afraid to lean back in case I touch something. So, head in my hands. For the first time since this kicked off I feel tears coming on. I'm glad we're in separate cells. Jesus Christ how has it come to this? I feel surrounded by guilt. Literally in the cells next door are lads who would not be in this mess if it wasn't for me. None of us would be here if I'd just kept walking the other night. Why could I not have waited to buy a flag? You could get one in any of the tourist shops on Florida Street in downtown Buenos Aires. You could probably buy one in the gift shop in the airport on the way home? But no. I had to jump the gun. I had to act on impulse. We were on tour and I was the big man having the craic.

God knows what the price of this will be. And the cash is only the half of it. I borrowed from my brother-in-law to make the trip. There was no question of: 'I don't have the cash for this – I'll not go'. I hit Dad for some money as well.

This will be all over the papers. What will it do to my mother? Her health is not the best anyway. What will they think? Maybe they'll think this is Willie being the big man, ploughing on without looking left or right, doing what suits him. And they'll have to clean up the mess.

I don't know how long we were there for, but this was Argentina so it can't have been too quick. Then it's upstairs again, more press, more flashing bulbs and shouting, and outside where there was a prison van waiting in the yard. The door was at the back, in the middle. I remember walking around there and waiting for it to be opened. I expected seats to be along either side, a chance to chat to the lads and see how they were getting on. When the door opened there were no seats, just these long, skinny cubicles like the sort of lockers you'd get for your clothes in a gym or a swimming pool. I'm 6'5". Davy is about 6'2". If they were designed for anyone at all then it would have been someone around the six foot mark and pencil thin. We were jammed into one together. It was fucking unbelievable.

There were three Koreans ahead of us and they were jammed into one. I honestly don't know how they endured it. The van pulled off on a tour of the police stations and lock-ups of Buenos Aires, collecting and dropping off as we went. All we could see through the cracks at the bottom of the side panels was kerbstones spinning past. Every stop was a chance for the driver to have a smoke and a natter or take a leak or whatever the fuck he was doing. It must have lasted about two hours. It was unbearable. Then we arrived at our lodgings. It wasn't the Shelbourne Hotel of South America.

Detention Center, Camara Criminal Building, Vaimonte 1155
Wednesday 13ᵗʰ August, 1980

Dear Mum, Dad & Oliver

I am writing this letter from a holding centre in Buenos Aires. I suppose by now you have heard what has happened and are worrying what is going on. Well, at the moment I am in the dark as much as you are. Please forgive me for the anxiety I have given you all but it's very hard to explain all that has happened. At the moment I am living on my nerves and have never felt so bad in all my life.

It's times like this that you really think of home though you all have never been far from my heart. I love you all and wish to God that I was home. There are three of us and we all hope to be deported tomorrow. If we are not I don't know what will happen. I can only hope and pray we will all be home soon.

It is very hard to know what to say to make you understand but try and believe me, I haven't let you down and hopefully it will all be a big misunderstanding. I'm sure the news and media said a lot but I can say no more than them. I have thought of nothing else but you since I got here as I felt terrible about leaving you all to do the hard work and it was as if I was running away from it all but I wasn't, believe me. I do wish I could be there now and even though sometimes it seems that I give the impression of being distant or self-centred that is not me. You know I couldn't have asked for a better home and upbringing and sometimes it seems I have let you down (but) you have always accepted me. I don't expect you all to forgive me as it again seems I've let you down but if I could just talk to you all for five minutes it would be the greatest thing of all.

Although Dad and I have never had a heart (to heart) I have known that he has always been behind me in all I do. Me playing rugby is not just a self-centred thing and I have always thought about you all when I play as I know you have always backed me. Please back me now as I think the bottom has dropped out of my life. You can't understand the feeling until it happens to you but my God I never want to go through this again. I leave you with these words that I hope you never have to read this and if you do please forgive me as I wish to be home again so much.

I love you all.

William x

At last, a shower. Not the kind of loud, laughing and slagging episode you'd have after a game, but a chance to wash. The atmosphere seems OK. The Director is quick to make himself known to us. He has a little bit of English and I think he sees us as a good chance to improve his language skills. Fine.

They feed us straight away. Steak and salad. Things are looking up. Over the next while we'd be seeing plenty of kidney beans and drinking lots of Maté, their favourite brand of tea. We each had an individual cell on a floor with maybe 16 cells and they all opened up onto 3 corridors that lead to a communal area with a big table. Our section is called U22. A blanket, a pillow, a stone bed. Hole in the ground for a toilet. Then, next morning we were all up and getting our bearings when John Palmer's name was called out. Over he went to the barred doors and he was taken off. Basically he'd been released.

Even that wasn't straightforward though. It wasn't like they opened the front door and waved him off down the road. No, back into the paddy wagon and off around the streets of Buenos Aires again. He was jammed into a locker with a local fella. It was a warm day and there was some guy screaming, John said, all the way through the trip. Seemingly he couldn't breathe. When John got to whatever lock-up was the destination he was put in a big cage with about 12 others. One of the prisoners had been badly beaten. John got talking to a Brazilian lad who had been arrested when his car was stopped after driving over the border. He had cigarette papers on the floor of the car, which the customs thought was suspicious. So he was arrested and remanded in custody and hadn't been given access to a lawyer. And that had started a year earlier. The good news, this guy told John, was that everyone in the cage was being released. Sure enough he was. Embassy staff drove him to the airport and he got the next flight out, to anywhere. It was Brazil. John said that everyone in the airport knew who he was, as did everyone on the flight.

Back in the Camara Criminal Building we weren't too sure what to make of John's release. First off I was delighted for him and relieved because he hadn't been within a country mile of anything on the night in question. But the penny was starting to drop a bit: OK, there's now three of us. There had been a group of three on the scene for the liberation of the flag: myself and Mr A taking it down, and Frank nearby but uninvolved. Davy was looking like the fall guy to complete the party. As we settled in we got a handle on the ructions around the case. We were referred to as 'Los Tres Ingleses'. They really didn't get the bit that we were from Ireland.

Between Carlos and Dudley Ankerson, and our daily chats with the Director, it was clear we were a golden opportunity for the Generals. Never mind that we were from the island of Ireland, we were British subjects and the Argies were embarked on an anti-English journey that would explode 20 months later around islands in the South Pacific that we'd never heard of.

Our chats with the Director would get longer and turn into daily sessions in his office. He said he had a qualification in psychology. He explained to us about the history of the Malvinas and how keen the Junta was to get them back off Britain, who referred to them as the Falklands. It was interesting, but all the time we would bring it back to our case. He had this phrase that struck a chord with Frank.

"For every day of rain there are two days of sunshine," the Director would say. And one day Frank shoots back: "Mate it's pissing down now, believe me. When is the sun going to shine?"

"It will," says the Director, all wise and knowing. "It will."

We couldn't be sure when we would be brought before the judge again, but the message was to keep our heads down and say as little as possible. The longer it went on the more heat would go out of the situation. That wasn't what I wanted to hear. I wanted to get out. I wanted to get back to the farm I had been so keen to escape. If you look at a map of Ulster you'll see

Sixmilecross is bang-on in the heart of it. I spent a fair while trying to get away from it, but I'm consumed now with the effect all this is having back there. I'm praying all the time. The kind of prayers that start with: 'Dear God, if you get me out of this I'll...'

Things were moving at home. Davy's dad George is a professor of general practice. I think he's the best placed of the parents to lead the charge on the lobbying front. My father, on the farm in east Tyrone, isn't very well connected. Frank's dad Charles works in Short Brothers and Harland. So George is doing a lot of the heavy lifting around contacting people who might be able to help us. I'm not sure how well this sits with him because he hadn't budgeted for this, and his son is blameless. Wilfie Wright in Dungannon is doing a terrific job on the fundraising front because this was obviously going to cost a lot of money to put right.

Harry Cavan in the IFA is also trying to help. I think there are a few avenues leading to him, one of them from Malcolm Brodie in the *Belfast Telegraph* who is following the case closely. The story was that Cavan had been supportive of Argentina's bid to host the 1978 World Cup, and was in a good position to help.

Meantime in Buenos Aires we were getting to know our neighbours.

They were in for all sorts of stuff from murder down to petty theft. Most were locals, apart from the three Korean sailors who had been done for selling ghetto blasters around the town when their ship had been docked in Buenos Aires port. What kind of country would put you behind bars for that?

One of the Argentine lads was in for stealing cars. He said he had been given the water treatment as well as electric shocks to his eyelids and balls. Through pidgin English and whatever we got to know these folks. Davy taught me how to play chess. We would have Northern Ireland versus South Korea chess tournaments, with neither of us sticking to the same rules.

We settled into prison life. It's amazing how quickly you can adjust to something so alien. It helped enormously that we had each other. There was a routine that would start with cell inspection every morning. There wasn't much to inspect but this particular prison warder took it very seriously. I think it was Frank christened him Bilko, after the character on the Phil Silvers TV show. He was a hateful wee bald fucker. About 5'5" or 5'6", he tried to make up for his lack of height by dandering about the place with a big attitude.

So every morning you'd have to spring up and straighten out the bed. This meant making sure the blanket had no creases in it and the pillow was in place. Then you'd make sure there was nothing on the floor. When the job was done you'd stand to attention outside your cell door for Bilko's inspection.

Davy's cell was the first one so as soon as he'd pass the test he'd be winking and making faces behind Bilko's back when the wee shite was moving on to Frank and myself. The routine would start with him staring you out and then running around the cell in a jiffy, waving the baton he always carried. He was forever poking people with that fucking baton.

One day he had Frank and myself carry a table from the communal area down the corridor and up the stairs. He was prattling away with his instructions in Spanish and poking me at the same time with the baton.

The corner at the end of the corridor was right angled, and tight enough if you were trying to get a table around it. We were making a hames of it. He kept shouting, and poking. Frank is half laughing, half trying to keep me calm. Eventually I dropped my end of the table and turned on Bilko.

"If you poke me once more with that fucking stick I'll shove it so far up your arse you'll have splinters for a week!"

Bilko loses the head and hustles the pair of us up the stairs, looking for one of the Argentine prisoners who has a bit of English. He's shouting and roaring and waving the baton.

"He wants to know what you say," the lad says. "He think you insult him."

"God no!" I said. "I was angry with myself for dropping the table. I was asking for his help to get around the corner."

He explains this to Bilko. "Ah si, si," he says. Wee shite.

By that stage we knew all the other prisoners well enough and they were pretty sound men. There was actually a bit of team spirit about the place. Aside from the three Korean sailors, the local guys would get food parcels delivered regularly enough. Whatever came in would be shared out among the whole group. We really appreciated that kind of togetherness.

There was one guy in there for armed robbery. He's chatting to myself and Davy one day and he has a sock in his hand. And there was a thread hanging out of the top of the sock, and he starts to slowly unravel it from the top down. So he ends up with a big ball of thread and a smile on his face. Davy looks at me.

"All right big man, where's he going with this?"

Then he starts stringing the thread across the room we were in, from one bar to another, back and forward, working away. When he had finished he had woven a small crucifix on a sort of a necklace and gave it to Davy as a present. As solid Ulster

Prods we wouldn't have had a crucifix on our Christmas list, but it was a lovely gesture and it meant a lot.

There wasn't a lot to do, so we kept fit. Press ups. Sit ups. Pull ups. Whatever we could do we did it, and it always would turn into a contest. Myself and Davy are working our arses off one day and Frank is looking on.

"What are youse boys at?" he asks.

"We're staying fit, what does it look like?" I say. "It's all right for you Frank. You've played for Ireland. You've done it. My time hasn't come yet. And I'm ready to answer the call!"

"If playing for Ireland is the top of your list of priorities right now Willie you need to reassess!" says Frank. We all laughed but it was a life raft for me and I was clinging to it. The physical exercise was important in keeping us sane and tiring you out in the hope of getting some sleep. And that was always a battle.

When the cell door would close at night I would have visions of it, running out in green in Lansdowne Road. My father there to see it. I was so desperate to give himself and Mum something to be proud of. Then those visions would be overtaken by the reality of being locked up in Argentina with no idea how this was going to end. The guilt of being the cause of the other lads being involved would visit me every night, no matter how hard I tried to dodge it. The selfish part of me thanked God that I wasn't alone. I could not have coped with that.

Tuesday 26th August, 1980
After two weeks in the Detention Centre we're due to get the decision from the judge today. Usual start: out of bed 6am, tidy the cells, mop the floor, have breakfast. All we're talking about is what comes next? At 11am we are brought down in the lift

to the Director's office. We're told the Judge's secretary is to come with the decision. The Director is reassuring as always. We're sitting there for an hour with him jabbering away, and our hearts beating out of our chests. At 12.00 the secretary eventually shows up and a man from the Embassy is with him.

After a lot of dandering about the secretary gets to the serious bit. Instead of referring to the three of us together though he's talking now about "Meester Weelsohn and Meester Earween". Where the hell is Meester Andersohn?

When it's translated it's confirmation that the two boys are free to go. Frank leans over with both hands flat on the table and starts to weep. Great big sobs are pouring out of him. The valve has been released and the stress is just flowing out of his body on a full tide. I think Davy pulls himself in a bit or else the three of us will be all over the place. I don't know what to feel. I'm massively relieved that it's over for them.

A day didn't pass since 10th August without me wanting to turn the clock back and save these men the bother they've been through. But I'm on my own now.

The secretary tries to say something reassuring, that I could be home in 10 days but it comes out as 10 years. I can feel my stomach turn and the blood drain from my face in the seconds it takes for him to correct it, with a laugh and his hands up to apologise. Now there's a wave of relief flooding through me. I'm getting out on bail of £1,500 and will be under a sort of house arrest – I'll be back at the team hotel we used for the Banco game.

As with John Palmer it's not like opening the door onto the street and letting us go. The boys are taken out of U22, our unit, at 2.40pm. We're hugging and shaking hands and saying our goodbyes and then they're gone, just like that. Ten minutes later I'm taken out. I have said my goodbyes to the Director and the other prisoners and am led downstairs and out to a prison van. The two boys are in the back of it!

Off we go, for some reason back to another court building where we are put in the same cell with a stinking blanket each. We're there for nearly five hours. We talk about home and rugby and manage a bit of sleep before we're out the door and into the back of one of the dreaded paddy wagons with the lockers. A journey of one hour and 20 minutes and we're at the central police station.

We're put in lines facing the wall. It's like Gestapo HQ with police all over the place. Next it's upstairs with the other prisoners and there are pressmen there, snapping away. For some reason they take our prints again, and mugshots. Frank is 49008. Davy 49009. I'm 49010.

We've been there for eight hours by the time we're brought out and put into an Embassy car and taken to the team hotel where it all started. We're physically and emotionally wrecked at this point. There is a bizarre scene in the room where one of the Embassy staff puts his fingers to his lips, like 'don't utter a word'. He turns on the tv. He goes into the bathroom and turns on the shower and the taps. Jesus Christ are we in a movie here?

"We're probably being listened to," he says. "We don't trust the Argentinians."

We had a sandwich and a beer. At midnight I chatted to Oliver on the phone. It was so good to hear his voice. I give the lads a list of people to ring for me when they get back. Carlos took us out for a meal and I got to bed at 2am. Richard from the Embassy was sleeping in my room as part of the protocol and I was woken at 5.30am as he headed to the Embassy. He was back at 7am. I slept til 9.30am and the two boys got up and showered and were in great form. They lifted my spirits, as they had done so many times over the previous few weeks. We had a beer together at midday and took photos of each other on the balcony. When we went downstairs the Embassy officials had packages for them and statements to read to the press at Gatwick when they got back. The route was BA to Rio to Lisbon to London. And then Belfast. Then they were gone.

On the Friday morning the papers in Ireland are carrying pictures of the two boys arriving in Gatwick, blazers and ties, looking like they've just come back from a relaxing wee trip where everything had gone according to plan. Davy is quoted saying he hadn't been too keen on living in lock-up while a criminal charge was hanging over his head. Frank says that, with me still in Buenos Aires facing the music, he'll say nothing at all.

When Frank arrives back to his parents' house in Ballygomartin, in west Belfast, there is a banner across the road proclaiming: 'Wilson is innocent.' His mother, Mary, was mortified. I don't think Davy's dad was too pleased either with the way his son got caught up in a mess of someone else's making. I'm on my own now. That's how it should have been from the start.

2

The Flag, Part II

Wednesday 27th August, 1980

I'm in Room 409 of the Hotel Asociación Bancaria. My new home. I've been in Argentina almost a month now. I'm the only man left. Carlos Guarna is waiting for me downstairs. Davy and Frank have just gone to the airport for the long journey home. I'm looking around: my bag on the floor, a few bits and pieces on the chair and table. I'm thinking that if they're not going to move me I can do a few wee things to make it look more like a flat than a hotel room. But to be honest a part of me wants to curl up on the bed and cry. I'm telling myself to keep moving, keep talking to people, keep doing something that will postpone the reality of this situation. Yes, it's a nice hotel in a big, vibrant city, but it's a different kind of prison – just one with more comfort. But none of the company.

Carlos brings me to his house where we have a big feed of chicken and chips. Carlos had started out as our local helper on the ground when we arrived in Argentina. Now in these harrowing circumstances for me, he'd become an ally and a friend. He drops me back to the hotel where I nap for a few hours. Then I train in my room. He brings me to a park nearby where I run non-stop at a reasonable pace for 35 minutes. I didn't think I could manage that after more than two weeks locked up, but I fly along. I suppose it was the thrill of being out in the fresh air in lovely surroundings on a perfect autumn evening.

We got back at 6.30pm and Carlos went off to see his girlfriend. I showered and lay on the bed for a while and started fretting. So I went out for a walk. I'd hardly gone a few blocks and got the impression I was being followed, so I headed back to the hotel. By then I'd spent enough time in the company of Embassy staff to know that was more likely than not. They probably had tabs on us from the moment the Penguins landed in the country. You can't run a fascist regime without keeping an eye on everyone who comes in or out.

On the way back I ducked into a shop for a minute, partly to see what I could see when I came back out. I ended up buying a comb. It cost me $4!

When I was back in the room the phone rang and I nearly fell off the bed in my scramble to answer it. I had hoped for Heather or Oliver or one my friends from home. It was Peter Gould, a reporter from BBC Northern Ireland. I don't think I was much use to him on the news front but it was good to hear a friendly voice from home.

Later that evening Dudley from the Embassy picks me up with his wife and we go to Richard Gozney's house – they're both second secretaries in the political section. Lovely meal and great company. There are two other couples there and they're all very supportive. Home at 1.30am.

Thursday 28ᵗʰ August, 1980

I have a new routine now. My body clock is waking me at 6am but I try to get back to sleep and shorten the day a bit. No straightening the bed, no cleaning the floor, no Bilko like a bug up your arse.

When I get up it's to get stuck into my routine of press-ups and sit-ups. I aim for a hundred press-ups in sets of 20. Then it's downstairs for breakfast. Bacon and eggs or continental. It's bacon and eggs today and my appetite is good. It's not long before Carlos appears. Every time I see this man I feel grateful for his company and guilty that I'm taking him away from his normal life. He has a job working for his father's company, supplying parts for armaments for the military. It seems secure. He has a girlfriend. He has his club, Banco Nación. He agreed to be the liaison officer to the Penguins, not a babysitter for one of their players.

He will take me to the rugby club at least twice a week to train. I might get to play for them if it doesn't cause any fuss. The last thing I need is to draw the attention of the authorities to myself.

Friday 29ᵗʰ August, 1980

I get an early morning phone call from Ken Reid back home. Ken is a prominent figure on the Ulster rugby scene and, more importantly, headmaster of Grosvenor High School, as it was then, not far from Ravenhill.

Ken had opened the door for me there when I came out of

Stran and was ringing to tell me the door was still open. That was a huge relief.

John Palmer had been in the same boat in England. He had just done a PE degree in Exeter and was due to start in a private school near Bath. In the short bit of time we had together we compared some notes on that. Anyway, in fairness to Ken he put me completely at ease on that front. Mr A, who had feared for his job the night the police had come calling to our hotel, wasn't the only one suffering from career anxiety.

"The job is still there for you Willie," Ken says. "You just concentrate on getting yourself home."

It puts a spring in my step. I train in the room, go down for breakfast and then set off for a 10.15am meeting in the Embassy with David Dewberry, who is the Consul there. While we wait for the lawyer to arrive, David gives me a good background on Argentina and how tricky it is doing business there. As the meeting goes on my heart sinks: the plan is not to appeal for me to leave the country ASAP, but to sit tight and let the Prosecutor and the Judge have room to move and then see where we are. That will take time. Everything in Argentina takes so much fucking time.

The lawyer gives me a lift back to the hotel. I feel for him a bit because I don't think my case is going to rocket him up the popularity charts in Buenos Aires. We get lost on the way. No matter, I'm not going anywhere in a hurry. Carlos appears and we have lunch at the hotel. Then we go for a spin to a tributary of the River Plate and take a wee cruise to kill some time. I train at the club later and meet this guy, Alberto Fahey, a fine player who is really interested in my situation. And yes, with a name like that he's of Irish descent.

"My family – mother, father, sister, me – we worry very much for you and your family and every night we speak to God to help you," he says.

What a lovely thing to say. I train hard with him for an hour. I eat something at the club and go back to the hotel and wash my rugby gear in the bath, and hang it out the window to dry. Sleep is hard to come by tonight. It's well after midnight when I close the cover on this diary.

*****

The diary becomes my lifeline. Mostly it is written to Heather. Sometimes it's written to the part of my brain that controls how I feel about what's happening. So if I read back over something now, all these years later, I wonder what state of mind I was in when I wrote it. In the chain of letters and entries to Heather I'm having to apologise for being too honest when I've been at a low ebb. Control has never been my strong suit. Knowing when to keep my mouth shut, or to water down what I want to say, has always been an issue.

So, where does Heather fit into all this? When we met in Stranmillis I was immediately struck by her looks. Blond and bright eyed, she was beautiful without making a scene about it. There was a kind of an aura about her that said she was first and foremost a sound person, and good craic. It was an immediate attraction. I'd be lying though if I said she was the only blade I was chasing. But of the three I was after, Heather was the best bet. No question.

Mostly I think it was the fact that my bit of madness didn't put her off.

We had been seeing each other for a few months and it was going fine. The social life at the time centred around the bar in Stran, which was fairly lively, or The Bot or The Eg, both of which were big student hangouts near Queen's. I had been to her house in Antrim for Sunday lunch, and met her family, which had all gone fine. And likewise she had been over to Sixmilecross, where my mother managed one day to call her by the name of one of the other two blades. No harm done. So I was quick to send Heather a postcard from the early part of the trip. And in fairness she wrote back straight away. If she hadn't I really don't know how this story would have finished up.

With the Argentina diary, sometimes I squash two days into one. Soon enough my routine changes, as I get further away from the prison drill of getting up at 6am. Life on the outside in Argentina can start late and finish late.

Instead the new constant in my life is the battle with my mood. The least bit of good news lifts me up onto cloud nine. I can see the finish line. In my head I'm packing my bags for home. I'm on the way to the airport. Any sort of setback and I'm plunged into a depression. The walls begin to close in, and the more people are nice to me and try and support me the more I feel I'm a burden on them.

When I was growing up in Sixmilecross if someone was being dragged down by anxiety or depression they were said to be 'suffering with their nerves.' But by the autumn of 1980 I had become accustomed to the D word, and it was featuring more and more in my diary. It would be many years later before another life-changing episode led me to get counselling. Turned out my self-diagnosis of suffering from depression was on the money.

THE FLAG, PART II

Everywhere I turned in Argentina there were triggers to set me off. So, I'm in the cinema with Carlos one day. I'd wanted to see '10' with Dudley Moore and Bo Derek but it's run its course by the time we get there. Instead we end up going to 'Foul Play.' Goldie Hawn and Chevy Chase. It's subtitles and not dubbed, which is good for me. And we're laughing along and everything is going fine but the more I look at Goldie Hawn the more I think of Heather B. That's what Carlos knows her as now, to distinguish her from my sister Heather. It's like he thinks her name is Heatherbee. I have the ear worn off the poor man from talking about her. And when I think of her I quickly get overcome.

From day to day different people call from home. One day it's Jack Gough and another it's Dessie McCann or Bobby Mills – all Dungannon men. Or Wilfie Wright. Each and every one of them stalwarts of the club, very supportive of my situation.

"It's just so good to hear from you guys," I'd say. Then I'd get to think of what I was missing, and the hurt I was causing my parents.

My most frequent caller was not a rugby man, but a rookie reporter from the *Belfast Telegraph*, Martin O'Brien. I was very sceptical of him at first, but over time we struck up a good relationship. When he would get into the Tele office on Royal Avenue he'd crack on with the long-distance phone calling. Ringing Buenos Aires from Belfast was an obstacle course. The last hurdle was the receptionist in the hotel.

"Buenos dias senora. Weely Andersohn per favor."

It took Martin a while to whittle it down to that offering. Sometimes he would lose the connection and have to start all over again. Or if he got through the quality of the line could be awful. I was mindful in my letters to Heather not to curse all over the place, except when it came to the Argentine press. Then I would let fly. Jesus, I hated those fuckers. They were slaughtering me. Martin was the other end of the scale. Most of our conversations were off the record and he respected that. It must have been hard for him with his editor.

'Well Martin, what did you get out of him?'

'Aye not much that we can use for tomorrow, but it's coming along.'

He ended up becoming a confidant. What a sound man.

Most of the phone contact tended to be early morning calls, which would be the ideal start to my day. Depending on what happened next I would either stay on an even keel or start to slip under.

Thanks to Carlos a group of regulars developed around me, like a committee dedicated to keeping me sane.

I think at first his girlfriend, Sylvana, thought I was 'the other woman', he was spending so much time with me. But when we met we got on straight away.

The boy-girl thing in Argentina was funny. Carlos's best friend was a girl, Laura. And she had a boyfriend. That didn't cause any problem whatsoever with Sylvana. I couldn't see that working out so smoothly back home. Other prominent members of the Ladies Committee were Maureen and Adrianna. I spoke a lot to them about Heather, and I mentioned them a lot to Heather in my letters.

"I suppose you are wondering what's with the girls but they have been kind and very helpful and are my friends here," I wrote one day. "Maureen's surname is O'Keefe and has strong Irish heritage. She has been like a sister to me. Like you she cares deeply for people's feelings. But for the two of them and Carlos I would be lost."

Tuesday 2nd September, 1980

Heather I was so happy to talk to you again and but I didn't say the things I wanted to – like how much I missed you and how much I wanted to hold you and love you again. But I suppose I had to give you the situation here without any optimism. That is the reality for me now because before Argentina I always thought that when you're down you would be back up the next day. But here I found new depths. On some occasions I could hardly walk with fear and worry for home and you. Instead of being elated to the heavens I was sad after talking to you because I knew how much I wanted you but there was nothing I could do. I've asked myself a thousand times when would this nightmare end but I hope with luck things could change. I feel that tomorrow is vital for us. Maybe I feel I could be talking to you instead of writing to you. I will pray for you and my family tonight as I have done for 3 weeks. Please forgive. All my love

  Willie x

*****

I would go to Maureen's and Adrianna's houses for dinner and meet their families, and there was never any suspicion of me or my motives. The O'Keefe clan treated me like one of their own. When I would reflect on that I'd wonder was I worthy of their friendship and compassion. And that would lead to another slide in my mood.

The guys at Banco were great – despite the language barrier I felt part of the group when I trained with them. I actually played a game for their Second XV, but got a serious dunt in the back. A good while later I discovered I cracked a couple of ribs.

The case was dragging me under. In early September we thought there would be movement. Great, my mind starts to race about what that might bring. The appointed day comes and there is no news on any front. Two weeks later and we hear that the Prosecutor has asked for a sentence of two years. This needs some context.

According to their system, as explained to me by Mr Molinas and Carlos, anything up to two years and the judge can suspend the sentence if he sees fit. Anything over two years and either I'm found not guilty – which is not going to happen – or I serve the lot.

So if he asks for say 25 months and the judge says I'm guilty then 25 months would be what I have to serve. If it goes badly then I will be serving time and paying for the privilege on top of that. My bail money was £1,500, and the lawyer's bill will be coming at the end of it.

The Embassy staff explain the options: 1) Stay and face the music 2) Make a run for it. If I was going to choose the second then they could get me to the Falkland Islands by boat and a flight from there closer to home. Alternatively I could snuggle down under the floorboards of a bus going across the border to Uruguay. It was made absolutely clear that if I made a run for it and got caught then I was fucked. Whatever the Generals were going to do to me the Generals were going to do to me.

There were a few reasons to stay: 1) Carlos had given the court an assurance that he would vouch for my staying in Buenos Aires 2) If I ran then it would confirm all the lies that the press had been printing about us – and that meant me as

I was the only one left, and 3) The prospect of getting caught trying to escape was terrifying.

I decided to stay. The terror of the whole thing was brought home to me one Saturday when Carlos took me to a match between La Plata and Banco Nación. Carlos was unbelievably good to me, my lifeline in so many ways, but he never got too deep into the political situation in the country. I never got the impression that he was worried about the military lifting him in the middle of the night and taking him off to the Navy Mechanics School – over the course of the dictatorship an estimated 5,000 people were tortured and murdered there. He wasn't short of a few bob. His father owned the factory that served a purpose for the generals.

The day we went to La Plata I learned a little bit more about the local club who were in the eye of the storm. I didn't appreciate at the time that the players of that club had been victims of the regime. There was a lot I was slow to understand. Only a couple of years earlier, just before the football World Cup had kicked off, one of their players was murdered by the regime. He was a Marxist. And when his teammates protested they started disappearing as well. Yet the club kept going, kept playing.

What were we doing in a country like this?

Earlier in the tour, when we had got to Buenos Aires, we had seen the Mothers of the Disappeared protesting near the pink house, The Presidential Palace. These were the Madres de Plaza de Mayo, who would gather every Thursday in front of the Palace. It was almost like a tourist attraction except that lots of locals I think were looking the other way. It washed over us at the time to be honest.

We're talking about war crimes on a grand scale, except

there wasn't a war. The Junta had set out on what they called the Process of National Reorganization, which was basically a murder campaign against anyone who was left of centre, or had something to protest about, or just didn't think the way the Generals did. I couldn't get my head around it.

And I wasn't coming from a Utopian society myself. This was 1980. The Junta was in its prime, and I was on the wrong side of the law. So what might have happened if they caught me trying to escape?

There was a strong Irish community in Buenos Aires. St Brendan's College in the Belgrano district had been founded by an Irishman, JJ Scanlon, and his son JJ junior invited me one day to visit. It was more than a welcome break. It was a look at the life that could be ahead of me in Grosvenor Grammar School if ever I could get the fuck out of Argentina and back to Belfast.

I was blessed to be befriended by Paddy McLean, a Northern Irishman who had emigrated to Buenos Aires, married a beautiful Italian woman, and raised his family there. Paddy couldn't do enough for me. Years later his son Martin would spend a good few years in Northern Ireland working in the pharmaceutical industry. He became a regular at Ravenhill on Friday nights. He approached me there one night at a game. He was 12 when I met him at his father's house in Buenos Aires. I hadn't a clue who he was when he came up to me in Ravenhill. When he mentioned Argentina I shut the conversation down and moved on. I've since explained myself and apologised to him. Martin's parents showed me incredible kindness when I was at a very low ebb.

At one point, in the hope of moving things along in my favour, I wrote an open letter via my bosom buddies in the press. I sent it to the local English language paper, the *Buenos Aires Herald*, and the Spanish language *La Nación*. The *Herald* had been the first paper to write about the people being lifted off the streets illegally, interrogated and in many cases disappeared. Writing about that stuff was an incredibly brave thing in itself.

In the British Embassy's annual report for 1980, a confidential document that I got to see many years later, the following observation was made:

'Meanwhile the scars of the "dirty war" against terrorism are not all healed – and some of them perhaps will never heal so long as there are guilty consciences, prisoners who know too much and stool pigeons living in terror of both sides to provide arguments and excuses for putting off a return to full legality.'

Friday 5th September, 1980
Letter to Buenos Aires Herald, La Nación
This letter is not only for my friends and enemies in Argentina but for the whole nation because I feel that I have offended you all by my behaviour. This was never my intention when I came to this country for I can only use words like generosity, kindness and decency to describe the way which my friends and I were treated by our host rugby clubs (especially Banco Nación) and everyone involved with us.

When I took the flag, which on reflection was silly and thoughtless of me, never did the word disrespect cross my mind for the flag of your country. At the time it was only taken as a souvenir to be held by me in remembrance of a magnificent time I had on tour.

The course of events since then have made me realise my mistake and also from this solitary experience I have learned more about culture, politics and moral standing of this country.

Finally I can only apologise again for my behaviour and ask that I may be forgiven for a tragic mistake which I have made, which I know will probably change the course of my life. From what I have learned of your country I have liked and hopefully someday I can return to enjoy again the friendship I have received.

Yours sincerely

William Anderson

Wednesday 10th September, 1980
Diary entry

I slept well enough last night apart from waking up from a dream where my parents came over here to visit me. I was in prison. Heather, they said you couldn't come over. Then you appeared, and they were all laughing. Great joke! I was so relieved.

I'd thought you'd had enough of me over this whole thing.

I awoke again with the knocking at the door which was the signal that a call was coming through. It was Wendy Austin of BBC NI. I told her what I could, which you probably heard.

I was very tired so I kept the exercises down a bit, had breakfast and went for a walk. I bought a copy of Midnight Express when I was out. I read a bit of it and started comparing my case with William Hayes. Is that crazy? He's in a Turkish prison and I'm in an Argentina Hotel. But the lack of control over my life is hard for me to come to terms with. Carlos came over at lunchtime and stayed with me until 3pm when I was due to call the Embassy to hear what the Judge had requested. No white smoke for another few hours.

I went over to Banco with Carlos and bought four rugby shirts with the money I changed yesterday. One each for Frank and David, one for me, and one wee one for my nephew Stephen. Carlos wouldn't let me pay full price in the club shop. That's the kind of man he is.

He received a letter from Prof Irwin thanking him for all his help on David's behalf – and deservedly so. He has been a rock for all of us. Just reading that letter highlighted for me that David would never had had any bother only he was sticking up for me.

Eventually we get word that the Prosecutor is asking for the sentence we expected. Thank God for that. And Banco want me to play another game for them. Things are looking up.

*****

The following week summed up my yo-yo existence in Buenos Aires. It started with a trip back to the Detention Centre to visit the Director. He was delighted to see me, and again was very upbeat about the case. While I was there one of the judges walked past us wearing a Penguins tie. Maybe I should wear one when my case comes up again?

Then I get a call from Frank Wilson. It was like a tonic. Frank has a great ability to lift your spirits and he did the trick for me. We were mindful of not getting into too much detail over the phone, but it was great to hear from him. Then I had a meeting in the Embassy with Dudley Ankerson and David Dewberry, followed by a message from Paddy McLean when I got back inviting me to dinner, and a telegram from schoolfriends who were getting married. Just as I'm taking all that on-board Carlos says to stay put in the hotel, that the press have just been to his office and are certain to be on their way. Sure enough they're in the foyer 20 minutes later. That puts an end to my playing career with Banco Nación. Never mind my ribs, if I played the next game for them it would turn into a circus. The hunted feeling was back with a bang.

I'm accosted by one of the journalists when I try to get out and go to Alberto Fahey's house for dinner. Head down and plough ahead to Alberto who is parked outside. At his house there is a sign over the door: 'Welcome to our home. It is your home too.' That set me off, and I had barely got in the door.

On 16th September, I was pulled down to a new level when the Prosecutor asked to reopen the case. So suddenly it was no longer a matter of the judge deciding whether or not to accept the request for a two years' sentence, now they were looking to investigate it further. What the fuck did they hope to find?

The Embassy guys warned me it might take another six weeks to complete that investigation. They said the Prosecutor wanted me cleared through Interpol to see if I had any other crimes outstanding. When I heard that bit I knew that I was a like a cork bobbing away on the tide. Whether it was coming in or going out was well beyond my control.

If I had made a list of my fears at that time it would have started with some new scrap of shite being produced that would see me locked up for years. Neck and neck with that was never seeing Heather again – how could I possibly ask her to put her life on hold for some pawn in a game of chess being played out in a South American country run by psychopaths? The most immediate fear was that my Buenos Aires network would write me off as a lost cause, an inconvenience.

Thank God they didn't. They stood by me. And it lasted for weeks.

Hotel Asociación Bancaria, Suipacha 854
Thursday 30th October, 1980
Hello Heather

THE FLAG, PART II

Tomorrow I will be away from home for 3 months. I feel that I have aged 10 years and hardened likewise. I hope and pray this will be the last letter I write because about this time next week I should know my fate. I pray that it will mean my release. I must apologise for the previous two letters I've written because they were written in one of the many depressing times I've had. I can only say that I am up now and feel the inner strength I have had before. Again I must thank you for your letters because they have made me feel alive. Your sincerity and kindness in them shows that you are indeed one of the best people I've met. Thank you Heather. I also hope that you are fit and well and enjoying hockey/basketball etc. When we get together again I would love to train with you some nights.

Well, what has been happening? Last week nothing really much. I went to see the Fijians play San Isidro Club here. I spent Saturday with a fella called Giorgio. He has become a good friend. Carlos went to Chile with the English ref who is here now. I spent Sunday and Monday alone and trained on Sunday and Tuesday. I have sort of developed deep within myself and at times I have found it strange to have company and to know what to do with company.

In the last two weeks I wanted to isolate myself from everything because I felt that I was in the way and putting people out. So I enclosed myself inside a wall of distrust, worry and anger. This was totally wrong and as I had no vent except my writing it grew so large inside I felt so down I didn't know who to turn to or talk to. Since then I have realised that I am lucky and the cross I have had to carry may have been even bigger and that I could be in jail. I know now that the judge must make his decision next week, taking the full time to make his decision. This might not be bad as I might get a suspended sentence and get home soon.

The weekends here are the worst of times because I know there will be no news and I must spend them mostly alone. It's these times when it's hard to find logic and normality within because you wonder who the hell really gives a damn. No one really here because so many people have washed their hands of me. Yes I've seen a lot of different attitudes. Thankfully I've still got Carlos but he is the manager of this ref now and probably finds him less of a strain than I. I will however never be able to repay him.

You my love have seldom been out of my mind in the last three months and my love for you has grown very strong within. It is hard to imagine tenderness, kindness and love because I have not had any for so long by anyone.

Too many husbands and wives say after 10 or 20 years that they don't know each other. My God what a waste of life. Heather you have listened to my thoughts over the last three months and I hope you have not been too bored. It has been hard, as you have seen from my last two letters, to be reasonable all the time and not to have built up aggression.

I have been a messer but not to show disrespect to any nation but now I carry that with me. Not just Willie Anderson, but 'the one who stole the flag.' How sick I feel when I think of that and I want to live a normal life but can I be allowed to forget. Please God I hope and pray so. You will help me to restart Heather. Please give me a chance to start again and be accepted.

I hope when you are reading this letter one week from now I will have some good news. I pray for you and my family every day and hope we will be all together again. I love you.

Willie

*****

I will never forget the morning a few days after writing that letter when I was out for a run around the streets of Buenos Aires. My back had recovered and physically I was fit but my head was bursting. And then I had one of those moments of clarity. You might be lucky enough to get them a few times in your life, or unlucky enough never to experience the calm that comes with it. It saved my sanity. I knew that whatever was coming around the corner it was up to me to deal with it. I couldn't keep leaning on phone-calls and letters from home. I couldn't expect that my little BA network would keep me afloat. I would deal with it myself. And if the 'it' was a stretch then that's what I would do.

The Fijian national squad arrived into Argentina on tour and stayed at my hotel. They were fantastic people and I loved their company. I became good friends with their fullback Lemeki Vuetaki. The Fijians would be done and dusted with their tour, and back home safe and sound in Suva, before I was freed. So, as promised, Lemeki wrote to Heather to reassure her I was OK.

"Please reply so that we can know what is happening with my friend," he signed off. "Also we would like to send you some souvenirs of Fiji."

When the Fijian lads heard my story they were slow to go out around the place.

An Irish monk got in touch with me one day and I travelled across town to meet him and his fellow monks and see the work they did in the poorest favelas of Buenos Aires. They were such honourable men. Spending a wee bit of time with them gave me further insight into the crazy way society can be structured. The folks they were helping wouldn't have two coins to rub together.

I actually had a bit of calm about me when D-Day arrived, three months after I had said goodbye to Frank and Davy. But I was able to smile when I read this letter from my brother-in-law, Alan Bell.

15 Upper Green, Dunmurry
Sunday 9th November, 1980

Dear Willie

I am writing in the hope that you will not be in Argentina to receive this letter. Heather, myself and the kids just returned from Sixmilecross. We had a good weekend and everybody went to the rugby club last night. We had a 'siege' with Oliver and the girls.

I hope you will have had good news by now, but if not you must keep on going. I know none of us can really appreciate what you are going through. The uncertainty must be terrible. Just remember we are all behind you now and when you come home.

All the family are well. Your mum and dad are relaxed and being patient. Oliver and Helen are the same as ever and we are going to the rugby ...next Sat with them. Heather is well and training hard to pass the time. She baked you a cake which is in our house. I will try and resist testing it before you come home.

The feeling in the press and rugby world is that you should have been home long ago. I have enclosed a cutting from this week's Sunday News.

Ulster lost this weekend 21–10 to Munster. I don't think you will have too much bother getting your place back. Keep on training as hard as you can because I'm sure if you are in good shape it will help you mentally.

Perhaps you could let your Mum, Dad and Oliver know what you want to do about the press when you return. I am sure the media

*will want a 'big show' and if you could let them know what your
wishes would be we could organise things in advance. However that
will be a pleasant task once you are on the way home. Don't let them
beat you and remember we are all thinking about you all the time.*

Hoping once again you are on your way home when this arrives.
Best Wishes
Alan

Ps Oliver and Dad will do what YOU want

*****

Time was what nearly pushed me over the edge altogether.

Great big gaps to be filled all over the place. It got to the
stage where I would stop myself looking at my watch. I started
swinging from a positive state of mind one minute, believing
my Argentine friends when they would tell me I was nearly
over the line, to the other end of the spectrum, thinking I was
becoming part of the local landscape, some sort of clown who
went offside and wandered the streets for years. In the end the
legal stuff was like a marathon walk that turned into a jog for
the last 100 metres.

The Prosecutor reopening the case threw some more light
on his star witness: the night-watchman who reported the
incident in the first place. He had rung the police and it didn't
take them long to figure out who the culprits were. When they
rang the hotel the receptionist would have confirmed seeing me
dandering in the door with the national flag under my jacket.
Can you imagine their excitement?

As we dragged on into the third week of November we

were still waiting to see what the judge would make of the lawyers' submissions. The week before he finally dealt with me he sentenced a group of 'terrorists' who had been on remand for five years. Jeepers. I wasn't sure whether to be glad he was actually working or worried about what he might come up with.

Mr Molinas had gone to the scene of the crime and compared the position of the witness with the position of the flagpole and established that he couldn't have seen a whole lot. He had seen fellas running past his window but he didn't catch much in the way of detail. Mr Molinas also established that the flag shouldn't have been flying at that time of night, that it should be taken down at sunset and flown again at sunrise. That seems in hindsight like a dodgy case to be making to fascist dictators but it didn't backfire, thankfully. Maybe they were tired of it too, for there was no more bang to be got from this buck.

So the two years that the Prosecutor asked for originally was the two years I got, but on conditional release. It didn't mean I couldn't travel, it just meant you couldn't reoffend in the Argentine jurisdiction in that period. This was all done back and forth between the legal folks. I was in my room when I got the call from Mr Molinas, with someone helping with the translation. I sat there in a kind of twilight zone. It was unofficial but rock solid.

Carlos rang, delighted. He had gone on a wee cruise up the coast to Brazil for a week but was staying in touch. The Embassy lads were on quickly to confirm everything and to tell me not to hang around. Packing? I had done it a million times in my head and it took me about five minutes flat to whizz around the room and gather my stuff. I had thought about having everything half-packed but then knocked that on the head, in case things would go arseways again.

I can remember clearly looking around the bathroom to make sure I hadn't left training gear in the bath or razors on the washbasin. Was I insane? I wanted the room to be clean for the staff who would have to check it out. I had caused enough trouble already.

The Embassy sent a car over. It was waiting for me as I left the key at the reception desk. There was an emptiness that Carlos wasn't on hand but in a way I was almost grateful because I would have broken down had I seen him. We sped off to the airport. My instructions were not to run but not to linger either.

Suddenly the military presence became even more noticeable. They were all staring at me. Jeepers lads, I'm going! The next suitable flight out was to Rio de Janeiro and the Embassy had sorted my ticket. At check-in I got hit with an extra baggage charge of $200. I couldn't believe it. I didn't argue. Next I had to go through security, and then passport control. At that point a policeman came over and told me to follow him. My blood ran cold. He seemed pleasant enough but maybe that's part of the act? He went downstairs with me a few steps behind him. When we turned the corner at the bottom the O'Keefe family were all there. The waterworks started. I was still wiping away the tears going back upstairs. I passed a gift shop on my way to the lounge at Gate 6.

They had Argentine flags on sale.

I didn't buy one.

The flight to Rio took about three and a half hours. I had to change terminal when I got there, to catch the next leg, to Madrid. As I was disembarking with the rest of the passengers

I saw this familiar face up ahead, waiting. It was Carlos. How the hell he managed that I don't know, but I'd never been so glad to see anyone in my life. It was typical of him to sort that final chapter. His friendship and support had meant so much, and thank God he was on hand to say goodbye. We embraced, and cried, and went our separate ways.

Diego Maradona was on my flight to Madrid. I think he must have been going on holidays, or maybe it was a long negotiation before going to Barca in 1982. Whatever, he never asked for an autograph so I didn't ask him for his.

When I eventually got to Aldergrove I was exhausted. One flight after another and most of the time spent thinking of Heather, and what it would be like to hold her in my arms. I had gone over in my head a million times what that would be like. But from the moment I walked into the arrivals terminal there were airport police hustling me out of the line of passengers and down a corridor marked 'Staff.'

The next thing the two Heathers – Buckley and Bell – were in front of me, alongside Oliver.

It wasn't how I imagined it. In my head she had been running to meet me and I was sweeping her off her feet. Sounds like a commercial for aftershave, I know, but that's what I was thinking. Instead there were hurried hugs between the four of us.

"We need to hurry you up here folks, the press will be onto us," said a man in uniform.

Sure enough when we were hustled out a side door a few reporters were on our case. Martin O'Brien was one of them. I couldn't really give him the interview he deserved without feeding the rest of the press pack so I felt bad about that. I caught up with him years later. He's a sound man who treated me like a human being rather than a storyline.

Then we were away off in a waiting car to Sixmilecross. Things were happening so fast at that stage it was hard to believe I was finally sitting beside the woman whose love and support had kept me alive.

When I walked in the door at home I was an emotional wreck. My father hugged me. I'd say that was the first time we had embraced since I was a wee cub running about the place, throwing the discus with Oliver and getting up to all sorts. None of us could say much that made sense. We were busy mopping up the tears.

Later I resolved to sit down with Davy and Frank, but you know what? It never happened. I saw lots of Davy all right but in time Frank moved over to Exeter and then to Portugal. We – the three of us – never got around to sitting down and reflecting on what had happened to us. But we will. They have told me since that there were huge positives to take from living through an experience like that and coming out the other end in one piece. And they were right. But they could have done without the scar tissue, an injury sustained by supporting me. Truly they are special men, and I love them for what they did.

And the cost? In pounds, shillings and pence it was around £20,000. My parents paid half and fundraising looked after the rest. The rugby community in Ulster, driven by my friends in Dungannon, were extraordinary – a great help.

But in wear and tear on my parents you couldn't put a figure on that. Farming can be a lonely enough existence. My mother, especially, suffered when I was in Argentina. She relied on alcohol more than she would have wished. These were things

I needed to address before I got a handle on my rugby career at home. I had got a call one day in Buenos Aires from IRFU president Bobby Ganly, saying I hadn't been forgotten. It was good to hear from him but I wasn't exactly sure what that meant.

As for the Penguins, they went on touring. So did I. It's just that we never did it together again. They popped into my head a few times, one of them being in Bermuda when I was there for a tournament. I bumped into Denis Thatcher, husband of Prime Minister Maggie who went to war with Argentina over the Falklands. It wasn't long after that conflict when we met. He had a few drinks on him and so did I. He had given me the clear impression he wasn't too impressed with anything about the island of Ireland.

As we parted I confided the following: "If your missus had asked me in 1980 I could have told her there was going to be trouble over that place!" He wasn't impressed.

A few years after our experience in Argentina, Davy was over playing an exhibition match for the Wolfhounds in London Irish. It had all gone off well – it was for the opening of a pitch or something – and Davy was in the bar afterwards, waiting to get served. His attention was drawn across the crowded bar to a man he recognised. It was Tony Mason, now deceased, who had led the Penguins tour to Argentina. Or the Emperor, as I called him.

So Davy danders over and kind of works his way into Tony's company. They're chatting about the game just played, and Davy realises Tony hasn't a clue who he's talking to. Tony introduces himself. "Yes I remember you," Davy says. "My name is David Irwin. I'm one of the four lads you left behind in Buenos Aires a few years ago."

Awkward silence. Davy felt a wee bit bad about laying that one on Mr Mason, who was a very pleasant man and a good age at that stage, but I could understand completely where he was coming from. In the writing of this book a spokesman for the Penguins was adamant that every I was dotted and every T crossed in the preparation for that tour, and what happened afterwards. Maybe so, but I can't remember it, and neither can the lads. But they do remember subsequently getting bills for their Penguins ties. The same spokesman referred to me as "a part of the Penguins family." I'll just leave that one there.

Carlos M Guarna
Buenos Aires, Republica Argentina
Tuesday 2nd December, 1980
My dear friend:
This is not an official letter, this is only for enclose with your letters. Those are the only I have received up to date. I am working so hard. My father now is very strong. It is OK. My club is preparing our tour – I don't know yet if it will be to South Africa or to New Zealand. It will be behind the 2nd of March until the 22nd of March.

Willie I am very happy because you are OK home. It was made official yesterday that the lawyer has accept the sentence. The two years in suspend are confirmed. No more problems. The case is shut.

I am translating the sentence for send to you.

Don't be sad these months. I'll stay with you in spirit.

Best regards

Carlos

3

The Farm

Our Town
Sometimes in the darkness I dream
Of the Town that is home to me still,
Of the gardens that slope to a stream,
And the roofs on the side of a hill,
Of the rown where the slow waters steal
Underneath a half-circle of stone,
At the foot of the hill of O'Neill
In the middle of County Tyrone

When WF Marshall, the Bard of Tyrone, wrote that ballad about Sixmilecross sometime early in the 20th century, I don't think he was on a high stool in one of the half dozen pubs in the village.

It probably wouldn't have been WF's style, and anyway I doubt it would've been easy to pen your poetry in one of these saloons.

THE FARM

There was a touch of the Wild West about Sixmilecross on a Saturday night when I was a child. The locals would descend on the place in the early evening. By closing time they were well pished. It was noisy and messy. It left an impression with me that this was how you let your hair down when you were older.

They would be back again the next morning, all dressed up but looking rattled, and smelling of stale beer and hair oil. The pubs were run by Catholics so the Prods would have to suck that one up. The general policy was to park your religion at the door and worship at the altar of drink.

The picture would change on the Sunday morning, when churches were the attraction. Between the Church of Ireland at the top of the street, the Presbyterian church around the corner, and the Catholic Church a few steps out the road in Beragh, everyone was catered for separately. That's a lot of religion in one wee place. The tone might have been different across the churches but I think the messages were all on the same track: mend your ways, or get your arse burned in hell. This is where I grew up.

The Andersons came to Ulster a few years before the start of the Great Plantation. From Paisley in the West of Scotland, they arrived in Ireland in 1602 as part of a contingent of Scottish troops sent by Queen Elizabeth I to sort out a few problems on the ground. They settled.

"There were 12 tribes of the Israelites – but thirteen of the Andersons," according to a family history of the Andersons of Flush and Bawn in Co Tyrone.

Our farm was 80 acres of decent land, running close to the road as you head west from Pomeroy to Sixmilecross. It was our world. Not like *Little House on the Prairie*, but it was where we played as kids. We kept 200 fattening pigs, a dozen dairy cows and a couple of hundred chickens. It was a lot of work. In time the chicken business came to dominate, and we were up to a few thousand.

If you think about it, that's a lot of varying shades of shite. A lot of noise. A lot of looking after. The pigs were the ones in the line of fire.

In the 1960s there was a television ad featuring George Best plugging Cookstown sausages. After the meaty voiceover line came George's time to shine:

"What the man means is, Cookstown are the best family sausages!"

We supplied a fair few of those babies. Let me take you through the cycle. We reared them on turnips and potatoes that we grew ourselves, supplemented with feed bought in. When they were judged fat enough it was, as Andrea Bocelli put it, time to say goodbye. Sometimes we'd get a man out to the farm to kill one for us. He was an expert. The pig would be restrained and then BANG! He'd whack it on the head with a mallet, and then slit its throat. The blood would spurt out like a burst main.

You had to have lots of boiling water on hand to scrape the hair off it. Then the surgeon would go to work. The big thing about killing pigs at home was that night you'd get to eat the liver. It was absolutely delicious. The other bits and bobs would be taken away and we'd get bacon and sausages back.

If it was a job lot of pigs then we'd be away with Dad to Cookstown on a Saturday morning, trailer in tow. There would be a queue to get into the abattoir but they used to let myself and my younger brother Oliver in the gate to have a look around. The privilege of Dad being a good supplier.

The smell of the place was overpowering. You'd think you'd

be used to the noise from having pigs on the farm but this was a different level of action. There were the pigs and the machinery and the shouting of the men working there. Then there was the whoosh of the furnace. Doors open, rush of heat, off you go.

Unlike at home the pigs were stunned using callipers before they had their throats cut. Then they'd be hooked up and whisked off to the furnace for hair removal. We went along each step of the line, marvelling at the speed of it all. It was part horror show, part adventure.

There was less drama with chickens. Mum said during the Second World War they had been a vital source of income in her family home in Brackey, long before she got married. She had about two dozen of them. One day a fella stopped by asking if she had any hens that had stopped laying.

"Aye, we buried a couple of them the other morning," she said.

He dug them up, put a bit of lipstick on their combs, and away he went with them. Adding a bit of colour made them look fresh. They would have appeared on somebody's plate not too long afterwards.

The work bit always came first. Dad made that clear. He was born Thomas Steen Anderson, the youngest of five children to William and Eleanor McLaren of Sixmilecross. My grandmother came from just across the valley. Dad left school at 13, but could have gone much further if there was a mood for that. But he was needed on the farm. End of conversation. He resented the fact that he had to wade in to the daily grind while our grandfather indulged himself a wee bit.

Milking 13 cows twice a day on top of all the other stuff going on was hard rod for a child – which is what he was. I remember a friend of his telling me once that the hay barn was Dad's go-to spot for a nap when he could get it.

My grandfather was also a justice of the peace. In reality he was more of a JP than a farmer. He wasn't someone who sweated over the land. He showed horses and rode horses and jumped at shows around the province, and sometimes down in Dublin. Despite being 6ft 6ins tall he was an accomplished horseman. All For Ireland was the name of the horse that won him a few rosettes here and there. He got a bad kick off one of the horses one day which did for his knee, which he said curtailed his labouring on the farm. I'm not sure he was too keen in any case.

So Dad was left to care for the horses, and more besides. With three girls and two boys, he seemed to end up with more than his fair share. Horses are high maintenance. He had no interest in having them about the place when the farm became his. There was enough to be done as it was. As the youngest he was the last man standing. My three aunts had moved on – except for Aunt E, who never married and continued to live there. Uncle Bertie had no interest in the farm, so Dad inherited it.

Work. That's what dominated my parents' lives. When our mother Evelyn was a child she would have been given a week off school in October to help with digging spuds. Everyone did their bit.

She was a good looking woman. About 5ft 9ins tall with grey/green eyes and auburn hair, you wouldn't pass her on the street without noticing. Dad had been the only man in her life. I mean the *only* man. Once a friend of hers had organised a foursome with two local lads, to go to a dance in Omagh. They were to meet at the end of the lane. Mum got cold feet. That was that.

Evelyn was clever and worked hard in school. She was sent to agricultural school in Strabane. It had opened just before the First World War. Because the menfolk would have been slaving away out in the fields from spring onwards they decided to open up to girls. Specifically they were talking about: "Housewifery, cooking, sewing, hygiene and poultry-keeping."

On the face of it this would make her an even more attractive marriage partner than someone who wanted to be kept in cigarettes, nylons and high heels. It also tied her firmly to the yoke. She was so good at her job there would be no escape. Mum had a work ethic. She was organised and had an ability to crack on and get things done.

Every morning she would have a pot of porridge on the stove first thing before going to help Dad with the milking. Her job was to put on the clusters and pour the milk. It was physical and demanding. Milking was like the tides: it would come morning and evening and you couldn't dodge it, no matter how you felt. I remember if Mum walked half way down the byre she could see in the window of the kitchen from there. When she could spot three heads at the table she'd leave us to it. Heather the boss, then me, then Oliver.

She would bring us a cup of fresh cream, and a jug of milk, to go with the porridge. When she had got us off to school and cleaned up she'd make wheaten bread or soda bread. There'd be a pinch of this or a throw of that. It all looked so casual but in her head it was measured.

When we would get back from school there would be an apple or rhubarb tart on the table, fresh from the oven. We'd demolish it with a wee sprinkling of milk or cream around the side. I can still taste it.

By 10am she'd have been getting on with collecting eggs from the hens. When coffee became a 'thing' she would get to sit down and have a cup at 11. With the wireless turned on in the corner, that would be her first break in a day that started before 7am. Every day was much the same.

Over the years the farm became more about chickens. In 1966 we built a henhouse that held 1500. Another was added three years later, with room for 3000. They were kept in what was called deep litter. So, no cages, but a floor covered in peat moss. If you were a townie you'd be flabbergasted to walk into a scene like that. Our chores would have involved helping out there from a young age. Then we'd move on to the evening milking at five o'clock. Heather, myself and Oliver.

I remember it more as a daily routine than a grind. Heather was more sensitive, and being two years older than me she was quicker to pick up the cues. Like the message from my mother, who developed this weary mantra: "It's all about the men."

That went over my head at the time. Oliver too. But it struck a chord with Heather. I wouldn't say she was that close to Mum, but the message was conveyed right enough. Marrying a farmer meant chaining yourself to the yoke. There was a better life to be had beyond Sixmilecross.

Like Mum before her, Heather was handy at school. She was always going to come away with results that would open doors for her to third level education. Taking that route was something fixed in her mind from her early teens. Mum's road was straight and narrow and bound by high hedges on each side. That wasn't the one Heather wanted to travel.

THE FARM

As a child I suppose I was guilty of not stopping to think how hard my mother worked for us. She spent most of the time running around keeping the men in her life fit and fed and able to do their bit without hindrance. Evelyn had little time off, or at least not much in the way of respite. There would be the odd game of bowls in the church hall. Occasionally she went to meetings of the Women's Institute, which sounded like zero craic. There was no bridge circuit, which she would have been made for. The only break in the clouds would be paying a visit to cousins.

We would have called that a céilidh, an Irish word which worked its way into our vocabularies even though none of us ever had a lesson in the language. It became a verb for us. We're going to céilidh with so and so.

Years later, when Heather was living and working in Belfast, and I ran into trouble in Argentina, Oliver was holding the fort at home with the folks. It was a time when they should have been céilidhing left, right and centre. He became the link between them and me, filtering messages and trying to put a positive spin on things.

Argentina destroyed Mum. It was a dark time for everyone and she was frazzled by it. She was 54 years of age with her children reared and the farm about to be lodged in Oliver's safe hands. Dad was still very much involved in the day to day, but he was taking things a bit easier. She should have had her feet up, relaxing. Then I hit the headlines.

Mum and Dad were actually on a wee holiday in Scotland the day the news broke from Buenos Aires. They had finally started taking some time for themselves, which they didn't find easy to do after a lifetime of work. If they could have been kidnapped and taken to Canada to see Auntie Nora I know they would have loved it. But sometimes it was a battle to get them beyond the 'Cross.

As a family we had never been away together on a holiday, as such. That was fine. No one else around Sixmilecross had either. There would be Sundays spent in Portrush and Rossnowlagh, and with Uncle Bertie in Castlerock, up beyond Coleraine. Those trips to the coast were highlights, and all of us would have learned to swim in the sea. Myself and Oliver would have had our days down in Santry Stadium, in Dublin, when we started making strides in athletics, in our mid-teens. And Heather got around a bit through playing hockey in Omagh Academy. But family holidays weren't a thing.

So there were Mum and Dad in Scotland, original home of the Anderson clan, when their son – the Penguin – waddled his way into trouble in South America. Oliver was hoping I'd be home before the week was out, when they were due back. Jeepers, when I think of it. How simple that would have been. The whole experience burned her nerve endings. When the anxiety would mount she would lean on drink for comfort.

Farming back then meant living a lot of life in isolation. For Heather, Ollie and me that wasn't a problem. We got along fine. Summers would be spent working in the fields and then playing in the silo. It was about 16ft wide and 50ft long. We'd put planks between two swings and make a stagecoach. We used our imaginations. We would use the straw to make tunnels and build houses. We made our own wee playground from what was around us. It became a set for Indiana Jones adventures before Disney had invented him. We didn't feel the time passing.

Heather had her own room and I shared with Oliver. With

such a small age gap between us boys we were going to see a lot of each other. So it would be either war of the worlds or brothers in arms. We were pals from the start.

For Mum, life slowed to a grind by the time we had grown up and moved on. She started working as a carer for some neighbours because it suited her personality. In the end though it came down to just her and Dad.

There had never been much affection running through the house. There was love, surely, but not many hugs or physical demonstration of it either between parents or between parents and kids. But we didn't feel like we were living in a cold house. Emotion was tucked away in a corner with a lid on it. I never doubted that we were loved, it's just it wasn't exactly reinforced.

Instead our parents were mostly matter of fact. In our company anyway the only conversations were about what needed to be done about the place. Maybe a bit of local news on top. That was it. It was so structured and formal that if Dad wanted to correct Heather on something he'd get Mum to do it. If she was heading over to a friend and he didn't like the length of her skirt, or the amount of lipstick she had on, he'd get Mum to have a word. It followed that we weren't being showered with affection either. It was only much later in life I reflected on an emotional gap that should have been filled. At the time you didn't miss what you didn't know. We all evolve though. When our next generation started springing up, both Dad and Mum got full value from loving their grandkids. Dad especially became a more affectionate grandfather than he had been a father.

My parents met at a local dance during the war. If it wasn't in one of the local Orange Halls then they would have thought nothing about cycling the 10 miles to Omagh to a dance. It was a challenging time to be making a match because there were lots of Yanks on the scene. Carrickmore, Omagh, Enniskillen – there were pockets of US soldiers based around here, training away before heading over to Europe on active service. There would have been a few skirmishes with Tyrone boys, not keen about having their patch invaded by fellas with white teeth and fast talk. Women were hard enough to pin down as it was.

Of course the visitors were glamorous attractions. These boys had chewing gum and fancy clothes to complete the package. Auntie Nora was a nurse. My father said all she spent her money on was nylons and lipstick. Lassies were on red alert every time GI Joe came into view.

She worked in St Thomas' Hospital in London and ended up marrying a man she had nursed there. He was in the merchant navy and had all the moves. He promised her the earth. They ended up in a log cabin in Canada with bears outside. While he was at sea she had come back to live on the farm with their wee son, Robert. When it came time to reunite after the war my father drove them down to the airport in Shannon. That would have been at least a nine hour round trip at the time. Dad said it was the hardest drive he ever did in his life because he thought he would never see her again. It was rare to see him express that kind of emotion.

My father's moods were defined by how well things were going on the farm.

Even if it was good he wouldn't have been wild chatty with us. If Thomas Steen Anderson had been starring in a movie then he would have been cast as the strong, brooding character. More pictures than sound. When that sound was whistling it was never good. Dad was no Roger Whittaker. If he was whistling then it was to warn us we were in trouble and probably to keep himself calm. Cleaning out the byre could be a flashpoint.

We were put in behind the wheel of the tractor from a very young age. Your job was to nudge it forward as Dad shovelled out the dung. If you went too hard then the dung fell out of the box. Not good. You learned to get it right.

Heather was lucky enough to avoid that. She would have learned to drive the tractor in the summertime, out in the fields when we were baling hay. Good grass in the summer meant feed for the cattle in the winter. Otherwise you'd have had to buy-in, which was never part of the plan, and not easy to do in any case. It was all about hay. And there was always pressure. You could feel the stress coming off my father in waves if the clouds started rolling in. Farm life was one long battle against the elements.

When the sun was shining it was the best of craic. So a sunny June meant happy people. In the evenings our meadows would ring out with the call of corncrakes. They're funny birds: secretive but noisy. They would come up here to breed, from Africa, for about six months from late spring until autumn. That throaty, rasping call takes me home in an instant. You don't hear them now. Farming practice changed and crops would be cut earlier in the summer, destroying the nest of the corncrakes.

When the forecast looked good the grass would be mowed. After a few days the hay would be shaken out with pitchforks. There was an old man who lived very close to us, known as Big Willie Anderson. Of course he was related. We all were. But he was somewhere off in the distance. In keeping with the tradition of adding or substituting names to distinguish between an army of the same clan with the same name, he was known as Willie Charlotte – his mother's maiden name. We called him Willie Sling. No man could make hay like him. A blacksmith, he would have been in his 70s when we knew him. As we would say, Willie was a bit of a gag. Quick witted and great company, he loved being around people. The story goes that he was inside in a shop in town one day, smoking his pipe, when the local church minster came in to buy his newspaper.

"Ah, you're in to spend the church collection I see," says Willie.

"I am Willie," goes the minister. "And I don't see your contribution in here…"

He worked hard at the hay but it was the company he was after. When things were gathering pace Willie would shout: "Turn the green thing up!" Which meant flipping all the green grass so it would wilt in the sun. When we were young all we were fit for was rolling the bales into clumps for the men to load. As we got bigger we could lift and build the bales onto the trailer. Sometimes we would ride on top of the load on the way to the hayshed, dodging the overhanging branches. It felt triumphant. Like farming's ticker tape parade.

During hay days Mum would bring a picnic to the meadows with a can of hot tea and rough cut plain bread, smothered in jam she had made herself. It was a team thing before I understood anything about teamwork.

Wet weather meant a different mood. The hay would have to be lapped and lumped. That meant shaking it out and then gathering it up in your arms, and standing it up so the rain would roll off it. It was back-breaking work. Because of my long arms I was good at it. Strength-wise it did me a power of good.

THE FARM

The only thing worse than that job was having to clean out the sheughs – pronounced 'shucks', or ditches. We'd use a tool called a dredge to clear the weeds and overgrown grass, to allow the water to flow more freely. Oliver could spend all day hanging over the edge to catch sticklebacks. Sometimes the men would pull out eels, which were delicious fried on the pan. The odd time they'd pull out a newt, or a mankeeper as we called them locally. Willie Sling always told us mankeepers would climb into your mouth and pull out your guts, so we would keep our lips tight till we left the meadow. We did as we were told.

Thresher Day was a big event. Before the combine harvester came on the scene, corn stacks were built in the haggard. That's the name we give to a small enclosure close to the farmyard. With us, it was a wee hard, dry area. We'd park the thresher up close and the corn sheaves would be forked up to two men up on the thresher. They'd cut it and feed it into the machine.

It was a social event. Neighbours would come to help. Our job as kids was to chase mice that would scurry out looking for fresh cover. Our instruction was to stay away from wheels and belts. Any farm is a dangerous place. The day would end with a bonfire to burn the trash. There would be sandwiches and mugs of tea as the men swapped stories and laughed.

I'd say it would have been the mid '60s before there were big commercial suppliers where you could go for feed, but even that was an admission that the weather had beaten you. It was such a precarious business. I remember my father telling me that during the war he had to walk two heifers to a mart in Ballygawley one day. That's eight miles away. He didn't get a bid for them, and had to walk them back home.

His only break from the farm was to drink a few pints on

a Saturday night. While he was doing that Oliver and myself would be around the corner in the Orange Hall. That was our community centre: Cloughfin Loyal Orange Lodge 1277.

My earliest memories of being part of a gang were there. Not a *Bugsy Malone* outfit, but a group where you knew you belonged. For both of us the music quickly became the glue that bound us to the place. To be a part of the band when we were only seven and nine respectively was special.

Robbie Nixon was the man who organised the music. It looked good craic straight away, but the slots for drummers were the first to go. Soon we were directed towards the pipes. Ollie was a more natural musician than me. He would learn the piano at school and much later would play the guitar at home. I made up my mind early I was going to master those bloody pipes.

At first there were 10 of us learning them. Robbie brought a man in from Cookstown to teach us. He was strict enough but we both had an aptitude for it. You needed a bit of staying power as well as lung power. We had that. Over time the 10 became four, including the pair of us.

In those days the Hall was the nerve centre for Protestant social life. Harvest Queen dances came along every few weeks. As we got older Cloughfin was included on the showband circuit at a time when they were sweeping the country, north and south, like wildfire.

When we improved a bit musically as kids we used to be taken around to neighbouring towns to parade and play to raise money, in our tin boxes, for the Hall. There was a buzz to it all. You were on stage and getting a bit of attention. The big deal was to make it to the 12th.

THE FARM

The 12th of July is the Orangeman's big day out. I didn't have a great interest in the historical comings and goings of King William III. I understood the connection, and learned in school all about the Battle of the Boyne, but I was in it for the music and the craic. The 12th was pure, unadulterated craic. Or at least it would be when we were older, when pints were swilling around.

Our first experience of marching on the big day was in the Strabane Parade when I was 10 and Ollie was eight. It was abandoned because of a riot. Missiles were being thrown in by nationalists on top of the Orangemen and the RUC couldn't restore order. It all happened up ahead of us and we were taken back to the cars, and then back home. The adults were all giving out like fuck, but I don't remember being traumatised by it at all. We had ice cream on the way home and got over it. By then I knew there was a 'them and us.' Like lots of things that Dad didn't explain in any depth, that was how it was.

Years later we got another wee glimpse of how temperatures ran high at that time of year. I had married Heather Buckley and we were living near Magherafelt High School, where she was teaching. Along with a few other teachers they were taking a busload of their pupils to France for a week. I went along and brought our own three kids.

There was a lot of ferrying and driving and we covered a fair bit of France. Everyone had a great time. The last leg of the trip was the drive from the ferry in Larne back to the school. It was the 12th. We were driving through Toomebridge, no more than six miles or so from home, when the bus driver warned everyone to take cover. She put the boot down.

Sure enough we came under attack from a crowd who thought

we were an Orange Lodge on the way back from a parade. I dived over to cover Chloe, who was four or five at the time. Windows came in. The driver was hit by a stone. Somehow she managed to keep things under control, skidding the bus to a halt right outside the RUC station. It took a few minutes to restore calm in the bus. The kids would have ranged in age roughly from 12-16. There was no sign of anyone coming out of the station to investigate. Welcome home.

Dad was a fixture with the B Specials by the time our Strabane gig was coming to a premature end. It wasn't exactly a rite of passage but plenty of lads in the Orange Hall would have dads who were B Men. Or the Ulster Special Constabulary, to give them their official name. Depending on your standpoint they were either Unionism's stormtroopers or keepers of the peace. Catholics would have seen them as a Protestant Army. They hated the sight of those dark uniforms. To me they were more Dad's Army, at least the ones my father would go on patrol with.

The B Specials were the support act for the RIC originally and then the RUC. They had been set up in 1920 when the Irish War of Independence was going on. They were disbanded in 1970 on a recommendation from the Hunt Committee, set up to report on policing in Northern Ireland. In between they hadn't exactly covered themselves in glory. By the time the Civil Rights Movement was up and running in the late 1960s the B Specials were on the wrong side of the argument.

They would go on patrol a couple of nights a week, setting up roadblocks, stopping people and asking them their business. If you were a Protestant you would have found this reassuring. If you were Catholic it was a threat.

Many of the Protestant farmers in the locality were a part of it. I'd say there was a fair few of them enjoyed being awkward and causing trouble for Catholics, and another few just along for the spin that got them out of the house. I always had Dad in the second group. There was an allowance of some sort but it wasn't a big deal.

Being a B Special wasn't a topic of conversation around the dinner table. 'You won't believe who we stopped last night!' There was none of that. It was only later, when I started to look back on the madness of the way we were segregated from our neighbours, that I thought about how strange it must have been to be policing the community you lived in. A divided community.

How many times would he have stopped men he would meet at the local mart? How many times were there awkward exchanges with men he knew, to say hello to, in the village? Then he's part of a group of armed, uniformed men stopping the same folks that night, maybe a couple of miles away, on a dark country road? How could you have trust in a set-up like that?

Dad's uniform was hung up in the cloakroom at home. A shade of dark green/black, with a peaked cap. His boots would be sitting beneath them. He'd be shining them any night he went out.

I don't think the B Men received much training, but there would be an army boy along every so often to give them some instruction about what to do if they came under fire. One day Dad brought the Sterling submachine gun home and he showed myself and Ollie how to fire it. We had a barrel set up in the henhouse field and let off a few rounds. We would have been early teens at the most.

Dad told us a story of one night when they were in the B hut, as it was called – where they'd be based before going out on patrol – sitting around the stove. Clements Hutchinson, who was married to our mother's sister, Nora, was one of the group. He was a pretty cool customer, Clements. He took the ammunition clip from his gun and held it in the air.

"What would youse boys think would happen if I threw this into the fire?" he says to the others.

They were looking at him in disbelief. Then he threw the clip in the flames. Boys were falling over each other trying to scramble out the door. Cool as a breeze he picked up a set of tongs and fished the clip back out.

I said to Dad: "He must have had the bullets in his pocket?" He just shook his head.

Dad never got into any scrapes so it didn't present much of a worry to our mother.

He gave it up before the Troubles kicked off.

When the B Specials were disbanded they were replaced by the Ulster Defence Regiment. The B Men would have taken some intelligence with them I suppose, a lot of local knowledge gathered by fair means or foul. The UDR was an altogether more serious outfit. A fair few B Men made the transition from one to the other, which was putting themselves directly in the line of IRA fire. Dad was well past his sell-by date by then. He had no interest.

Tommy Irwin was not a B Man but he joined the UDR, and paid a price. His brother Fred too. Tommy worked as a farm hand with us for years. I remember himself and Fred sitting in to babysit us in the early days when Mum and Dad would be going out for a few hours. Tommy's three sons did a bit of work about the place as well. He was a quiet man, about 12 years younger than Dad.

When my mother was serving up dinner every working day Tommy would have been sitting at our table. Eventually he moved on and took a job with the council at the Treatment Works over in Mountfield, about seven miles from us. He was a part time private in the UDR, so it would have involved at least a couple of nights a week. Being in the UDR made you a target, plain and simple.

One day in March 1986 he was halfway down a service manhole at work when a couple of IRA boys appeared and shot him dead. A year later the East Tyrone division of the IRA attacked an RUC barracks in Loughgall, and walked into an SAS ambush. It was one of the most high profile incidents in the Troubles. Eight of them were killed. One of their weapons recovered on the night had been used to shoot Tommy. I didn't shed a tear.

His brother Fred had died in similar circumstances seven years earlier. He was a member of the local Orange Lodge, the same as us: Cloughfin LOL 1277. Fred also worked for the council in Dungannon. He too knew the risks of being in the UDR. He had received death threats, and used to vary his route to work. But there was no way around the last stretch, along Oaks Road. A few IRA men were waiting for him one day and opened fire. They shot him up so badly his family couldn't view the body. That was the East Tyrone division of the IRA for you.

They were kept busy. When we had been at primary school Ivan Anderson was the teacher for the middle years, and then took over from Master Sloan as Principal. He was shot and killed driving home from school one day in 1987. A prominent

Orangeman, chairman of the local branch of the Ulster Unionist Party, he was also a part-time captain in the UDR. He was shot a few miles from where Tommy Irwin had been murdered.

Willie McKee went the same way. He was the local school-bus driver. His killers had taken over a house at gunpoint to ambush him as he drove past. When that didn't work they hijacked a car and chased him for a mile and half, forcing him off the road near Omagh. Then they shot him. He was a corporal in the UDR.

Some were lucky to get away with their lives. Oliver was on the farm with Dad on a frosty morning in February 1983 when he heard shots ring out up the road. The sound of a shotgun being fired on a farm was nothing unusual, but automatic fire would root you to the spot.

Neighbours of ours, Robbie Gibson and Sammy Managh, were on their way to the mart in Dungannon, as they did most Wednesdays. Both UDR men, their routine was a danger. They came under fire as they drove the cattle truck up the road. They managed to return some fire with the weapons they carried for personal protection. Maybe that's what saved them. In Robbie's case there was the freakish element of having his cheque book in the breast pocket of his shirt. The stub of it took a direct hit from a bullet and changed its course. Both were injured, but survived. Robbie never quite recovered the full use of his arm. His hand was always cold. He would wear a sock on it.

As kids it never dawned on us that our whole society was roughly split down the middle. Before there was any pandemic we were cocooning among our own people. At least those who we were told were our own people. I thought of Catholicism as the Voodoo over the hedge. We weren't encouraged to play with them, not that there was much of a crossover anyway. It was bizarre. My father was a decent man who would help a neighbour regardless of his religion. If it was to bring a beast to market then he'd happily provide the trailer. Or saving some hay, he would help out. That's where it ended though. He picked it up off his parents, and without painting pictures or spelling it out, he passed it on to us.

Heather once told me how sorry she had felt for a Catholic neighbour of ours, the eldest of 12 kids. Because the house was so packed he was shifted up the road to live with the grandfather. There was just the two of them there: the grandfather and this lad of about 14. When she mentioned this to our parents she was told it was none of our business. It was over the hedge. Crack on.

Dad was a Unionist without being passionate about it. A conservative without being a rabid right winger. His sister Rose, who had a more liberal outlook on life, would try and broaden his views a wee bit. She had a grocery shop in Omagh. Between dealing with staff and customers across the religious divide she could see a bigger picture. With Dad though it was fairly small-frame stuff. Farm and family. I think the prospect of exploring beyond what he knew and believed didn't appeal to him. I think there would have been peer pressure as well. It wouldn't have made life any easier to come across as a soft Prod.

There was a fear element to it as well. When I was about 17 I went out a couple of times with a Catholic girl who went to the Convent in Omagh. She worked part time as a waitress in the Royal Arms Hotel in the town. She was lovely, a bit out of my league to be honest. Off my dance card as well, as it turned out. Mum called me aside one day and told me that

Dad had decided the curtain would be coming down on that little show. "He's afraid you'll be shot," she said. "By one side or the other."

We went to separate schools, played different games, mixed in different circles. They had big families. We had small ones. Our parents bought different newspapers. We would subscribe to the *Con*, the *Tyrone Constitution*; they would read the *Herald*. We would see each other every day and pass by without much heed. This started before you even went to primary school – the kids you played with. The primary schools were divided along religious lines. Ours was bang in the centre of the village. The Catholic one was on the outskirts. The schools were close enough for us to hear each other in the playground.

They didn't sound any different to us.

For secondary schools we would share the same school bus, never the same seats. The Prods went to Omagh Academy. The Catholics to the Christian Brothers, or the Convent, nearby.

The seating area would be defined by whoever got on first. If that was a Prod then it was straight down the back and the others would follow suit in dribs and drabs. The same applied to the Taigs. On the way to school in the morning this had a certain rhythm to it, broken if the boy or girl who normally got on first was out sick. Then there might be a swap, but one that followed its own natural order.

On the way home things had the potential to get messy, especially on the later bus which Oliver and I would be taking if we had rugby training after school. But it never got out of hand. There would be the usual horseplay such as firing wee missiles at each other from rubber bands, the kind of thing you'd get on any school bus.

THE FARM

But this was the complete opposite of natural. And it flowed perfectly from what we were taught, or not taught. Did I learn about Irish history in school? Did the Catholics learn about why we felt an allegiance to Britain, why the 12th July was the biggest day on our calendar? We each followed our own path from cradle to grave, which is how the messed-up system was designed.

Elements of it remain unchanged. Unlike the early days in Sixmilecross when there was a whiff of Dodge City on the Saturday night, there are just two pubs there now. It's not so black and white to say one is Catholic and one is Protestant, but there wouldn't be too many customers frequenting both. Ollie would be comfortable in either.

We had so much in common with our Catholic neighbours that we didn't know about, because we didn't mix. For example, we were both battered in school.

In our house we were never pushed academically. But there was enough pressure in the classroom to get things right, partly because our aunt taught there.

The local primary school had six classes spread across three rooms, with three teachers – including Aunt E. The boss man, Master Sloan, was a disciplinarian. Plain and simple. He was the enforcer. I don't think that was peculiar to our part of the world. Strap, cane, grabbing us by the hair – whatever. It was open season, no-holds barred stuff. The real victims were the kids at the back of the class who just kept their heads down to avoid the punishment, which of course didn't work. The more they struggled with the schoolwork the more they got hammered. Later in life I often wondered what kind of scars kids carried from those days when we were supposed to be learning.

I remember Oliver being bashed one day for getting a poem wrong. It was called '*The Sands of Dee*', by Charles Kingsley.

'*O Mary, go and call the cattle home,*
And call the cattle home.
Across the sands o' Dee,
The western wind was wild and dank wi' foam,
And all alone went she.'

Oliver was saying kettle instead of cattle. The more Master Sloan beat him the more he got it wrong. When we got to P7, our last year in the school, he would line us all up against the wall and go round posing maths questions.

"What's 27 multiplied by 6?"

The tension as it crept closer to your turn was gut wrenching. If you got it wrong you got battered. Primary school life was complicated by the presence of Aunt E. My Dad's sister, she was also an Evelyn.

In today's parlance she'd be described as being somewhere on the spectrum. Back then she was just peculiar. She was a spinster and lived in a wee cottage on our farm with Dad's mother. She was in her own little world. Often she would ring our house rather than call around. Her messages tended to be short and to the point. The phone would ring and you'd pick it up.

"Hello."

"There's a storm coming."

End of conversation.

She drove an Austin A40. I don't think it ever got into third gear. Her route was from the farm into Sixmilecross and back. I don't think she ever got as far as Omagh. If you were out in the fields you could hear her coming up the Altamuskin Road into the village. The car would be crying out to go up a gear, but it never happened. It was worse if she was giving us a lift to school. I would sooner have rolled around the henhouse floor than take a lift, but if she called there was no way you could refuse.

You'd be sliding down the seat, trying not to be seen because it was your aunt bringing you to school. Worse again because of the way she drove. There was a railway line that ran across the Strand Brae, into the village, so she'd have to give it an extra bit of poke to get up and over that. We'd be willing the car forward.

"Dear Jesus, don't let us die on the railway line."

Aunt E drove up to Castlerock one evening, which was a big deal. Auntie Rose, my Dad's sister, asked her how she managed the lights.

"What lights?"

The car was dark green. Everything Aunt E wore was some shade of green.

'I close my eyes and picture the emerald of the sea
From the fishing boats at Dingle to the shores of Dunardee
I miss the river Shannon and the folks at Skibbereen
The moorlands and the midlands with their forty shades of green.'

Larry Cunningham had a big hit with that *Forty Shades of Green* record back in the day. He could have been singing it for Aunt E.

She was the original Miss Marple: brogues, tweed skirt, twin set tops, pearls, a hat on Sunday and the handbag carried at an angle.

I think she had been engaged at one stage. It was one of those stories no one ever talked about. She became a bit of a recluse in later life, but she was a kind soul. I think she related to girls more than boys. She didn't have a lot of time for Oliver or me. She would bring Heather on nature walks, down by what we called the Pocket, a long, narrow wee field that was alive with wildflower.

All the fields had names – there was the Bush Field which had a tree in the middle of it; the Stone Field which had a Neolithic rock about six foot high. We had a right few wells on the farm. They were all built with a cover over the top. Inside the cover were all the different ferns, which were beautiful, complete with steps down to them.

Leaving the village school behind and going to Omagh was a blessed relief. To be free of the tyranny was one thing, but the adventure of the bus journey to Omagh, and meeting other kids, was enough in itself. Heather and I were well settled into the relative freedom of the Academy by the time Oliver joined us. His first day was like watching a child opening his presents on Christmas morning. "And we get to do this tomorrow, and the next day?" he said.

This was the big time. Omagh Academy was a co-educational melting pot of townies and rednecks, and a few others thrown in for good measure. Yes, it was more of the same in that it was Protestant, but it was different. My own journey there had been bumpy. The 11 Plus was something that melted my head in primary school. You needed it to lock down your place in grammar school. Otherwise you had to pay.

I was a capable enough kid but I struggled with English and getting my thoughts down on paper in a coherent fashion.

THE FARM

I read back now over my letters to my wife Heather – then my girlfriend and my lifeline – when I was in Argentina, and I wonder what the stress was about. But in school it was an issue.

I feared the worst when it came to the results being delivered. On the fateful day I was looking out for the postman. I was trying to work out was it better to try and intercept him or stay put? Whatever, it was bad news. Dad said he'd stump up the cash to send me to Omagh Academy. I was relieved he didn't make a song and dance about it. Issue sorted. Move on.

We lived fairly simple lives but we didn't want for anything material. Literally, we were comfortable. Most of the farmhouses around the area would have been a good age, passed down through a few generations, but Mum and Dad built a modern bungalow in the early '50s. It wasn't exactly the Southfork of Sixmilecross but it had all the basics, plus a few bells and whistles – like a bath and a washing machine. There would have been plenty of houses that didn't have indoor toilets.

The big events of the year were things we celebrated. If Mum had ever gone on Mastermind then Christmas would have been her specialist subject.

She would rear, dispatch and leave oven-ready a dozen turkeys each year. That's a bit of work. She looked after the presents for us. She sorted clothes, food, and anything else, on top of the farm work she had to do. Christmas Eve was a family outing to Omagh, to see the real Santa Claus. There was only one in those days, and he appeared in Omagh. We all went to JB Anderson's store – they were distant relations too – where there would be a fantastic display with an electric train set running round a big goldfish pond, and Santa was in his big blue sledge. Then it would be down to Uncle Bertie Pollock's store for biscuits, cheese and a massive ham.

By the time the three of us were in Omagh Academy the picture changed. Myself and Oliver were introduced to rugby and athletics, and that took over our lives.

Heather played hockey for the school and immersed herself in that. There was nothing around Sixmilecross to interest her. She gave the dances in the Orange Hall a wide berth. Heather really started to live her life when she left school and went to Belfast to study physiotherapy. I was next to go, heading to Stranmillis to do PE. Then Ollie went to Queen's for agricultural science.

Ollie left that early to take over the farm full-time. It took him a while to get the place running the way he wanted, but from the outset he had some invaluable first-hand knowledge: you run the farm, not the other way around. Get that balance wrong and your life loses its colour.

Without us knowing it we had all learned a lot.

4

The Field

THE FIRST GAME OF RUGBY I EVER SAW WAS with my father. My Uncle Bertie played for Dungannon, and one day he took the pair of us to watch a schools game between The Rainey and Methody College Belfast. I was 10 or 11. Everything about it looked impressive.

I didn't have much to compare it with. Gaelic football was alien to me because it was on the other side of the hedge, soccer I knew a fair bit about, and it was a lot better than that.

I knew very little about what was going on that day. Dad and Uncle Bertie were jabbering away during the game and I didn't ask them too much. There were lots of other lads, older than me, watching it. They all seemed to know exactly what was going on, and who was who.

The initial fascination was around flattening lads on the other team without getting into trouble. You could run as far as you wanted with the ball so long as you didn't get flattened yourself.

You could pass it or kick it or fall over the line with it and score. The other line, not your own – I got that straight away. There was stuff going on around the fringes of the action that seemed crazy, and involved lots of people in the same place at the same time. Understanding that would come later. I couldn't wait to get to big school and actually have a go at it.

In those days that's where everybody started the game. This was before the mini rugby revolution created a new bottom rung in Irish rugby. There was no rugby in primary schools. If you went to a rugby school for second level then you were exposed to it for the first time. If not, then you're next hopping-on point was joining a club when you left school, at 18 or 19. There was no attempt to fill the gap. Youths rugby in clubs had not been invented.

For me, big school would be Omagh Academy. That's where my game kicked off.

I was wracked with nerves on my first day. Part of it was making the jump from the small village primary school, and the farm, to a big deal in the town. I was incredibly naïve. There was a lad, Karl Lipsett, in first year and he seemed to know his way around. With a swagger he looked at me on day one and made the two fingers sign. Like, fuck you pal! He was just being cocky and announcing himself. I hadn't the first clue what that meant.

Mostly my lack of confidence was about having got into the school without my 11 Plus. Basically if you failed it you were a second class citizen.

Its official title was the Qualifying Exam. Or the Qually as it became known. It not only opened the door to a grammar school but it was free passage. Some doors could be opened if you stumped up the fees.

THE FIELD

I remember the day the postman came up the lane with my 11 Plus results. If he had to wedge a fat envelope through the door then it was good news – it would have been stuffed with all sorts of booklets and information. If it was skinny as a rake then it was a Dear John letter. I hadn't been expecting flying colours. In fairness to my father, he accepted the shades of grey without too much fuss. He wrote the cheque. I was put in the C class. Down the back of the plane, a long way from business. I was reminded of my place on a daily basis. The 11 Plus Club had free passes on the bus. I had to pay.

There were three streams in first year. I remember the A and C classes mixed in together for music lessons. It was all about getting in the choir. From my grounding in the Orange Hall I had a feel for music. By then I would have been decent enough on the pipes. I could sing OK and enjoyed it. Some of the lads couldn't hold their breath, never mind a note. I seem to recall the A class pretty much filling all the places in the choir. I didn't get a look-in. My place in Omagh Academy society was set.

Then we started to play rugby. From the first whistle I was stuck into it. I hadn't had my growth spurt yet. I was gangly, but I was strong enough and had confidence out on the field even if I didn't know what I was doing. Neither did anyone else. I could hold my own. Knowing that was a tonic for my self-esteem.

Passing a rugby ball is one of the first skills you learn. For some it remains a mystery throughout their careers. I got it quickly. That opened doors on the field, and in that first year of feeling your way around I had a good touch. So it was a toss-up whether I should go into the forwards or backs.

It was a while before we started playing games against other schools. Our dance card would have been against the likes of Armagh, Portora, Enniskillen, Banbridge and Portadown. There was a top circuit involving the big Belfast schools and a couple from outside, but that wasn't for us. If Ulster schools rugby was a beauty contest then we would have struggled to get on the catwalk.

It didn't bother me in the slightest. I was getting better all the time, and loving it.

The Campsie playing fields used by the school were down by the river. It was a bit of a walk away, and if you weren't pissed on making your way there then you were likely to sink on arrival. It was usually a quagmire. I'd say there wasn't a school in the province who fancied the idea of playing us down there on a shite day. It didn't knock a feather out of me. Better still, I loved seeing other lads struggle with it. I understood early that I wouldn't be dandering around Sixmilecross with schools medals pinned to my chest, but so what?

The whole package of farm life shaped me to play this game. A bit of hardship? I didn't mind getting out of bed early to help with the milking. And in those days you didn't use a tractor to dig out the silage. You used a kind of fork, known as a grape. You cleaned out the byre with a shovel. You dug holes with a spade. You didn't have all the machinery. That hardness – your fingers sticking to pipes in the winter time – that hardness stood to me. That strength. No matter what weights you did you wouldn't have that. It stuck with you into adult rugby. I would have worked on the farm every summer. That was my training ground.

The teachers who influenced me in those years were Jackie Reid, a physical education teacher who had spent many years teaching in Africa, and Dick Hinds, a big rugby man who taught Latin. Both coached Oliver and me. Jackie only arrived to the school in my last few years there but immediately he opened the pair of us up to athletics. Much as I loved rugby from the start, it was athletics that put the notion of representing Ireland in my head.

Jackie got us started on discus and shot putting. Soon he was giving us a discus to take home. We would spend hours perfecting our technique in the stone field. The challenge was two-fold: launch the flying saucer without committing a foul; and land it somewhere other than Planet Cowpat. Fishing it out after a direct hit was a nightmare.

We both represented the school in Ulster competitions, and were good enough to head down to Santry Stadium in Dublin for the nationals. If I was blessed with long arms, strength and a bit of technique then Ollie was better again. He competed at Intermediate to start with, winning the shot in his first year and coming second in discus.

It got him a weekend in Cymbran in Wales, representing Ireland. It might as well have been the Olympics. He was an intermediate socialising with the seniors but he was well able to hold his own on the party front.

The discus was my main event and I was 5cm off winning the title at senior level in Santry while Ollie was at intermediate. I didn't mind the bit about not winning, but when I saw the tracksuit Ollie got I was transfixed. I was just mesmerised by having a uniform that said: 'This cub plays for his country'. I was a long time staring at that crest. Jeepers, that had huge appeal.

So did the craic. Athletics was no use as a team sport but

Ollie and me knocked full value out of it. The best bit was the days out in Santry. Dad brought Ollie down the first year when I hadn't made it, but then Jackie Reid brought the three of us along the following year. It was like a mini tour. Mum naturally would make enough food for an entire team but part of the enjoyment was having a meal in Kealy's Pub in Cloghran, not far from the stadium.

When the competition was over it was about getting home as fast as possible and getting on the monumental pish, over in Omagh Rugby club. I was your standard Irish teenager of 17: drinking pints when I could and courting girls at every opportunity. Supporting the school hockey team helped on the second front. So did driving my father's car. I'd say I was 17 years and 30 seconds old when I got in behind the wheel of his Triumph 2000. Not for the first time, but the first time legally. Farm kids can all drive not long after they learn to walk. Despite all the drink-driving, which no one passed any heed to, my only mishap was being rear-ended one night when I stopped to pick up a pal on the Broad Road, near Ballygawley. The car looked like an accordion after it. I was fine, thankfully, and the other driver was paying the bill.

On the academic side of things I had to work hard for whatever ground I gained. I was conscious of that in first year especially. I kept the head down and got into the B stream for second year. Along with my prowess on the rugby field that did my self-confidence no harm. It also made me feel like I was paying a wee bit back to my parents. Of course I eased off on the books after that.

The craic was always good. Lads like Tom and Ivor Clements – second cousins of mine – Eddie Gibney and Adrian Heuston.

They all contributed to me spending a lot of time laughing. We weren't winning medals on the playing fields but we were world class at enjoying ourselves. In my last year there we had a good side, good hardy boys and lots of them went on to play afterwards in Omagh RFC.

We actually did a bit of doubling up when we were in school, playing a few games for the Accies, one of the adult junior sides in the club, in our final year. There were times you'd play for the school on a Saturday morning and then line out for the club – playing with and against real men – in the afternoon. That was where I met Mickey Harte.

He's from Ballygawley, just over the hill from Sixmilecross. He would have gone to Omagh CBS, but ended up playing a bit of rugby alongside his GAA commitments. In fairness to the club, there was always a decent mix of Catholics and Protestants wearing the jersey. Mickey played on the wing. It was the start of a long friendship where we would swap plenty of coaching notes across the codes. Our family have knocked great craic out of Tyrone's success in the All Ireland.

When they beat Armagh in the final in 2003 it was a special day north of the border. It was the first of three titles in six years, a terrific record for a county who hadn't been mapped for so long. We're still in touch today, I'm glad to say. Mickey is a very sound man, with a great feel for high performance sport.

I made a point of standing my ground in those Accies games, without fully thinking of the consequences of going toe to toe with adults. I got away with it. There would usually be a dance in the club on a Saturday night, so that would be lit up brightly on our radar after a day's sport.

It was no great surprise that I came up short on the O Levels front. I nailed down just two subjects. Dad took me aside and said he'd be happy for me to leave it at that, and get stuck into farming as a career. It was great to have that as a fall-back but I was all about going forward: rugby, college, travel. Like my sister Heather, I needed to escape. But I needed a few A Levels for that, so first I had to clean up the O Level mess by repeating the year. In the heel of the hunt I got good enough grades for a ticket to Stranmillis College for a Certificate in Education course – short of the target, which was a physical education degree, but at least I was on my way.

That seemed like the best choice. Jackie Reid had been encouraging and it suited my talents. I liked the idea of teaching. Jackie had allowed me help out with PE classes for younger kids in the school in my final year, and it had gone well. I could find a balance between keeping control of a group and having a bit of craic. When it came to the interviews for Stran I did well, compensating for a history of ordinary exam results. They liked the idea of having men who were actively involved in sport, teaching PE and coaching teams after school.

There were other attractions for me too: a staff room where there was bound to be some craic and summers free for touring the rugby world. What's not to love about that?

*****

If Omagh Academy was a whole new experience from Sixmilecross then Stranmillis was another life. First off, it was a beautiful setting: about 45 acres of mature woodland in a secure campus near the centre of Belfast. I arrived there in the autumn of 1974, just as the leaves were turning to gold. It was an oasis.

THE FIELD

It's hard to imagine how secure it felt given the madness that was going on around the city. The sound of gunfire, or bombs, or both, was like a soundtrack in the mid '70s. Bizarrely we cracked on without much bother.

I loved that place. Omagh had been co-educational but it wasn't boarding. This was different. It was one long sleepover. The ratio of women to men was about 5:1. It was the challenge of gaining access to the dorm of a good looking girl. It was the challenge of avoiding detection when the morality police came calling. It was the challenge of looking like part of the furniture when the wardrobe door was opened by one of the college wardens and I was wedged inside.

"Oh, hello!"

That was a conversation I had one night with a lady by the name of Beulah Watt. We were all in halls of residence and Beulah was the warden in one of the girls' blocks. It was a grand set-up. Everyone had their own wee room, enough space to swing at least a couple of cats. Access by day was via the front door. Access by night depended on your athletic ability and enthusiasm. I was a good climber. I hadn't great boundaries when it came to safety. And I was keen.

Beulah was a short wee woman, no taller than a few clumps of turf, with firm ideas on following the rules. Having done the hard part – in getting access to the maid's chamber – I was at a loss when Beulah opened the wardrobe door to find me squeezed in like a sardine. I could see the lassie in question over her shoulder, fighting back the laughter and doing her best to look surprised.

"How did he get in there!!"

A few years later the same Beulah would be kind enough

to ring me when I was at a low ebb in Argentina. She went to some trouble to get the number of the hotel in Buenos Aires, and had the patience to persevere until she caught up with me. Calls from home kept me going. It was a lovely touch.

By that stage she was teaching in Friends' School in Lisburn, alongside one Barney McGonigle, a rugby nut who was serving a life sentence to Ulster and Irish under age rugby. Barney had been a few years ahead of me in Stran. He became a good friend.

Stran was also the turbo boost I needed for rugby. Unlike school, rugby was a big deal there. They would put out a handful of teams every week. Rugby there had a profile and playing for the King's Scholars was a big deal in Ulster. The name sounded very grand – originally students would have applied for a King's Scholarship to get in. Being on the first team could get you noticed. It was technically a junior club, but we were good. There were a few big names had passed through the club ahead of me: Stewart McKinney, Ian McIlrath and Roger Clegg all went on to play for Ulster and Ireland. So did Jim Stevenson. Like Ian McIlrath, Jim put in many years on the Ulster branch and the IRFU.

I was physically fit going in the door there. Between farm work and then running up hills with bags of meal on my back I was in very good shape. I'd say there were very few days in my three years in Stran where I wasn't out playing with a ball or doing strength and fitness work. You were surrounded by like-minded people. It was as if we were all on a mission. The college was serious about its role in the education system: to generate a steady stream of teachers keen to coach as well as teach. The motto was *docendo discimus*. By teaching we learn. I liked that.

From the first training session for the rugby club I was in

my element. There were lots of good players. It was my first time mixing with guys who had come through the big rugby schools. Lads like Glenn Aiken from Inst, an Ulster Schools player who had played football for Northern Ireland under 18. Stevie Graham, who went to Dungannon Royal, had also played on the wing for Ulster Schools. Modelling ourselves on the Welsh legends Stevie became JJ, after JJ Williams, and I became Mervyn, after Mervyn Davies. Both had starred for the Lions in South Africa the summer just before we arrived in Stran. I had the moustache, the headband, the long lanky frame. In my head I was Mervyn Davies.

I also had some playing gear to get started. To this day young players climb over each other to get rugby gear. I had an Ulster tracksuit top from my athletics competitions. It didn't specify which code in Ulster sport, just the key word plus the non-negotiable: the Red Hand. I wore it to my first training session in Stran and they thought a messiah was walking amongst them. Well, a high-ranking disciple.

Barney McGonigle wouldn't have been long setting them straight but he would have given me a good report. Barney knew everyone and everything that moved on the rugby scene in Ulster. After the arrival of the internet I christened him Google, for his treasure trove of information. He was fully involved in the college as well. We both played a bit of basketball there, and Barney would drive the minibus for our jaunts to venues far and wide across the province.

It's funny, but despite my near obsession with rugby the game that stands out in my memory was a dodgy night playing hoops in Limavady. We had a decent enough team. I had good hands, long arms and sharp elbows. And I could get up and down that court all day. I think we were expected to fold early but we played really well, spurred on by the rising temperature among the locals. By the time the fourth quarter started we were in the lead and getting stronger. Limavady would be roughly a 50-50 split between Protestant and Catholic, but it didn't feel like many Prods were in the hall that night. It had a hard edge.

Basketball in theory is non-contact. As the locals became more agitated about the scoreboard things cut up rougher. No problem boys: welcome to my world! We won the game on the buzzer and things were boiling over by then. The next target was to get to the bus in one piece. I agreed with Barney that when we were leaving as a group he should slip out ahead of us, get the bus started up and reverse it close to the door.

The row kicked off as we were heading for the exit. As the biggest man on our team I was the mother hen, minding the chicks on their passage to safety. Literally I was swinging, with my back to the door, as the rest of the team barrelled through it. Then I raced out after them to see the bus pulling away slowly and the door left open for me. Sprinting was never my forté but I was out one door and in the next like a scalded cat.

On nights like that, bus trips were the best of craic. We laughed and sang all the way back to Belfast, dropped our gear off and got out on the pish. As students it was mostly about swilling pints and having a laugh. Gathering souvenirs along the way was important too. For example there is still, I hope, some shrubbery in the beautiful grounds of Stranmillis that started out life over in the University of Ulster in Coleraine. They used to host a universities and colleges rugby tournament there every year. Making another hasty escape from there one night I got

Barney to stall the bus while we liberated some plants to bring home to Stran. On the way back the weather took a bad turn and the wipers were struggling. I climbed out onto the roof rack and tried to manually operate them from there while Barney ploughed ahead. We had got to the intersection of what is now the M2, below Ballymena and Antrim, before I got back inside, soaked to the skin but feeling very little pain. We would have sorted a stash of beer as part of the logistics of the trip. Drive on Barney.

On our triumphant arrival back at base I fished out the pipes and led the group, minus my clothes, on a musical parade around the grounds. I was like the Pied Piper. I think the college authorities looked on me as missing a few links upstairs, but overall being good for morale. For me, I suppose I was savouring every moment of my new-found freedom. I'd say the first person to get a hold of my head was Jimmy Davidson.

My first contact with Jimmy D was when he was coming off a pitch in Omagh Showgrounds after a game for Dungannon. I was getting his autograph. He was an Ulster star at the time, a big attraction to myself and a few pals. He taught Geography in Dungannon Royal. His move to lecture in Stran coincided with my arrival there in '74. The planets were aligning. This man would be my mentor.

Jimmy Davidson was the hardest man on the face of planet Earth. He recognised pain all right, and he respected it. It was just when it arrived, screaming through his nerve endings, he parked it. He would never let it put a halter on him. He was astonishing.

Jimmy turned up for his first lecture in Stran in shorts and a t-shirt, absolutely ripped. There wasn't much body fat testing going on in those days, but facing a test wouldn't have kept him awake at night. He called me up in front of the class one day to use as a guinea pig. When I say class I mean the Magnificent Seven. There were only seven of us on the certificate course – a fraction of the number doing the degree. I think they did away with the lower course altogether soon after we graduated. Anyway, Jimmy told me to strip down to my underwear. I'm not sure if this is how lecturers nowadays go about establishing the difference between endomorph, ectomorph and mesomorph shapes, but back then nobody passed any heed. I was in decent nick so I didn't mind. As it happens I was somewhere between ecto and meso: lean and muscular but struggled to gain weight.

Between practical sessions on the field or in the gym, along with training and playing for the King's Scholars, I saw a lot of Jimmy. It was an interesting experience having one of your lecturers lining out alongside you on a matchday, as Jimmy did on tour. It only added to my motivation to impress him. If he gave you some praise then it was like an adrenaline shot. If he gave out to you then you were desperate to fix things straight away. He had a great ability to read things on the field and give simple instructions to follow.

And Jeepers he could put up with any amount of punishment. As a wing forward there was always going to be a bit of pain. That said, on the Ulster club scene he was giving more than receiving. I think he would have liked to be more a Fergus Slattery model – a tall, top of the ground player – but he didn't have that height. Instead he developed a hugely powerful physique and was an expert around the tackle.

In my second year there we went on tour to British Columbia.

I was a few months past my 20th birthday. It was my first time on a plane. I struggled to sleep with excitement the night before we flew out of Belfast. I didn't sleep much for the next three weeks either.

Touring in those days was about getting back what you put in. Jimmy had instilled in us the importance of respecting our hosts. And the power of song. That was massive. Pity he wasn't looking after the school choir in my Omagh Academy days. Genuinely it's a powerful tool. We would have a repertoire we sang post-match, which our hosts loved as much as we did. It would finish with Jimmy's routine from Snow White and the Seven Dwarves, leading us out to the bus, walking on his knees. We followed dutifully, singing along: *Heigh-ho, heigh-ho, it's off to work we go.*

We'd sing on the bus. Music lifts the spirits. When you'd be half dead with a hangover, having arrived back in the nick of time from a very late night, you could be called upon to pipe up. It was our medicine. I couldn't get enough of it.

By the next year I was getting picked for the Ulster junior side. They made me captain. Jimmy of course was a veteran of five Ireland Tests, but his career there seemed to be over. His last cap had been against the All Blacks in 1973. Opportunity was about to knock again.

Ireland were touring New Zealand and Fiji in 1976: seven games in NZ and then sign off in Fiji on the way home. Shay Deering and Stewart McKinney were selected as the only two specialist flankers. That's a heavy workload for two men.

"I'll be going on this tour," Jimmy told us as it was leaving without him.

"Right, OK," we said.

"I've got my clock changed to Kiwi time and I'm training during the night so when I get to New Zealand I'm ready to go."

"Right, OK."

Sure enough, half way through, Shay Deering got absolutely melted. Tour over for him. Jimmy had the bag packed, ready to go. His flight had a few stops along the way. In Hong Kong he was running up and down the apron, getting some speed work in, waiting for the next leg of the journey to take off. The other passengers thought he was insane. Jimmy arrived in New Zealand ready to hit the ground running.

He got there in time to watch the Canterbury game, a filthy affair where Ireland were well beaten. McKinney had his nose broken and six stitches over his eye courtesy of Canterbury prop Billy Bush.

Jimmy decided on the spot to write an assessment of what needed to be fixed. It ran to many pages. He shoved them under the door of coach Roly Meates's room that night. With Deering gone, McKinney had taken over as pack leader. Tom Grace, a senior player at the time, approached McKinney soon after.

"Jaysus McKinney," he said. "Could you not control your man for fuck's sake!"

McKinney knew better than anyone that wouldn't be happening. Southland, down in Invercargill, was the next game – Jimmy's first on the trip. As McKinney recalls:

"That was my first day leading the pack, and beforehand I brought the forwards into the showers and told them to take off their shirts. Everyone had been badly striped by that stage from stamping.

"'I never took this in South Africa two years ago and I'm

fucked if I'm taking it now,' I told them. 'I'm going to start a fight today.'

"Pa Whelan got a bit carried away and he kicked Jimmy accidentally in the head at a ruck. Nearly took his ear off.

"'Jimmy that's serious – you'll have to go,' I told him.

"'I didn't come 10,000 fucking miles for five minutes on a rugby pitch!' Jimmy said.

"He was back on the field five minutes later with great swathes of bandages. We won 18-3."

Jimmy had 13 stitches down the side of his head, running roughly north-south. The next week they were travelling back from training on the bus when the team for the Test was read out. When Jimmy heard his name he jumped up to punch the air in delight. There was a baggage rack running overhead and he whacked his head on it. That gave him another 12 stitches running roughly east-west. When they bandaged him up again he looked like Vincent van Gogh, only worse. Did it bother him? Did it fuck! He had an obsession with the All Blacks. He had an obsession with rugby. This trip could restart his international career.

Much as I loved Stranmillis the idea was to leave it one day. Via the front gate. That meant passing exams. My history on that front over the years, from the 11 Plus to O Levels, had been a saga.

I never considered myself slow but I wasn't exactly quick to join the dots between hard work and getting good results. If you were offering me a choice between a good time now and maybe a better time later on I was pushing the button on the first option.

There were a couple of essays that were deal breakers. One

of them was titled 'To be in authority, or to be an authority.' Right. My first effort at putting manners on the distinction failed miserably. The more I looked at it the more I couldn't see the wood for the trees. Along came Ian Grimason. My saviour.

Grimi was from Portrush. Unlike me, soldiering along on the certificate course, he was with the elite in degree land. He played on the college third XV and I gave them a dig out one day when they were stuck in an important match. We became pals after that. The rugby teams used to train over in Shaws Bridge, on a Wednesday afternoon, and Grimi would squeeze me into his Riley Elf – a cool wee motor that was a bit bigger than a mini. How did a student have a car like that? Because he had worked his backside off in Atlantic City on his first summer at college, saved up, and got the second hand runaround when he got back. That level of organisation and planning was beyond me.

Just as the essay issue was beginning to melt my head, Grimi was badgering me to go to a dance on campus one night. Normally I would have been top of the queue.

"I can't, if I don't get this essay done I'm out on my ear," I told him.

"What essay? Show me…."

He took the jumbled mess I had offered up the first time and straightened it out.

"Did they not teach you structure in Fivemiletown or Sixmilecross or wherever you're from?"

I had to suck it up. He worked a minor miracle. We made the tail end of the dance as well. I strutted in like John Wayne the next day and submitted the essay. It came back without any red lines through it. Grimi went on to become vice president of a school in Glengormley. Many years later, after retirement, he took up a job in retail with Marks & Spencer where coincidentally he was working alongside my wife, Heather. I was collecting her one day when she called him over.

"Heather," I said. "This is the man who saved my teaching career!"

If Grimi helped get me into the race then it was Ken Reid who fired the starting gun. He offered me a job in Grosvenor, where he was headmaster. Ken was another big rugby man, whose career path would take him through Ulster to manager of the Ireland team and then president of the IRFU. It was all sorted. I had a job. And I had a rugby target: get into the Dungannon back row between McKinney and Jimmy D, and ride that baby all the way to Ravenhill and the Red Hand.

5

The Red Hand

TOWARDS THE END OF MY TIME IN STRANMILLIS, in 1977, I was included as a travelling reserve for the Ulster senior side heading over to play Bègles Bordeaux. Playing for the Ulster juniors was on a different track to the senior outfit. You'd be codding yourself if you thought one opened the door to the other. So I was jumping about the place when I got the call. There was very little chance of me playing, but just to be in the mix – and to get a wee trip out of it – was a real feather in my cap. I remember sitting beside Colin Patterson, from Instonians, on the flight over. He was already a highly rated scrumhalf but hadn't been capped yet for Ireland.

"If you don't mind me asking, what's your plan?"

"My plan?" he says.

"Yeah, I mean how far do you see yourself going in the game?"

"I'll be a British Lion."

Jeepers, OK. Colin was a pretty determined character. He had been picked along with Alistair McKibben to play for Ulster when the two of them were on the Instonians seconds team. I never heard of that before or since. It caused consternation in the club. To have a player on the seconds leapfrog the guy on the firsts to play with Ulster? Instonians continued picking Willie Oakes on the senior club side. Ulster kept picking Colin on the interpro side. He kept his head down and ploughed on, which was a real test of his character. Sure enough he was on the Lions tour to South Africa three years later with all the biggest names in the home countries. Given the shit he had to put up with I was delighted for him. Sadly, a knee injury on that trip would kill his career. The timing was cruel because he remembered Mike Gibson telling him at the outset that the first target was to get through two seasons without being turfed overboard.

"By that stage you'll have been to the other big grounds in the Five Nations and got a feel for things," Gibson told him. "Then you'll be able to settle in and enjoy it."

Colin had just completed that two-season introduction when he was away with the Lions. One busted knee later and both Ulster and Ireland had lost a very good little operator.

So I'm sitting on the bench in Bègles, with Colin's career plan still registering in my brain. Next thing Stewart McKinney is in trouble with what looks like at least one broken finger. You can tell it's killing him but he's sucking it up. If this plays out then I will come on and win my first cap for Ulster.

I'm trying to process all this information. Subs don't often get a run. Lads don't like coming off injured, which is the only way for subs to get on. But McKinney is struggling. He gets the fingers strapped and cracks on.

Jesus Stew, could you not have walked? Afterwards he danders over to me.

"Well, did you think I was going to come off and give you a cap that easy?"

I wasn't sure what to say, apart from not looking stupid and saying yes.

"You will *earn* your first cap for Ulster. And you will earn it the hard way."

He wasn't messing around. If he had pointed to the Bay of Biscay I would have swum home without question.

The fact that Ulster were not exactly shooting the lights out in those days didn't matter. Your province was your province, and Ulster meant a huge amount to everyone who played club rugby in that part of the country. I just wanted to wear the jersey. I was fascinated by the Red Hand emblem, which dates back hundreds of years to the O'Neill clan who once ruled Ulster. Northern Ireland being the place it is, the Red Hand has been claimed by both sides to suit themselves.

For me it's convenient that it's common to both Tyrone GAA and Ulster Rugby. *Dextra Dei* in Latin: the right hand of God. It was a symbol of power and protection. On good days at Ravenhill you'd hear the cry 'For God and Ulster.' Leinster have a harp on their chests. Not really what you're looking for, is it?

Dungannon would be my launch pad. The transition from Stranmillis to the club was smooth and well mapped out. Omagh was my local club, where I had done my socialising and carrying on when I was growing up, but Dungannon was the nearest senior club to us. They brought me on tour to America when I was leaving college. That was a bonus. The prospect of playing in the same team as McKinney and Jimmy D was like a dream come true for me. It worked on two levels: the buzz of being involved in a good club side who had great pride in being Tyrone men and the profile it gave me towards selection for Ulster.

There was a fair bit of hero worship from me for McKinney. If Jimmy D was the straight and narrow then Stew was the sideroads, with a bit of cross country thrown in. He was the wild side. He was dangerous, and I loved that about him. I knew by then I had my own difficulties with boundaries. McKinney recognised that straight away and took me under his wing. That didn't mean curbing my mad tendencies. It just meant company. We were a potent combination.

Stewart McKinney is a horse of a man. I don't think anyone or anything scares him. He would be up for everything and would remain utterly without regret if it went arseways. McKinney's code does not allow for complaining. He's had a brain haemorrhage. His sight is badly affected. He's had a broken marriage, a few legal issues, his fair share of assorted setbacks. At one stage in his career he was vice principal of one of the biggest primary schools in the UK. At another point he was kicking his heels on freezing winter mornings on one of London's broadways, queuing for work on a building site.

Stew was at the tail end of his representative career as mine was starting out. He went out of his way to teach me valuable lessons in surviving on a rugby field. Off the pitch he never slowed down. We did a fair bit of drinking together. Pints on a Sunday afternoon were especially enjoyable.

One time we were nicely settled in the York Hotel on Botanic Avenue. McKinney was just back from Bermuda where he'd been playing in some tournament. He brought back a bottle of 151 proof rum. It was rocket fuel. Who walks in the door only the bould Alex 'Hurricane' Higgins, the Belfast hustler. Snooker's original wild child. He was playing in the Irish Professional Championship the next day, and was loosening up with a few drinks. Higgins comes straight over and looks Stew, the British and Irish Lion, in the eye.

"I believe you're a good drinker?'

"Yeah I can drink."

"I'll put you under the table."

I went out to the car to get the rum. They started drinking half pints of Guinness topped up with the rum. Soon enough I could see McKinney wavering a bit. The next thing Higgins fell over. He was blessed he didn't break his skull the way he landed. I put him over my shoulder and carried him outside while the barman called a cab. He was just skin and bone. It was like carrying a wee bag of spanners. Stew had tickets to go to the snooker the next day in the Ulster Hall. Higgins is signing autographs as he walks in, and spots him straight away.

"Fuck you! I lost the first seven frames this morning because of you… So where are we going tonight to drink the rest of that stuff ?"

The truth of it was there wasn't much to like about Higgins.

McKinney actually did him a big favour once but steered clear of him thereafter. It was when Stew was in London, working with John Murphy & Sons, the big building contractors. John Murphy, the boss man himself, wanted Higgins for a gig in the Forum, a massive dancehall in Kentish Town. Murphy and McKinney went to see Higgins play one night and he was so bad the promoter wouldn't pay him. The fella who Higgins had with him to look after the business end of things started to cry.

"Are you going to pay him or not?" Murphy asked the promoter.

"No, I'm not."

"Well my name is John Murphy, and I'm going to make a phone call, and I'll have 200 Irish labourers in here and they'll wreck the place."

Higgins got paid. Himself, Murphy and McKinney then went to a pub called the Spotted Dog, on the other side of Camden Town. Higgins started playing pool and tried to hustle Murphy for the gold pen in his breast pocket. Murphy had saved his bacon an hour earlier and here was Higgins, busy trying to rip him off.

Stew's sign-off with Ulster was against the touring All Blacks in 1978. Munster had beaten them the previous week, and then Ireland had gone close at the weekend. They weren't even halfway into the tour so they were desperate not to get another blot on their copybook. We were poor that day. Well beaten, which was a pity for McKinney as he never subscribed to the idea that the All Blacks started every game with it half won.

When it came to the Test match, Billy Bush, who McKinney had plenty of previous form with, started the game with his knee heavily bandaged. At the first opportunity McKinney shoed the fuck out of him, with the knee as his bullseye. Instead of running off to take cover, he bent over with a message.

"Billy, that's for last week. We'll start again now."

At the next lineout Ian Kirkpatrick went to number one and Billy came to mark McKinney at the tail. It was clear what was coming. Willie Duggan turned to McKinney and said in a loud voice, "Stew, I think you're fucked."

"Willie, I think I am."

"Well he's fucked as well if he touches you."

That had the desired effect. Bush went back to the front of the lineout and Kirkpatrick came back to the back.

Willie Duggan was a good man to have in your team.

Ulster were not a dominant force when I got into the side but we were always better if McKinney was on board. I inherited some of his willingness to put up with pain. That started with my first cap, against Yorkshire in 1978. I needed to take deep breaths to calm down when I was named in the team. My only problem was a worsening cauliflower ear that afflicted a fair few scrummaging forwards. One medic who looked at it was fairly frank: "Jesus, you've got a deformity there Willie."

We had a scrummaging session early in the week of the game which left me in a bad way. I went to hospital the next day and they gave me a local anaesthetic. Then they put a kind of foam down the side of my ear and sewed my ear around it. The idea was to stop it bursting open when the friction started. When it came to match day I was a mix of nervous anticipation about realising my dream of playing for Ulster, and worry about the state of my ear. I had so much strapping around my head I looked like Jimmy D in New Zealand a couple of years earlier.

At the first scrum I was focusing hard on getting my bind and body position right, trying to not to think of what was coming. Sweet Jesus it was the worst pain I've ever endured. Like a red hot poker being wedged to the side of your head. The only way I could scream was if it was related to something else. Like a roar of anger. Except it was a friendly against Yorkshire and we were going fine. I had been nervous about being off the pace on my first run at that level, but once I got my second wind I was grand. Except for the bloody deformity on the side of my head.

The coaching set-up back then wasn't great. Cecil Watson was the man when I arrived and he was replaced by Willie John McBride. You'd be mesmerised listening to Willie John speak in the changing room, but he was a player and a leader, not a coach. Our sessions were mostly running up and down the pitch in Ravenhill, stopping for exercises on the 25, then the half way, then the far 25. The tactical side of things remained a foreign language.

After Ulster lost to Connacht in Galway in 1983/84 – our first defeat in the fixture in almost 20 years – something had to change. The chat on the journey home was that Willie John would be stepping down. Sure enough, he was replaced by Jimmy D.

The process of change was gradual but the impact was immediate. I had a fair idea what to expect from being exposed to Jimmy in Stran. By 1984/85, his first year at the helm, I was a lot surer of my ground than those early days under Cecil. Jimmy always saw provincial rugby as a model that could work wonders for Ireland, if only the provinces could get a few more games. Back then the staple diet was the Interpro Championship – the be all and end all – spiced up with a few games against Scottish districts or English counties. Or tours, both incoming and outgoing. It wasn't a lot to sustain you so his attitude was to make the most of every moment. So, get fit, figure out what we wanted and then focus on it. We wanted the picture he painted: Club Ulster.

Jimmy's arrival came as Leinster were on autopilot, winning a record five interpro titles in a row. Under Mick Doyle they had got themselves sorted out. He was a refreshing change for them. They always had good players but Doyle repackaged what it meant to wear the Leinster shirt. He was rewarded in spades.

Jimmy's approach had bits in common with that, but, naturally enough, was more scientific. Doyler was good craic but there was a fair bit of spoof about him. You just didn't get that with Jimmy.

Also he had a big advantage when it came to identity. Ulster are unique among the four provinces given our political history. The Ulster rugby team became a symbol of an embattled corner of Ireland. Well, one half of it anyway. We were conscious of being a good news story when there was so much muck and bullets flying around.

It helped that Jimmy D inherited Davy Irwin as captain. Knowing him from Queen's, Jimmy understood his good fortune. I had become close to Davy through the Argentina experience so I knew what he was like under pressure. He was every bit as passionate about Ulster as I was. He understood Jimmy's vision. He could see this had the potential to be something bigger than a collection of footballers.

Davy was from a family of high achievers, academically, and he was articulate. He could hold a room. And he was hard as nails. He could have hopped into the back row, no problem. I would be his vice-captain. We would refer to each other as 'C' and 'VC.'

The first thing on Jimmy's to-do list was to park club loyalties at the door. There was always some bit of bad blood on the go between a couple of clubs. I'd have got into plenty of scrapes, verbal or physical, so Jimmy impressed on me the need to embrace this change. It would have been a harder sell if the prospects weren't so rosy, but Jimmy knew he had the makings of a very good squad. He got to work straight away with very demanding standards in fitness, and complemented it with building our identity. Ultimately that would be about Ulster being the best in Ireland, and good enough to worry anyone else who knocked on our door.

He was blessed to have a clutch of talented lads coming through Queen's University where he was coaching the side. Derek Aldred had been coach there before Jimmy moved up from Stran, and had done a good job.

There was a seam of talent running through the team. So Kenny Hooks, Nigel Carr, Trevor Ringland, Davy and his brother Alan, Philip Matthews, Chipper Rainey, Rab Brady, Brian McCall – they were all part of a fine Queen's team and they all brought quality to the set-up.

Nigel was a very impressive player, an impressive man. It was funny, Regent House would have been on the edge of the schools rugby solar system but they produced two guys in the one team – in the same area of the one team – who would become stars for Ulster and Ireland. What were the chances of getting a Nigel Carr and a Philip Matthews in the same wee place at the same time?

I remember one day the pair of them came to train with me, just the three of us. There was plenty of that going on behind the scenes that I don't believe the other provinces were doing.

Nigel got on the treadmill and he started doing miles: first one was 4.58, then he gets off for 5 minutes. Next was 4.59; he gets off for 5 minutes. Next one was 5.00; he gets off for 5 minutes. The last one was 5.01. And I said fuck me. This guy used to run with weights in his socks and leave lads for dead. He was phenomenally fit. Nigel set a savage standard. I remember one day at an Ulster session we were the last ones left doing a bleep test. We got to 146 and collapsed.

I was nuts about being the fittest forward in Irish rugby. When New Zealand toured here in 1978, Graham Mourie was their captain. They were training in Bangor one day ahead of playing us in Ravenhill. I was talking to their liaison guy and he said Mourie wouldn't be playing in the Ulster game but he was training away OK with the squad. According to your man this was his routine. He stood on the goal line, sprinted to the halfway line, and then he jogged to the other goal line. And he did that 50 times. So, of course, I started doing the same thing. After a few years of trying I still couldn't get past 48.

The quality of conditioning in the Ulster squad before Jimmy took over was woeful. With the younger crew driving new standards, that changed. That allowed him to focus on the tactical and team-building stuff. He got players to start analysing their own performance. Keith Crossan for example had become an experienced Ulster player, having served under two coaches, before anyone actually coached him. Jimmy questioned him about the usefulness of a left winger being unable to kick properly with his left foot. He explained to him that he could get even quicker if he stopped trying to take such long strides. Keith was quick and brave and thought those two tricks would be enough.

Jimmy's routine for home matches was to gather us all at Stranmillis a couple of hours before kick-off. He would have a video presentation, and then he would have a wee message for each individual. It was more about what you could bring to the group and how highly he valued that contribution. Everyone left that session feeling better about themselves. Once we got to Ravenhill then he'd gradually fade into the background and let Davy and me do our thing.

A lot of my approach was predicated on savagery, plain and simple. I wasn't alone. That's how rugby operated. One day in Musgrave Park I took our outhalf Ian Brown aside before the game. I was like the racehorse owner and he was the jockey, getting his riding instructions. A lovely, dinky wee footballer, Bruno was very popular in the squad – partly because he was great craic, and partly because he was a matchwinner.

He came late to the Ulster side but made up for lost time. Himself and scrumhalf Rab Brady were parachuted in as halfbacks in the wake of the defeat by Connacht under Willie John. They would have fitted in your saddle bags, one on each side, steering you around the course. For Bruno the drop goal was his party piece. He sickened more opponents playing for Malone than even he can remember. I still have a vision of him dropping two – one in the first and the other in the second half of injury time – in a cup tie between Dungannon and Malone at Stevenson Park. The Reverend Des McCreery, a staunch Dungannon man, had done the honours at Bruno's wedding. He had christened their kids. As I was hurling abuse at Bruno on the way off the pitch the Rev Des was asking his forgiveness for wanting to join in with me.

Bruno's most important drop goal for Ulster saved us one day against Leinster in Ravenhill. It was the Centenary interpro between the teams, so there was even more riding on the result than normal. I don't know how long the ref played into injury time but the Leinster lads were very pissed off about it. When Bruno dropped the goal it was as if time stood still while we all waited to see if it was going over. As it sailed between the posts Willie Duncan already had Bruno picked up by the legs and was running up the field with him. Bruno, triumphant, arm in the air, saluting the crowd.

"For God and Ulster!"

Every time I came up against Donal Spring at Munster or big Mike Gibson at Leinster my plan was to try to beat them up. Plain and simple. They were in my way and I had to get past them. It was easier to get after Springer because with Munster it was always a war. It was a case of: Gentlemen, choose your weapons. Leinster usually wanted to play rugby. So for this mission to Munster I was going straight for the jackpot. It didn't really matter that I liked Springer. A few years later, having swallowed a rake of pints after playing Munster, he came back and kipped in the house I was sharing around the corner from Ravenhill. But this was business.

"If we win the toss we're kicking off," I said to Bruno. "If you don't get the ball into touch straight away then the next time you get it I want a lineout as deep into their half as you can get it."

Bruno obliged. Packie Derham, the Munster hooker, had barely let the ball out of his hand when we just whaled into the Munster forwards. The plan was no more sophisticated than to attack the man opposite you. I looked at the state of Springer when the dust settled and reckoned we had made a good start. Marker laid down.

The beauty of any away game was the bus trip. It's a wonder how we never came to more grief given the stuff we got up to. The most dangerous was the time we lost a player out the emergency window, somewhere on the road between Jedburgh in the south of Scotland and our team hotel.

The thought of arriving in the same clothes as we wore getting on board was an alien concept. It could be fishing a teammate's underwear from a refuse sack – which you would then have to wear – or a Little and Large fashion show. Bruno and second row John Rogers were a match made in heaven when it came to the second option.

On this particular bus trip, himself and Long John had been despatched to the on-board bathroom on our fancy bus to swap clothes for the catwalk. Bruno had managed to get John's gear on first and then came out looking like he was caught up in a tent. But something had gone wrong. He seemed panicked. Davy Irwin was sitting straight opposite the toilet door. I can see him looking at Davy with his hands turned upwards, empty.

"He's gone. John's gone"

"You what?"

"He's gone. John's gone!"

Davy hopped into the cubicle to confirm the news, and then runs out shouting to stop the bus. In the struggle to fit into Bruno's boy-sized clothes John fell against the emergency door as the bus went around a corner. So long John!

We ran back along the side of the road, calling his name.

"Jesus, he must be dead!" someone says.

"I'm not fucking dead!" came the reply from further down the road.

John said the sweetest sound he ever heard was the noise of the bus braking. We found him limping along like the Wile E Coyote after another explosive episode with the Road Runner. Buck naked, he was blessed it didn't happen on a motorway. Everyone was falling about the place laughing as he struggled back on board, to wild applause. He was picking bits of gravel and tarmac out of his backside for weeks afterwards. We called him Rawhide. He went to get checked when we got home and the doc couldn't believe the story. I think it became the standard in Scotland after that to put a bar across the emergency windows in buses.

*****

Success with Jimmy D was like travelling first class after being bumped up from economy. He wanted to lay down a marker. And who bounced up the Ravenhill Road in November '84 only the Wallabies, chasing their Grand Slam goal of beating Ireland, England, Scotland and Wales. In keeping with the ambush that awaited them the weather was pure pish. Jimmy D, only settling into the job, was rubbing his hands.

"This is not their kind of night boys."

He got that right. It was so bad the only thing good about it was knowing your opponents hated it more than you. There was a lot of value in that. I remember feeling so happy and proud for Nigel who was playing his first game for Ulster in 18 months, after massive knee issues. He typified the kind of work ethic Jimmy wanted to promote. I can't remember much about the game aside from the fact that even when we were 13-6 down in the second half they didn't look comfortable and we didn't feel rattled. In the end it came down to Chipper Rainey kicking a penalty conceded by the star of their tour, David Campese. Bruno had chipped away with a couple of penalties to get us back in the game, helped by the crowd, but this needed a bigger boot.

Many years later Barney McGonigle told me he had just

got back from England with an Ulster Schools side he was managing, and made a beeline for Ravenhill the moment they landed. They got there just in time to see Chipper land the kick that won the game. Can you imagine the impression that would leave on a teenager?

A week later we had Leinster in Ravenhill. They were reigning champions, going for a record eighth win in a row over us. History was going to be made one way or another. Over the years we had won 43 games, they had won 43 and 11 had been drawn. We got after the Leinster pack that day and drove them out the Clock End of Ravenhill. We followed soon after, on the pish in a big way, celebrating the start of something special.

On it went. There were changes in personnel but anyone who came into the set-up understood what they were signing up for. If Leinster had set the bar pretty high then we raised it another few notches. Kicking off with that win we went 28 games unbeaten in the interpros, until Leinster caught up with us nine years later. It was the most rewarding time of my rugby life as a player. We felt we could win every game we played. Because we had confidence in our fitness we made a point of playing to the final whistle. It was a mantra: the last minute is as important as the first. I had a 'Turbo!' call that I'd holler sometimes going into the last 10 minutes of a game, and every man had to raise the tempo of his game, mentally and physically. There were times I'd call it knowing that the opposition understood it as well as us. We would celebrate every win like it was our last. Jeepers, I loved that craic.

You could pack the Ulster experience away in three drawers: the interpro series to establish Ireland's best province, the challenge of big touring teams coming to Ravenhill and then us going on the road. A key to the middle bit was the start of Friday night rugby at Ravenhill. Tommy Lindsay was president of the Ulster Branch in 1982/83 when the decision was made to install floodlights. They were a godsend. Suddenly the door opened to Ulster playing on a Friday night, so supporters could come along to watch us without interfering with their club commitments on a Saturday afternoon. When Jimmy took over and the results ramped up it was just added value. Friday night was a big deal. It fitted perfectly with the Club Ulster ideal. It was about building the brand before we knew that was even a thing. So we had to send touring teams away with their arses in a sling. Beating Australia was the biggest statement we made, but over the years we managed an impressive list: Canada, Samoa, Italy and Fiji as well as some high profile provinces like Wellington.

When it came to exploring pastures new we went to the likes of Italy and France as well as our regular visits to England and Scotland. We even went to Zimbabwe. In 2009 McKinney put together a priceless book called *Voices From The Back of the Bus* where he got contributors from all over the world to share special memories of life on the road. Ulster's own Stevie Smith, a quiet but hilarious man who I had the honour of playing alongside, provided the following snippet from that trip to Africa: '*Travelling across the highlands on another interminable bus journey we happened across an army roadblock in the middle of nowhere. Being from the North we were well used to this but, nevertheless, in a foreign country ... you never quite know. There was a definite air of tension as an Idi Amin-like officer boards the bus, demanding to see our papers. To his eternal credit Jim Stevenson, our tour manager, leaped to his feet and welcomed the officer on board, presenting him with a tour brochure and commemorative plastic keyring – a must for any modern Marxist freedom fighter! To this day it intrigues me what might have happened to that keyring. Did the officer throw it away, show it to his mates in the pub, or is he perhaps still driving around Bulawayo with it dangling from his ignition?'*

The tour that set the bar sky high though was Romania. It was on Willie John's watch, a couple of years before Jimmy took over. It was so awful it became the gold standard in character-building experiences. An iron curtain country under the rule of a madman like Nicolae Ceausescu would be nobody's idea of craic. But it was monumental. From the moment we touched down in Bucharest to the uplifting feeling as the wheels left the ground 10 days later, it was us against them.

We weren't the first Ulster side to go to Romania. Portadown College went there in the late '70s for a wee tour. When I heard that I wondered about the shock it must have been to their system. It was a credit to their rugby coach and mentor, Jack Mulligan, who ran the PE department in the school. What a great way to show kids the other side of life.

Romania was an awful place.

Miles and miles of fertile countryside, full of crops, and no chance of a decent meal. The image of old women slaving away in the fields, with no machinery to be seen, stayed with me. Most of the shops were open but had virtually nothing to sell. The ones with food had queues that snaked around corners. Everyone smoked like they would never see another packet of fags, and drank like it was last orders in the only saloon in town. Why? Because it was allowed. The beer was cloudy and smelt like it came from a waste pipe. But if you had the stomach it took the edge off.

Romania was the only country where I came across a hotel with no kitchen. Like lots of buildings in Bucharest it was massive. The president's palace was close by. That was like an aircraft hangar. I only discovered years later that whole streets were flattened to accommodate officials of the Communist Party as well as extensions to the Palace itself. Basically the folks were told to clear off to the outskirts, or further. Lots left their dogs behind them, and so Bucharest developed packs of territorial, feral dogs. You'd see a gang and wonder what was the story.

We would be collected in the morning from our kitchen-less hotel and taken to the local Police Academy club for meals. All transport was in a bus that spewed as many fumes inside as outside.

On arrival we'd sit at long rows of wooden tables, set up with a bread roll at each place. The rolls were rock hard. Naturally enough we'd throw them at each other. They'd be reproduced at the next meal. They liked their fish head soup in Romania. And for mains there would be a serving of something that might once have been beef, or mutton.

There was a heavy French influence in Romanian rugby in those days, but it stopped on the pitch. You couldn't find two more different countries. Romania was grey and poor and depressing and downtrodden. Great swathes of the streets were not lit at night. In the hotel the lighting was a watery yellow. It would really get in on you after a while. Holy Moly, if this was Communism in the shop window then it was a shite look.

Our first game was supposed to be in Constanta, on the Black Sea. It sounded nice. At the last minute they told us it was closed. Change in plan. We were taken to Iasi – pronounced

Yash – about seven hours away on the belching bus. We stopped to see a few monasteries and have some fish head soup. Many hours later we arrived in Iasi, within sight of the Russian border. We pulled up at a soccer pitch with two-by-fours added to the goals to make longer posts. For a dead-ball area there was a gravel run-off. The pitch was like a rock.

Right lads, this is us.

It's the only time I've ever shaken hands with my opponent on the field before a game, and been presented with a flower. Lovely gesture. From the kick-off the shit started. By the fifth minute I'd say there had been three bust-ups. That was OK if you knew what was coming, and if you had guys who could deal with it. Our pack would have included the likes of Stevie Smith, Willie Duncan and Jimmy McCoy. They weren't taking many backward steps. Willie John was looking on and smoking his pipe, contented with the lessons being learned.

It was hard to find something to spend your money on. Ken Reid was managing the trip. We had only arrived in the country when he went to change some sterling into Lei, the local currency. He got a bit of local knowledge on the best deal. Good man Ken. He came back with a fat wad of notes, quite pleased with himself, only to discover that once he had reeled off the few notes of Lei on the outside he was into toilet roll and newspaper. He was haunted after that.

"Ken, you wouldn't change a few quid for us there would you?"

Towards the end of the trip we had won our few games and were on another epic bus journey when the two security officers – sorry, tour guides – who went everywhere with us, told us the bus had a mechanical problem and wouldn't be able to stop. No cement rolls and fish head soup then! It all fed into us being galvanised for the last game, which of course we won. The ref had created a new world record for penalties in an effort to give them the game. Again, things got very heated, but we held out. More waste-pipe beer followed. More Mars bars that we had brought with us. We had given some of them to local kids who thought all their Christmases had come together.

The local players were very keen to swap gear. We gladly would have given them the cheap slacks and sweaters we had. For an earlier tour to Italy the Ulster squad had been given Nottingham Forest tracksuits tops with the Red Hand plastered over the Forest logo. Ulster used to ration out playing gear like it was designer issue. It would be spilled out on the floor early in the season and there would be a scramble to hoke out something the right size. If you were foolish enough to swap a jersey with your opposite number you'd get a bill from the Ulster Branch. If you didn't pay it pronto you'd not get picked the next day. I think Nigel swapped a pair of Ulster socks with one of the Romanian lads and got ones in return that had no feet in them.

There was a loud cheer when we took off from Otopeni Airport for the flight home. Not so much to be escaping such a sad country but because we had been cheering every calamity the whole way through. It stayed that way through my time with Ulster. We had a knack of making a silk purse out of a sow's ear. In fairness, we had a lot of silk as it was.

My race was run by the time Ulster's interpro streak came to an end, in 1994/95. I wasn't slow to remind lads I was off the premises when that happened. They were quick to point out I had hogged the limelight long enough. I'd have to admit there were times when I was playing to the crowd – well, a certain section of it. At Ravenhill the selectors would sit in the committee box on the halfway line. Best seats in the house. If I was at number eight then there was a good chance John Rogers and Colin Morrison were in the second row. If we had Philip Matthews on board at wing forward then we weren't stuck for lineout options. The lads would testify that the closer the play got to the committee box the more likely I'd call the ball on myself.

"Every fucking time bar none!" Rogers hollered at me, years later.

There was one night Colin Morrison's mum was at the game and she went through himself and John afterwards. She knew her rugby did Mrs Morrison.

"Youse two big softies!" she says. "Why do you let Willie call everything on himself when he gets in front of the stand? Yisser big blouses!"

The boys were mortified. John also likes to remind me of the time we were playing Munster away and they were getting stuck into us. In later years when I'd finished with Ulster, and was involved in coaching the Ireland team, I struck up a great relationship with Peter Clohessy. The Claw, as he was known, was in the eye of a few storms in his time. When we were on the same side we had no problem relating to each other. When we were going at it on the pitch it was usually hot and heavy. We would have traded a few insults. One day, as Munster were on the charge, Claw called me a "black Protestant bastard." I turned to John, a Catholic, and said: "Did you hear what he said to me?"

John looked at me like I'd just landed from Mars.

"Will you clock him for fuck sake!" he said.

Referee Gordon Black, a good Campbell College Prod who had migrated across the border, was unimpressed. "Do you realise you've managed to offend this referee and the officials as well?" he said to Claw. Rogers was having a laughing fit.

It sounds a bit of a rugby cliché that what happened on the field stayed on the field but it was mostly true. The sessions we'd have with Leinster, Munster and Connacht lads were the best of craic. You'd part on great terms and then meet up the next season to beat the shite out of each other. The reward for all of this was the taking part, the belonging. And for that Ulster team of the 1980s there was incredible pride in being part of a ground-breaking group of men. We still meet up a couple of times a year.

It bothered me that the Ulster Branch didn't have any sort of mementos for guys who had put in time on a lot of those days. I remember Keith Crossan saying to me one day when we were still involved that he had caps from school and club and from Ireland – but nothing from Ulster. I was working then as an IRFU development officer, based in Ravenhill, and came across a bunch of embroidered Red Hand crests in the office. I got them cleaned up and framed and gave them to guys who had played 50 times for the province. I was struck by how much they appreciated the gesture.

Many years later when I was working with the Ulster Academy I was able to compare the new Kingspan with the old Ravenhill. It looked completely different, but much of it felt the same. Walking under the War Memorial towards the back of what used to be the old stand is a pilgrimage I made countless times. In the new tunnel area is a list of all the players who have represented the province in the professional era. I'm immensely proud to see the name of my son Thomas up there. And, I'll admit, a bit sad that I'm not up there with him. Ulster Rugby didn't start with the Heineken Cup win in 1999. It started with the first interpro, against Leinster, in 1875/76. It cracked on with the start of the official interpro series in 1946/47. It hit a purple patch in the 1980s: champions for nine years running from 1984/85. No one, from any part of the world, came to Ravenhill expecting to get out in one piece. It feels good to have been a part of that.

6

The Prize

IN SEPTEMBER 1977 I SWAPPED THE WILD LIFE of living on campus at Stranmillis for the unbridled mayhem of sharing a house with a few other lads. Yes, I had just become a graduate, a teacher, a man with responsibilities. So were the other four, which quickly enough became three, all of us starting our teaching careers: Stephen Cherry, a Stewartstown man who I became good pals with in Stran, along with Clive Russell and Mike Dallas. We were all new to our schools, but traditional in the way young men lived together.

The house was in Ravenhill Park, a matter of yards from the main entrance to the Ulster ground. So in autumn 1978, when I was still wet behind the ears as a provincial player, my address saved my bacon. There I was in the changing room before we played the All Blacks, by a country mile the biggest challenge of my young sporting life. It was a good hour to kick off, but already you could cut the tension in the room with a knife.

Some lads were already getting changed, going through their own wee rituals. I opened my kit bag to set my stuff out on the bench beside me. No boots. Oh fuck, how could I have left the house with no boots? How could I have taken them out last night to clean and polish them, and somehow forgotten to put them back in the bottom of the bag?

A wave of nausea spread up from the pit of my stomach. I felt my cheeks flush. I became short of breath. This was the first time in my life I had a panic attack. I said nothing, got up, and tried to breeze past the coach Cecil Watson at the door.

"I'm just stepping out for a minute to get some air."

He was too busy to notice. Strictly speaking that was true. How much air filled my lungs on the sprint out the gate, then hard left and around to the right, and a 40 yard dash up Ravenhill Park, is open to question. Thank God I had my key with me. I charged in, saw the boots on the kitchen floor, grabbed them and repeated the journey without dropping the pace. I was desperately trying to compose myself as I walked back in the door.

"Left them in the car!"

No one batted an eyelid. There was central heating in that house but I don't remember it being turned on. Ever. There were two electric heaters. They were on all the time. I'd managed to snaffle one of them for my room.

Our neighbours avoided us, until the first bleak winter had passed and we went to clean the garden up a bit. Suddenly they were handing shears and all sorts of garden tools across the hedge. We discovered a bin, hidden in the undergrowth. And a greenhouse that had collapsed in a storm. Indoors wasn't much better. We used to chuck our shirts in a communal cardboard box on the landing, and you would fish out whatever one was the least offensive. Eventually we'd concede defeat and put on a wash. Like the heating, there was a phone but it didn't get much use after a chunk of plaster came down from the ceiling above and demolished both the phone and the table it had been sitting on. We locked the door and didn't use the room again.

Eating was haphazard. On my trips home to see the folks in Sixmilecross, Mum would make sure to fill the boot of my car with food. So I'd walk in the door of Ravenhill Park with bags of vegetables and trays of cracked eggs – perfectly edible but not good enough for sale. And there'd always be a chicken that a few hours earlier had had its neck wrung. We'd eat like kings that night. At breakfast the next morning Steve and myself would crack on with our routine of raw eggs beaten up with a wee bit of milk. It was horrendous. Like me, he was always on a fitness kick. We had toured Canada together in Stran, and would share lifts to Stevenson Park when we graduated to club rugby with Dungannon. We were convinced the raw eggs were the business.

I tried to keep Heather away from the place. We met in Stranmillis in 1978. I was teaching PE in Grosvenor, but I was still using the Stran sports fields to get in some extra fitness sessions. And I was still pally with a lot of the rugby lads there, so pints in the campus bar were a regular thing. When I saw Heather Buckley first, literally across a crowded room, she was striking: blonde, beautiful and with a glint in her eye. She was with a group of friends and seemed to be having a great time.

There were a few big cliques in Stran. The rugby crowd was one. The arty crowd was another. I was in the first and Heather was in the second. There was some crossover but at the same time you could retreat to your own wee planet if you wanted. I got it into my head early on that Heather was a bit stuck up. When we would end up in the same group socially I'd be more likely to slag her for that more than anything else. I suppose I was a bit intimidated because I was fairly sure she knew more than me about lots of things. I was half intrigued at the same time. Despite my caveman approach she didn't run a mile. I think she saw me as a challenge.

Heather was actually going out with my Ulster teammate Chipper Rainey when I first saw her. Not long after that the relationship finished up. So I asked her out for a drink. She made like she was giving it a lot of thought and then said why not. We started stepping out together. She was in a residence hall in Stran, and I was across the road in Ravenhill Park.

On the face of it we didn't have much in common. Heather was solid Antrim Prod middle class, still teaching in Sunday School thanks to the Methodist upbringing of her mother. Her dad, Jim, and mum, Norah, were from the North of England, both near Manchester. Jim was a very creative man, a textile designer whose talent earned him the offer in 1957 of a big job in Riverside Textiles, owned by Samuel Lamont and Sons. Heather's sister Jane was a toddler when they moved over. It set them up nicely.

Her parents were driven. They wanted to provide for their own family, their parents, for themselves. They had met in a factory where Norah was a seamstress and Jim was the chief designer. When they moved to Antrim, Norah got a job in Maryville, a clothing manufacturer. She made all Jim's clothes. That included an all-in-one protective outfit for riding his motorbike, so when he arrived at work he could whip it off to reveal a well cut suit. Jim had a bit of style about him.

Norah was the financial engine in the partnership, so she did the sums on Jim's scheme for some long-term security. When they came over to Northern Ireland Lamont's had already built two semi-detached houses at the top of Moylena Road, in Antrim Town.

The family moved into one of them as part of Jim's work package. But he didn't like the idea of being so dependent on the company. The prospect of losing both home and job at the same time, if something went wrong, bothered him. He bought the vacant field next door, and built a house on it. So Heather was born into the company house, and she was still a toddler when they moved in a few yards away to their own place. As it happened, Jim stayed with Riverside Textiles the rest of his working life, but the message wasn't lost on his daughter.

Heather was very much his wee girl. Jim was a handy footballer who spent a season with Wolves. His career was just kicking off when the Second World War broke out. He was based in Scapa Flow in the north of Scotland, working with naval mines. When the war ended he took his navy uniform and put it on the fire. His best footballing years had been taken. He managed Chimney Corner FC when he came to Northern Ireland, and Heather would be perched on his shoulders as he patrolled the touchline.

The pair of us had mighty craic together. Our backgrounds might have been poles apart but we had a love of music and devilment. Heather had talent and loads of personality. She played the clarinet from the age of eight through to 18. She was a member of the Ulster Schools Youth Orchestra. Someone suggested the bassoon at one point. Her dad told her to bring it back to the school inside 24 hours. It was back to the clarinet, and then violin.

Drama was Heather's passion. It started when she went into Cambridge House Grammar School, in Ballymena, and continued through her years in Stran where she played the lead in Hobson's Choice. She was in her element on stage. Her degree there was English and Drama but she would have done it the other way around if she could. And she would have continued with a career on the stage after college if it wasn't such a tough gig to get into. Her mother called off that search soon enough. Unlike me, with my King's Scholars grant, Heather's folks were paying for fees and halls of residence. She got a job teaching in Parkhall secondary school in Antrim Town.

So it would be amateur dramatics from then on. Not long after we started going out, Heather joined the Oriel Players, a theatre group based in Clotworthy House in the Castle Grounds in Antrim. The army barracks was next door and a couple of British Army officers, from the Royal Engineers, signed up as well. They inveigled Heather into giving a couple of English classes each week to the sappers on the army base. The plan was for them to sit their GCSEs.

She brought a teacher friend, Fiona Marks, along as a chaperone and they really got to enjoy the bit of diversion. We were invited to dinners in the officers' mess in the barracks from time to time. They'd all be in their regimental gear. It'd be 'pass the port from the left hand side' type of shite, but great craic all the same. Free food and drink and a look at life behind the security barriers.

There was quite a little social life going on in the officers' mess.

That place was their escape from the world outside. I found them fairly regular guys with a very good working knowledge of the terrain. For example they had intimate knowledge of the lie of the land even in my home place, so if they had to land a helicopter in a hurry they would know the orange fields from the green ones. There was a lot of green.

I never felt any threat to Heather or myself for opening this wee window to army life. It was only 45 miles from Sixmilecross but this was a game with a completely different set of rules. In the 'Cross you were likely to be shot or blown up for having anything to do with the security forces. Antrim Town was staunchly Protestant though. The looneys in that part of the Northern Ireland asylum were loyalist paramilitaries. They had no problem with the army being here.

My relationship with Heather was a game of two halves. The first, pre Argentina, was a casual enough affair where we were dating and seeing a fair bit of each other, but we weren't exactly planning a wee house with a white picket fence. She had been home to the farm to meet my folks, and got on famously with them. They loved her from the moment she walked in the door.

In that summer of 1980 Heather was heading off to Greece for a sun holiday with a few girlfriends as I was going on the Penguins tour with the lads. My plan had been to stay in touch with her while I was away, then pick up where we left off when I got back. The nature of the 'staying in touch' was more than she bargained on.

The weeks after I got home were a whirlwind. Everywhere we went we were recognised. Any conversations quickly turned into questions about being locked up and what was it like, and what was it like for Heather et cetera et cetera. When it all calmed down we settled into a full-on relationship, but there was something bugging me at the same time. I had bombarded Heather with love letters from Buenos Aires. I was in a desperate state there and clung on to her. Did she feel differently now that I was back safe and sound, teaching in Grosvenor again and playing rugby for Dungannon and Ulster? Did I?

*****

Part of the price I paid for Argentina was a delayed start with Ireland. I was playing for Ulster again a couple of weeks after getting back home, in November 1980. I was 25. It would take another four years before I could get a green shirt on my back.

It wasn't that I was a slow learner – the Argentine experience was character forming, but career threatening. Lots of people felt I had paid over the odds for a stupid moment where no one had been hurt. A fair number of others reckoned I was a loose cannon. OK, who wants to pick a wild man who is likely to go off half cocked? Let's see if he can stay out of trouble. Let him serve some more time. It was hard for me to plot the route ahead. Play well for Dungannon and Ulster, and keep my bib clean. I focused on that. I never stopped working on my fitness and my game. I never stopped waiting for the call.

Dungannon in the early 1980s were struggling. McKinney and Jimmy D had moved on and we found them hard to replace. I was missing games through my involvement with Ulster and we were relying on a very young, talented halfback pairing of Ashley Blair and Mark Jennings to steer the ship. My eye was off the ball a bit as well, which might explain me throwing the toys out of the pram one Saturday morning when I was asked to shift from number eight into the second row because of a late withdrawal from our game against Instonians. I saw my future with Ulster and hopefully Ireland as a number eight. What were the club doing messing with that? Anyway, I played second row. And, I hope, got over myself.

There was always a bit of craic around the club even if we weren't shooting the lights out. Heather threw herself into the rugby scene there without getting lost in it. She had been a keen hockey player in school but as much for the social side as anything else. She fitted in to the Dungannon set where there was a strong crew of wives and girlfriends going to our games, but there was a side of it she never got her head around. I suppose like all clubs there was a country mile between the mood when we won and when we lost. Blame was handed out in hefty portions. Years later, when I took over as club coach, she saw it full on. Heather's attitude was if you couldn't handle defeat then don't make such a big deal out of victory.

Years later, in May 2001, Dungannon won the All Ireland League title for the first time. It was the most fulfilling day of my coaching career. We ran Cork Con off the field, playing rugby I was hugely proud of. It was an epic day all round. But the prospect of listening to me being slated by other Dungannon folk, if the game went sour, was a risk Heather didn't want to take. She watched it on TV in Davy Byrne's pub on Dublin's Duke Street, and joined me for the celebrations later. I was happy that she was happy.

By late 1982 I felt we were approaching a crossroads in our relationship. Heather had moved to Glengormley High School, in Belfast, and I had changed job as well. After six happy years in Grosvenor I spotted an advert for a Head of the

THE PRIZE

PE department in Rainey Endowed in Magherafelt – or The Rainey as everyone calls it. I applied in hope, knowing it would be a good fit for me. I was absolutely thrilled to get it, a perfect next step in my teaching career. It was a bonus that The Rainey had won the Ulster Schools Cup the previous year, only the second time in their history.

There was added value too in the school's 300 years of history and location. It was built on land owned by the Salters Company, who had a big presence in the town. Salters had formed themselves into a fraternity in the 13th century, and developed into a powerful outfit, like any other important trade. They would give land to causes they favoured, set up Alms houses, and generally have an influence in society.

As for the location, Magherafelt is a vibrant town with a great social and religious mix. The school reflected that diversity. On our rugby senior cup team you could have Derry and Tyrone GAA minors playing alongside classic rugby Prods. So I was a Head of Department in a progressive school who had won the Ulster Schools Cup the previous year, only the second time in their history.

I remember feeling that pieces in my life were slotting into place, and I needed to figure out where Heather and myself were going with our relationship. For a couple in love we never spoke much about the future.

One Saturday morning coming up to Christmas in 1982 the pair of us were dandering about in Belfast city centre when the subject came up. The conversation went from nought to 60 miles an hour very quickly. Basically, the choice was to commit to each other formally or leave it at that. I pulled a few coins out of my pocket.

"Will we toss for it?" I asked.

"Are you serious?"

"Yep. Why not?"

"I can't believe this. Go on."

"Heads we get engaged now, this morning, or tails we call it a day."

I flicked the coin, caught it in the palm of my right hand, and slapped it on the back of my left. I left my right hand there, covering it, for a second or two. Even now I can feel the unease of the moment. If I delayed any longer it would betray the uncertainty I felt. How would that look to the woman whose love and support had kept me sane when I had needed it most?

I suspected Heather had doubts of her own but felt unable to put them into words. If she opened that door then the bond we had built up through the Argentina ordeal would be broken. So I went for it.

When I lifted my hand we were looking at the fine head of Elizabeth Windsor.

All this took place on the pavement, around the corner from Malcolm's Jewellers on Chichester Street. The shop has been run by the Watt family for generations, and I knew Ned Watt through Dungannon. We had the ring picked out and paid for inside half an hour. Then we went to Heather's family home on Moylena Road where I asked her dad for permission to wed his daughter – as you do. With the decision made we cracked on and got married the following summer. We moved into a flat over Billy Campbell's TV repair shop in Magherafelt. I was coaching Billy's son Chris in school at the time. There was Heather, me, a big gas heater that could suck the oxygen out of a ballroom, and a family of mice who were liable to race across the floor at any moment. We made good friends locally through Billy, and the favourite night out was a dinner party of four courses where each one would be in a different house. Our target was always to get the cheese and crackers bit at the end because everyone was so buckled at that stage they didn't care about the state of the place. Instead we ended up, as often as not, with the main course. Our only source of firepower was a Baby Belling oven, a wee thing the size of a modern microwave, perched beside the sink. It was a challenge. And it was great craic.

It was in Magherafelt we bought our first house – in Coolshinney Heights, a grand spot where we met Ben and Marie Glancy, who became our closest friends. They lived up the road from us. Ben's dad Hugh was the local GP, and like father like son. The funny thing was I'd met Marie back when we were schoolkids in Omagh: her in the Convent and me in the Academy. I only half knew her back then, but one day I was on the bus, looking flustered having managed to lose my money, when Marie and her mum came to my rescue straight away. The apple didn't fall far from the tree in that family. They are wonderful people.

*****

As I watched Ireland's Five Nations campaign in 1984 I was jumping out of my socks to make the step up from Ulster. It wasn't straightforward. In those days pretty much everything in rugby involved a committee. Including picking the team. At national level the coach was one of five selectors, spread across a few provinces. Getting the best 15 players on the field wasn't always the top priority. There were provincial loyalties. It was the same selecting provincial sides, where every selector had club loyalties. Colin Patterson had become an Ulster selector when his playing career was cut short. He gave it a season and then hopped back over the fence, to retain his sanity. I remember him telling me how he resigned. "I rang Willie John to say I'd had enough," he said. "The politics was unbelievable. He just laughed! He was well used to all that stuff and thought it was hilarious I didn't want a part of it. That's how it was."

In summer 1984, Mick Doyle had taken over from Willie John as Ireland coach. Doyler had been a very good flanker in his day and had become very sure of himself as a coach. He had done wonders with Leinster before Jimmy D came along and changed the provincial picture. He also considered himself a bit of a character. I'd say he had paid his subs in the narcissists' club. Doyler had Mick Cuddy as chairman of selectors. The Cud made people laugh, often unintentionally. He had a special talent for mangling sentences so what came out of his mouth wasn't the message sent from his brain. It never knocked a feather out of him.

Both Leinster men, and good pals, their plan for Ireland would be to agree the team they wanted in advance of the selection meeting. They knew there was no chance of the other three selectors, with horses to trade, ever agreeing to the point of overruling them. Doyler had got the coaching job in the first place on a split decision. He was a very intelligent man who understood the system.

I remember him coming up to Ravenhill to talk to the Ulster players not long after his appointment that summer. Himself and The Cud were on a tour of the provinces, setting out their stall. Doyler knew there would be a fair sprinkling of Ulster players in the Ireland side so his strategy was to calm the natives by putting me on a pedestal, just in case any noses were out of joint about a Leinster man shoving an Ulster man out of the way for the coaching job. There weren't. In Ulster we were wide open to the idea of Doyler taking over.

And if he was going to cap me then all the better.

Mick Cuddy spoke first. No one was any the wiser by the time he finished. Then Doyler followed up, zoning in on me, how I should have been a seasoned international player by that stage, with a sackful of caps. Sure enough, my Ulster teammates all agreed, and he had completed his home run. He knew his audience that night, and got the tone right. That wouldn't always be the case. He was notoriously off colour when it came to after-dinner speaking. I'd say women would have left the room wondering why he felt the need to demean them, but that was his style.

Coincidentally my second cousin, Hugh Gibson, who grew up across the river from us in Sixmilecross, got to know Mick Doyle before I did. Hugh was in the agri/pharma business and reckoned Doyler, a vet based in Kildare, was ahead of his time in promoting probiotics for animals – mostly ruminants. They met at the National Ploughing Championships in Carlow, the mecca for farmers north and south. This festival for country folk was ideal for getting business done on the back of some brave craic, as we would call it.

Doyler wanted to set up an agency for a UK probiotics firm, and Hugh helped establish a manufacturing plant in Omagh. They were well matched, but Doyler was fairly disorganised. He was a demon for drink, and further along the road with it than me at the time. Hugh remembers them, early in their business partnership, stopping for a pint in the Halfway House, between Omagh and Fintona.

"Jesus Mick I have to get up early in the morning."

"One pint."

That was around 7pm. It was approaching midnight when the landlady was trying to close the shutter with Doyler's arm wedged underneath it.

"We'll just have the one we came in for."

Mick really loved the after-dinner speaking, which really fed his ego. One night he was proposing the toast to the guests at The Rainey Old Boys annual dinner. Jim Neilly was making the reply on behalf of the guests. Jim has been a good friend of mine for years, a great man to fly the flag for Ulster players in his BBC match commentaries. By the time Doyler finished and Jim got to his feet the bread rolls were flying. He wrote to the club to thank them for inviting him, but noted he had been due to speak on the 11th but didn't get a chance to address the guests until the 12th. It was a good line. Doyler could go on a bit.

He picked me for the Test against Australia in November 1984, four days before Ulster would play the Wallabies midweek side in Ravenhill. It was a crazy time. Our first child, Jonathan, was born six weeks earlier. The poor wee lad had infantile eczema and cried non-stop. Between Ulster and Ireland I was being dragged all over the place when Heather rang the school one day to say she was feeling awful. Well, even more awful that you'd feel with no sleep. It got worse. She spoke to our GP, Ben Glancy, and he asked her to drive over to the hospital in Ballymena. By the time I got home she was minus one appendix.

The sense of achievement at having realised my childhood

dream washed over the fact that, at 29, I was late to the party. It was all about what I did when I got there. But Jeepers, the nerves. In the days before the game I developed flu symptoms but knew I didn't have the flu. Mick Molloy, the team doctor, was trying to pin down what was wrong with me. He had to rule out a virus that could have head heart implications, and took me off to St Vincent's Hospital.

They stuck me on a treadmill to put me under stress in controlled conditions. I flew through it, but felt no better. In desperation I got a number for a woman in Aughnacloy, who gave out charms to eejits like me. I told her I was at panic stations about the game and needed to calm down. She whispered some hocus pocus down the phone line and that was that. By the time the referee started the game I was grand.

I was massively relieved that my parents were alive to witness that event. After all I had put them through, I felt that standing there in Lansdowne Road, with the Wallabies in their huddle and me in ours, was deliverance. Dad and Mum were sitting up in the West Stand, their first time in Lansdowne Road.

This is what all the fuss was about.

Over the years I had been guilty of putting my ambition ahead of all else. I couldn't wait to join them for a drink in the Wanderers bar after the game, with the two Heathers, Ollie and my brother-in-law Alan Bell. It was rammed. I felt like the Rhinestone Cowboy. Instead of 'getting cards and letters from people I don't even know' I was getting clapped on the back by total strangers. I could see the look on Dad's face.

"This is why I couldn't farm Dad," I said. "This is why I had to chase the dream."

They headed back up home, content there was an end to the

means. There were cows to be milked the next morning. And for me there were pints to be drunk.

The Wallabies were a brilliant side then. I got over the defeat easily enough because of my own personal breakthrough. And I played well enough, alongside Donal Lenihan in the second row. Brendan Mullin, Michael Bradley, Philip Matthews and Willie Sexton all earned their first caps alongside me that day.

At the official dinner that night captain Ciaran Fitzgerald mentioned us all. Honestly, I could have cried.

To top it off I got to play for the Barbarians a few weeks later, in Cardiff, when they were the final opponents on the Wallabies' tour. The 1973 thriller between the Barbarians and the All Blacks was the first game of rugby that really turned my head. I was 18, and already well stuck into it, but between Cliff Morgan's commentary and the sheer adventure of that occasion I was inspired. A year later the Lions became heroes in South Africa and every young man with an interest in rugby wanted to be a Lion. But for me it was the Barbarians. There was a style and personality about them that I just fell in love with.

Fast forward 11 years to 1984 and that breakthrough season with Ireland. Five weeks after that debut I was over in Liverpool with The Rainey, playing against a local school, when I got a phonecall.

"Can you get down to Cardiff as soon as possible to play for the Barbarians on Saturday?"

I was gone like a shot. It was the first of 10 caps for that wonderful club. That's where I got to know Serge Blanco, who became a great friend. Many years later myself and Heather took off camping to Biarritz with a few friends and a small army of kids. Serge invited us down to his hotel and spa at Hendaye, near the Spanish border. He put on a banquet for us. There were five adults with 10 kids in tow. It was an unbelievable spread, all on the house. I wonder is there another sport where you make friends like this.

So there we were, relaxing and looking out at the ocean, but of course the kids were yamming and gurning and driving us mad. Poor Heather was skundered, as we'd say, with their carry-on. That's when she came out with a line we'd refer back to many times over the years:

"Give me another drink – I can still hear them!"

*****

It's one of the great conundrums of Irish sport that you can be raised in Northern Ireland, in the Protestant tradition, with an allegiance to the Crown, and be obsessed with playing for a country that wants to reclaim the land that reared you. I didn't get hung up on it. So the anthem was no more than an irritant. Better men than me had coped with it. It didn't stop the looneys on my side of the fence letting me know how they felt.

Belfast Road, Bangor
Dear Mr Anderson

The other Saturday when I was with a group of people, a loud cheer arose when it was announced that the Ireland Rugby Team was beaten again. You do not realise how much the Ireland Rugby Team is reviled. There are tens of thousands in Northern Ireland who actively hate this team. It all comes about by the reason that the Ireland Rugby Team stands to attention for the Soldiers Song and plays under the Tricolour. Gerry Adams, Sinn Fein and the Irish

Americans would be proud of you all. What do you think about when you stand to attention for the Soldiers Song? This anthem glorifies, praises and honours the IRA. Do you ever give a thought for its victims; Shankill Road and La Mon House etc? The UDR men killed and maimed especially in Tyrone and Fermanagh? The next time you stand for it, give a thought. There are tens of thousands of people who do not consider themselves to be Irish but Ulster British. We would love an Ireland Rugby Team to be thrashed every time. Finally there should be an enquiry into how the Rugby Mafia controls education in Northern Ireland and how it manages to get soccer banned from grammar schools. Rugby cannot accept a challenge from other games. The only way it can succeed is to prohibit the playing of other games, especially soccer. It is illegal to discriminate on the grounds of sex, religion or race. How about sport? It is about time the matter was raised at the European Court of Human Rights.

Yours truly, Anti Ireland Rugby Team

I appreciated the letter, because it taught me to be grateful for what rugby was giving me: a window on the outside world. In time I got to understand a bit more about life south of the border. Playing for Ulster against the other provinces was about representing a place and an identity we cherished. We'd play, beat the lard out of each other, drink away happily, and then head our separate ways. Playing for Ireland broadened my horizons.

In the early days I roomed with Hugo MacNeill. What did I have in common with Hugo? Sixmilecross and South County Dublin could have been different planets. He had come through Blackrock College, one of the biggest and best-known rugby schools on the island. Omagh Academy wasn't mapped.

He was a mass-going Catholic. I didn't go to anything by that stage, but I was still a Prod. Our only connections were a love of rugby, fun, and a passion for representing Ireland. From there we developed a friendship that is as strong now as it was then. Hugo would ask me about the great divide in the six counties, what it had been like growing up in a system like that. A lot of the time I couldn't get past an answer that went: "It's all we've known."

He was fascinated by the Orange tradition, so it wasn't long before I brought the pipes down to give him a flavour. Over the years he came up to stay with us regularly. Initially though our conversations would take place either in the shared room at the Shelbourne Hotel or nearby in Strings Nightclub on Leeson Street. It was run by a lovely Donegal woman, Ann McGettigan. She reckoned a steady flow of Irish rugby players in the joint would be good for business. We worked our way through a lot of champagne and steak sandwiches there. Any Ireland squad session in Dublin would involve meeting up on a Saturday night after our club games that afternoon. Then down to Strings. Followed by training the next morning.

I remember one Sunday session after we got back to the hotel closer to breakfast time than midnight. We weren't feeling the best. The sessions wasn't long on when somehow Hugo took a high ball safely and then collapsed to the ground while we rucked over him. I looked back a while later and he was still there, hoping not to be noticed.

I was lucky that my time with Ireland coincided with huge change in the game. It started with the radically different approach from Mick Doyle, which pointed us towards a Triple Crown in 1985.

My only regret from that whirlwind first season was stopping short of a Grand Slam. Two years later I was off to the first ever Rugby World Cup – unthinkable for rugby when I was growing up. A year after that I was captain of a winning Ireland side in France, a highly significant event hidden in plain sight. And the following year, 1989, I was sailing the good ship Ireland into the storm of a Test match against New Zealand in a packed Lansdowne Road. It was a phenomenal few years. I am from a farm in Sixmilecross. This was what living the dream looked like.

7

The Rugby World Cup

THE TRIPLE CROWN WAS A WHIRLWIND THAT had blown itself out long before we started preparing for the inaugural Rugby World Cup in 1987. But we were eyeing it up from a long way out – it was going to be a game-changer for the sport of rugby union.

Just the thought of it had us salivating: a competition that brought together the best in the world – and a few who were well off that pace – in New Zealand and Australia for over a month? This was a whole new ball game. It would be a tour like no other.

It was touring with the prospect of medals at the end of it. Well, maybe not much chance of medals. The journey with Ireland from 1985 through 1986 to the Rugby World Cup in 1987 was a steady slide downhill.

I couldn't believe that just four months after making my debut against Australia I was winning a Triple Crown with Ireland.

Years later I read a line from Ronan O'Gara that your first 10 caps are spent trying to figure out what's going on. Then you begin to settle in a bit. In my case I was conscious of making up for lost time. I had lots of experience at club and provincial level before getting the call, so I wasn't clueless. And physically I was able to cope with the step up.

I made mental notes before going out to play in Murrayfield or Cardiff for the first time. I'd seen games there often enough on the telly. I'd go over it in my head that the pitch wherever we were playing was roughly the same size as any pitch I played on, so it wasn't a leap into the unknown. The in-goal area might have been deeper in Murrayfield than anywhere else, but that wasn't likely to keep me awake at night. This was rugby. It was something I could do.

Mind you, it was different rugby. Quicker, because it's the top end of the game, but also different because Mick Doyle was on a mission. He picked a team to run the ball. It became a story in itself, the whole notion of playing fast, open rugby, but it was the pragmatic option and he had the determination to launch it. If he was presented with mountainy men who could knock seven shades out of all before them then the ball wouldn't have been given any air. I was a country boy but I wasn't a mountain of a man. Fast and open suited me fine.

There was other stuff I had to get used to as well. I knew most of the players already from the interpro circuit but there was the 'plus ones' club to consider. Rugby was so far up its own chauvinistic rear end in those days, the wives or girlfriends were an afterthought. They would dine separately to the menfolk at after-match dinners. They'd have to organise this themselves. Then we'd all hook up later on. Heather is an outgoing, confident woman, but she wasn't a big rugby fan. I was a wee bit afraid that she'd be uncomfortable in this new environment.

Because I was about five years older than a lot of the lads, and married with a child, we gravitated towards Phil Orr and his wife Anne, who was a more experienced head. Anne knew her rugby but it wasn't her specialist subject. The matchday drill would involve Heather travelling down to Dublin with a chaperone – at her mother's insistence. This was an attractive wee jaunt for either my brother Oliver or Heather's brother-in-law Brian, or his younger brother John. As players we were given two free tickets, but that was the end of the jolly.

So typically they'd stop off in Balbriggan, in John D's pub, for a pint before hitting Dublin. Then they'd head for the Shelbourne and try and stash a bag somewhere because there was no accommodation for the wives and girlfriends in the team hotel. Usually one of the Leinster lads would give up his bed in favour of staying at home on the night of the game. That way one of the Munster or Ulster lads could swap rooms and have their partner stay the night.

For one game Brian took Heather to Davy Byrne's pub for a pre-match pint. She was struck by a cool looking fella they got chatting to, who had the letters 'EC' embroidered on his socks.

"Who does that?" she asked.

"Elvis Costello, that's who," says Brian.

There was always an interesting range of musical and arty types floating around that part of Dublin. It was a completely different scene and atmosphere to Belfast. Heather loved getting a taste of it. Having survived against Scotland and Wales the Championship showdown was at home, against England. Around lunchtime that day Heather and John had a drink in

Bruxelles pub off Grafton Street. She was waiting at the bar and this guy asked was she going to the game.

"Of course I am, I'm going to watch my husband play!" said Heather proudly. So a big conversation started up. The company included Marie Heaney, wife of Séamus. Heather had been teaching one of Séamus's poems in school the day before so herself and Marie had lots to talk about. They got on famously. A few months later, having beaten England and won the Triple Crown, there was a dinner to celebrate it in Dublin – the same June night that Barry McGuigan beat Eusebio Pedroza in London to become featherweight champion of the world. Along with a few others I'd ducked out to watch the fight on the telly, abandoning Heather. She was chatting with Ciaran Fitzgerald when she says to him: "You'll never guess who I met having a drink in Dublin the day of the France game? None other than James Joyce's wife!"

Fitzy, deeply impressed, leans back in his chair and shouts over to our resident literary expert, Hugo MacNeill.

"Hey Hugo, how old would you say James Joyce's missus is now?"

"Hmm, she must be 101," says Hugo.

Poor Heather was mortified. It was late. We were all tired and emotional after reliving every moment of a great campaign. Our squad and coach were the toast of Ireland. I was delighted with the way things were working out on the field, but still shell-shocked by what had just happened off it.

*****

In the week leading to that Triple Crown decider I had lost my job in The Rainey. To be honest the timing left me in a spin. My boss had asked if there was any chance of tickets to a game the whole island wanted to witness first hand. I played down the chances but managed to square away a ticket for him. He was delighted. A few days before we played England I was told I was being made redundant. I waited for the punchline and realised I was it.

I was doing a good job there. I got on very well with my pupils and colleagues. There were no problems with parents. Quite the opposite. The problem wasn't me. In fact, I was the solution. Cuts were being made across the education system and it was a numbers game. The most important bit for me was the subtraction: last in first out. Bye Bye Big Tam. It was the first time in my life I had been on the wrong end of an accounting exercise like that, and I was deeply hurt by it. Without being too precious I had bought into the ethic in Stran that teaching was a vocation where you didn't switch off when the bell went at 4pm. You took a team and coached them to love and respect the game as you did.

Heather stared at me open-mouthed when I told her the news. She was working in Glengormley High School at the time, but with incredible fortune a job came up in Magherafelt High School which she applied for, and got. It meant we didn't have to move from the town. But I still needed a job. Where the hell was I going to get one of those?

As luck would have it one night I was doing a fitness session in the local GAA club in Magherafelt, O'Donovan Rossa, when I bumped into a man I knew well enough to see from rugby and GAA matches. Patsy Forbes is a legend in Ardboe, and beyond.

There is a place in Heaven for folks who grow up and become major employers in their locality. St Peter will be tipping his cap when eventually Patsy shows up at the Pearly Gates. We are from opposite sides of the religious fence but share a love of sport and physical fitness.

Patsy is steeped in the GAA, through a lifetime with the Ardboe club and two decades with the Tyrone county side. He was recently installed as Tyrone GAA president on a five years stint. He'll be well into his 80s by the time that number is up, and hardly thinking of slowing down by then. Patsy's years after 'retirement' as a player saw him attack the running track. He has more Irish Masters sprint titles than you could shake a stick at, as well as two silver medals in the World Masters games in Turin at 100m and 200m. When I say Patsy is quick I mean Patsy is quick. He is a great man. So we got chatting that night about GAA and rugby and when he asked about schools sport I told him that had come to a sudden end. He paused for a moment.

"Give me your telephone number there and I'll see if we have anything for you."

The 'we' was Forbes Kitchens. Within a week he was back to me offering a job as a sales rep. It was common in those days for GAA intercounty players to have jobs on the road, selling, but not so much rugby men. I was a Protestant going into a company run by Catholics and staffed by Catholics and selling mostly to Catholics.

In a company of roughly 140 people there was one Protestant on the factory floor, Joe Patterson. And then there would be me.

The penny dropped that Patsy wanted me to break new ground with my brethren. My knowledge of kitchens extended no further than sitting at the table, eating and drinking. That was about to change. I started on the factory floor, got a handle on the manufacturing process, and got into the social life of the place. This was fundamentalist Gaeldom. I knocked great craic out of it.

The top salesman there was Donal McElhinney. He could charm the birds out of the trees. If Donal had to stay on the case, chatting and drinking tea till midnight with potential clients, then that's what he'd do. I just didn't have his staying power on that front.

Like any rookie salesman I kicked off on familiar territory, nailing down Nigel Carr and my brother Oliver as my first two sales. The floodgates didn't exactly open after that, but Patsy was happy enough with my efforts. I got paid by the week, had a car under my backside and a full tank of diesel every Friday.

When I'd settled in, a few of the lads suggested I join them one night for a gig in the Battery Bar on the shores of Lough Neagh. Paddy Reilly, one of the most popular folk singers on the island, was playing. The place was already rammed when along with Jim Curran, who was a well-known referee on the GAA circuit, and the Devlin brothers, Christy and Henry, we wedged our way in. Paddy was working his way through the crowd as we were tucking into the first round of pints. Jim introduced me to him. We chatted away for a minute and when he asked my favourite song I came back with *Spancil Hill*. Sure enough, he wasn't not long into his set when he introduced it with:

"Now, this is for the big man at the back there," nodding over towards me.

I felt like the cowboy who just walked into the wrong saloon in the wild west as everyone turned to look at the stranger. We had a great night. One of many with the Forbes crew, who did me the honour of hanging a picture from one of my Ireland games on the wall in the office. After two years travelling the highways and byways of Ulster and beyond I had learned more about people but maybe not that much more about selling kitchens. I had also calmed down a bit on my anger at the teaching profession, which I felt had ditched me when I was working away productively and happily. In 1987 a job came up in Magherafelt High School, pretty much on my doorstep. I thanked Patsy for rescuing me, and much more, and went back to school.

*****

Mick Doyle's coaching career with Ireland had three separate phases to it: the first was a breath of fresh air that carried us to the Triple Crown; the second was a pause where things started to go wrong; the third was a slide into something a long way from the first. By the end he was resentful of us for not winning games. We were making him look bad. Some of us were resentful of him for being resentful of us. Doyler's best intentions, which had been a shot in the arm for Irish rugby, turned into a bit of self-pity.

Did we appreciate how neatly things had fallen for us in 1985? Jeepers we had been blessed. Wales's goal-kicker Mark Wyatt not being able to hit a barn door in the game in Cardiff. Outhalf Rob Andrew missing a penalty that would have finished us against England. The longest couple of minutes I ever spent on a rugby pitch were between referee Jim Fleming blowing for the penalty – against me – and Andrew pushing the ball wide. The relief was euphoric. I always think fondly of Jim. Late in that game, with us needing to score to win, I asked him how long was left. He looked at me and winked. Long enough for Mick Kiernan to drop the goal.

Even the Scotland game, the one that got the ball rolling. Trevor Ringland's second try has been replayed a million times, and every time I watch it I wince when Paul Dean has to dip and pick up Michael Bradley's pass off his toes. He actually catches the ball at its top end, and then sets in motion a rehearsed move that needed skill and luck to work. It got both. And it came very late in the day to win the game. The buzz in the dressing-room after that was electric. Everyone knew how close we had come to getting done. You can get a coat of Teflon off something like that.

The next season, 1986, we thought the pieces would all slot into place again. When they didn't we looked at Doyler, who struggled to fix it. He wanted us to give it another lash. Everybody had copped the way we were playing though. We needed to kick a bit more ball, play some territory, but it didn't happen. It certainly didn't happen in Paris. France were gunning for us after the 15-15 draw in Dublin the previous season. I remember trying to get air into my lungs at one point in that game and I felt I was in a tumble dryer. Our preparation for that game had been awful. They hammered us. Doyler had to do something, so he dropped Phil Orr and me.

Heather still laughs about seeing the pair of us together in Phil's house soon after, huddled in our coats in front of a piddly wee fire, gurning and giving out about Doyler and the unfairness of life. Typical players. Wales were next up, at home, followed by England in Twickenham. Both games were lost. Phil was out of the squad altogether; I was on the bench. For England I wasn't sure if the game would go ahead. It was so cold in London, and there were doubts about the pitch. The replacements had been given thermals specially for the honour of warming the bench – Marks & Spencers finest. The night before I gathered the group of extras: Jimmy McCoy, Harry Harbison, myself, Rab Brady, Tony Ward and Chipper Rainey. I suggested a quiet drink in the Turks Head – a spot recommended by Stewart McKinney. The Guinness was not bad at all. We each bought a round, which was way more than Wardy had budgeted for. He's not a big drinker. I slept like a baby that night. Wardy looked like death in the morning. As the game unfolded in the ball-aching cold, and England's Dean Richards was driving over for his second try, the phrase 'be careful what you wish for' sprang to mind. The Irish scrum was being mangled. As a young lad on the farm in Sixmilecross, dreaming of playing for Ireland, this scenario never entered my head. I was happy enough on the bench that day.

I was back in harness, along with Phil, for the Scotland game, and was still there when Doyler dropped Fitzy against Romania in November 1986 hoping it would be the spark to wake us up. Sure enough we put 60 points on them, a record score at the time, but it had nothing to do with Donal Lenihan taking over as captain, or Harry Harbison, Fitzy's replacement. Harry was a good hooker – technically strong and playing well for Leinster – and Donal did a fine job, but Fitzy was a born leader. I would have followed him anywhere.

By the time the Rugby World Cup year rolled around in 1987, I felt we were all over the place. It mightn't have looked that bad from the outside, with wins over England and Wales to start and end the Five Nations campaign, but you could feel it in the changing room and at squad sessions. After we lost the opener to Scotland, Doyler announced to us a week later that he didn't want to be known as the coach of a lucky Triple Crown winning side. If you're a nailed-on narcissist then you won't be able to help yourself coming out with shite like that. That punctured the balloon for sure. I don't think there was a man in the room who didn't stop and think about that line as soon as it had fallen from his mouth.

I was still living the dream of playing international rugby but my expectations changed after that.

I've often wondered why we didn't get a better hold of things ourselves when there was nothing coming from the coach, who had admitted he was concerned about his own legacy. Look at the personalities we had in that team: Donal Lenihan, Nigel Carr, Phil Matthews, Michael Bradley, Brendan Mullin, Trevor Ringland, Hugo MacNeill, Keith Crossan. Although I was late to the party I wasn't shy, so I have to take my share of the blame here. We let it happen.

Yes, we suggested Doyler give us more access to Syd Millar, former Ireland and Lions legend, to help with the scrum, and that certainly helped. But looking back now we should have done more.

By their nature players are selfish. They use people around them to make sacrifices so they can prepare to play. And if they keep getting selected to play then they tend to focus mainly on that, and not on the shortcomings of the man selecting them.

There was also the prospect of Jimmy D succeeding Doyler. Naturally that idea had huge appeal to me, but I knew it would be a harder sell to the Leinster and Munster lads. The last game of the Championship was away against Wales. We knew by then we'd be meeting them a few months later in our opening game of the Rugby World Cup, in Wellington.

It was a shite day in Cardiff and the pitch was so bad you knew anything could happen. In those circumstances I always felt it was about being positive. When it came to rugby I had a PhD in positivity. Why not? Mick Kiernan was a big game player and the surface didn't faze him when it came to kicking. Everywhere I looked on our side I saw guys I trusted. Even when Wales exploded out of the traps I wasn't worried. We reeled them in. Sure enough when we got ahead we stayed ahead. You could see it in their eyes as we shook hands after the final whistle. Two teams were hard to tell apart because of the mud. We were the ones smiling. Roll on New Zealand.

*****

Our preparation for the first Rugby World Cup was a joke.

The plan was to curtail our game time before the tournament to avoid injury. So for the six weeks leading to the tournament we couldn't play for our clubs. For anybody. Sure enough we arrived in New Zealand undercooked and limp instead of battle hardened. The travel arrangements to get there were not designed to have you in good nick. To this day the marathon of getting there is the longest I have ever endured: 36 hours from Gatwick via Los Angeles and Honolulu, with a curve ball at the end when Auckland was covered in fog, so we left the holding pattern there after a couple of hours to fly down to Wellington to refuel, and then back up to Auckland where the tournament dinner would be held.

Missing the dinner was not an option. We had barely checked in when we were straight out the door for a marathon training session. After being folded up like a deckchair for what felt like a week, and then run ragged, I couldn't wait to get to bed. The mattress was soft. My back was fucked. I spent the first few nights on the floor.

It felt like nobody had sat down and figured out how we could attack the Rugby World Cup. That was evident from the haphazard training schedule we'd been on since the last Championship game against Wales, on 4th April. Three weeks later we had a squad session in Wanderers' ground on Merrion Road. I travelled down on my own. Jimmy McCoy and John McDonald drove together. Davy Irwin, Nigel Carr and Chipper Rainey were in Davy's car. Nigel remembers all the red lights on the drive from his house in Newtownards over to Stranmillis where Davy's parents lived. Davy remembers all the green lights after that. They had planned to be on the road by 8am. A wee bit behind schedule, they set off in Davy's Ford Orion with Nigel in the front passenger seat and Chipper in the back.

When they got to within a few hundred metres of the border they passed the Ford Escort of Lord Justice Gibson and Lady Gibson travelling in the other direction, coming back from Dublin. Even though Lord Gibson had been a specific target of the IRA, and had his holiday home in Donegal torched three years earlier, he and his wife regularly travelled across the border. This time they were coming home after a holiday across the water. They had taken the Liverpool to Dublin ferry, before driving up north.

There was a time lag in between the Garda escort seeing them to the southern side of the border and the RUC picking them up on the far side. I don't imagine the RUC presence would have changed the picture had they been there, but when they arrived on the scene it was carnage.

The 500lb bomb, detonated by a radio signal, blew their car across the road into Davy's, heading in the other direction. Davy thought it was his own car that had been blown up. Miraculously he suffered very little physical damage. Nigel, beside him, took the brunt, and was badly lacerated around the head. He lost a lot of blood and suffered a few fractures on top of ligament damage to an already dodgy knee. Chipper was knocked out by the blast, but otherwise was pretty much OK. The Gibsons were killed outright.

There were no mobile phones in spring 1987, so no footage to post on social media which hadn't been invented. Meantime down in Merrion Road we were wondering what had happened to the three lads. By the time word filtered through I was taken aside by management and they explained to me as much as they knew. I was numb. I don't remember if we did any training at all after that. I drove to Newry where Nigel was in hospital, and reports of the incident were all over the radio.

I remember thinking on the way up the road, I'd been a part of this Ireland squad for two and a half years. That was 14 matches including the 1985 summer tour to Japan, where we played two Tests for no caps. That's a lot of time on the training field and on the pitch, a lot of time eating, drinking, singing and swapping stories. A lot of time understanding more about the men you played with and them getting to know more about you. But those lads from Munster, Leinster and Connacht didn't appreciate how close we lived to death up north.

On the day of that bomb I was three weeks past my 33rd

birthday. From the time I was 13 the Troubles had been the soundtrack in my life. We used to joke about it: if we weren't young and foolish we'd never have been able to cope. I wasn't sure what to expect when I got to Daisy Hill and saw Nigel. As you'd expect, the poor fella looked awful. There's not a lot you could say to make the situation better. I was so glad he was alive. Jeepers he was unbelievably strong mentally. I was there telling him he'd be brand new in a wee while and maybe fly out late to the Rugby World Cup.

"I need to get out of here first," he said.

*****

There is a horrible feeling you get early in a game sometimes when you know it's going arseways and you can't fix it. Ireland's first ever Rugby World Cup game against Wales was the first and only time in my rugby career where I felt helpless.

When people describe out of body experiences in sport they're usually talking about being in 'the zone' where everything they touch turns to gold. I think back to that windy day in Wellington when we couldn't raise a gallop, and I'm looking at myself from above, telling my tired limbs to move a bit quicker!

There was a bad feeling beneath the surface in the squad that we were hopelessly short of match practice. In fairness to Donal Lenihan, he sorted a scrummaging session for the forwards against the Scotland pack, who were staying across town in Auckland. How did Donal do this? Well the Scots, Welsh and Irish had all been down the back of the same plane, in the cheap seats, flying out of London for the marathon journey south. He got chatting to the Scots' hooker, Colin Deans, and sorted it.

Literally we were making it up as we went along. Then we were hit with a couple of sidewinders.

The first was Mick Doyle getting his heart attack. He was in awful shape making the trip, carrying a ton of weight. He decided to use the tournament to get fit. A bit like us, you could say. It all proved too much for him and he was hospitalised in a hurry. Syd Millar, our manager, took over the forwards while George Spotswood, the IRFU administrator, helped with the backs. This happened in the first week.

Then there was the matchday drill – in other words, the anthems. *The Soldiers' Song* is only ever played in Lansdowne Road because it's seen as the anthem of the 26 counties and obviously Lansdowne is in that jurisdiction. When we would play away in the Five Nations there would be the home anthem, and then the game. I don't know how much thought the IRFU gave it for this new-fangled creation that was the Rugby World Cup, but the policy was to continue with dead air where our anthem was supposed to be. So, of the 16 nations on this stage for the first time, rugby's brave new world, one of them would be mute. Jaysus!

Donal, as captain, was horrified when he discovered this by chance leading up to the game. Along with myself and Phil Orr the three of us represented the players, who had no issue with *The Soldier's Song* being played. It turned into a shit-show. Policy was policy, so the IRFU were not for turning. The compromise was to play a version of *The Rose of Tralee*, which Phil had on a cassette. *The Rose of Tralee*. On the day when it crackled into life over the tannoy in Athletic Park I remember thinking: 'Oh fuck, that's for us.'

It was an acutely embarrassing moment. What do you do?

You make like it doesn't matter and you get on with it. Had we been fitter and better prepared we might have had the tools to fly over it, but it felt like another rug pulled from beneath us. Then we lost Phil Matthews early on when he got a serious seeing-to at the bottom of a ruck. We had the gale-force wind in the first half and couldn't use it. We were pish.

Typical of the times we went on the lash after it. There was a reception of some sort on site and I slipped out and reappeared with the pipes. With anthems a hot topic at the time I played a medley of them, which went down very well. We had a few pints with the Welsh lads the next night as well. That was where their winger Glenn Webbe announced to the group that he had something important to say. I think that may have been a watershed moment for Glenn.

"When I die," he said. "I don't want to go to Heaven, I want to go on tour!"

I could identify with that.

The Welsh were usually the best of craic. I look back now and think if it wasn't for rugby I'd never have met Jonathan Davies. His nickname among the Welsh lads was Jiffy, but I called him Wizard. I think most of the Irish lads called him that, and understood why. He was terrifying to play against because of his skill and pace and ability to magic something out of nothing. But he was the number one man to spend time with afterwards. Between games for the Barbarians and Irish Wolfhounds over the years we had plenty of that.

The Hong Kong Sevens, with the Wolfhounds, was wild stuff. We brought him along as a guest because he was the only one who could play Sevens. He was handed a bottle of Baileys Irish Cream Liqueur in Heathrow and told to have it drunk by the time we landed. In fairness, we all had one. We weren't long in Hong Kong when he says to me, "Come on Willie, I'll bring you to a decent Chinese restaurant."

He sounded like a restaurant critic. The place was nothing special though. We'd finished our meal and after-dinner drinks when he looks at me and goes: "Willie...?"

There was something about his tone that spelled trouble.

"Willie, we're doing a runner."

I'd say Wizard could have run the 100m in around 11 seconds, regardless of his condition. At my peak I'd have added five seconds on that. With a bellyful of local beer and chop suey I didn't put myself in that category. You could hear the noise coming from the busy kitchen: men with meat cleavers who naturally enough wouldn't take too kindly to someone doing a runner on them. Having seen the inside of a jail in Buenos Aires I wasn't keen to follow up with one in Hong Kong. Of course the wee fucker slid out the door like a ghost and was gone. I paid the bill. I found him a few minutes later down the street, hiding behind a wheelie bin.

A few years later, by chance, I had my revenge. We were with the Barbarians on the Easter tour, playing in Leicester. The pair of us, and scrumhalf Robert Jones, were stumbling back to the hotel at all hours when Rob takes off at a sprint, just about ducking under the sign on the lawn welcoming you to the Travelodge, or wherever it was. Wizard followed him, but being maybe two inches taller he got levelled by the sign. It caught him clean in the forehead and put him on the flat of his back. For Rob and I it was the highlight of the tour!

The two of those boys were playing for Wales that day in Wellington, and were looking smug as they prepared to head up the road to Palmerston North, with morale sky high, to play Tonga. They were sure to top the pool, and play England in the quarters. We were off to Dunedin to play Canada, knowing we had no form and no room for mistakes. The best-case scenario at that point would be a quarter-final against Australia, in Sydney. It all felt like a different world to when we were walking off the field in Cardiff six weeks earlier.

The Canada game was confirmation we were in trouble. They had beaten Tonga well in the first game, but they were miles behind us in the pecking order. To put it in perspective, Canada had one match before the Rugby World Cup. That's one game between January and May in the lead up to the tournament. And that was against USA. This was the type of opposition we should be beating without breaking sweat.

After the non-start against Wales we were loading the games against Canada and Tonga to try and play our way into some fitness and form. It was the direct opposite of what you want on tour.

Bringing Tony Ward in for Paul Dean was one of three changes. The time to play Wardy would have been in Wellington when the gale was blowing and he could have done what Deano was not very good at – kicking the ball in behind the opposition!

Canada caused us a fair bit of grief without ever looking like winning. So, back on another plane and across the Tasman to play Tonga, in Brisbane. It was my first time in Australia, a country I had been keen to tick off the list. It would have been better if we were still following the plan. Doyler was securely back in harness and his health seemed fine, which was a relief, but by then he was like a spare wheel on a racing bike.

We beat Tonga handily enough, and the Blackrock boys Job

Langbroek and Neil Francis got their first caps. That was also Davy Irwin's first – and only – game of the trip. The two of us raised a glass to Nigel that night, not knowing at that point how badly he would be affected by the bomb. He spent a week in Daisy Hill immediately after the incident but struggled badly after that. He listened to the Rugby World Cup games on the radio, unable to get out of bed without help.

We flew down to Sydney for the quarter-final, match-fit at last and OK on the injury front. If you went back to the Triple Crown clinching game against England in 1985 you'd see the entire backline was still in place. Half of the pack though had been moved on, one way or another: Fitzy, Jimmy McCoy, and Nigel, while number eight Brian Spillane had lost out to Frano.

The game was played out in the Concord Oval on a shitty day, which you'd think would have suited us. Even the start went our way, with Phil Matthews clobbering their scrumhalf Nick Farr-Jones in the first few minutes. On came a guy we'd never heard of, Brian Smith, who bizarrely would go on to play for Ireland himself a few years later. His ties to Ireland were as close as mine to the Vatican. Smith played like he should have been on from the start that day. The Wallabies were sharp and skilful and we were shite. Trailing 24-0 early in the second half, Donal and myself ran out early on their star outhalf Michael Lynagh at a short penalty, thinking he'd tapped it, and levelled him. He got up and kicked the penalty. 27-0.

We got a couple of late tries through Hugo and Mick Kiernan to take the bare look off the scoreboard but it was cosmetic stuff. This was the day Mick Doyle came out with the quote that would follow him for years like a stray dog.

"At least we won the second half."

Jeepers, what a way to finish. We were going home. On the stopover out of Sydney I had a drink with Doyler while we were waiting for the ball-busting 12-hour leg to London. We had always got on well even if I no longer rated him as a coach. Everyone was knackered by then, especially our coach who was struggling mentally as well as physically. He didn't sound like he was up for more of it. I felt for him because you could see he thought the Triple Crown honeymoon of '85 would have turned into a happy marriage.

"You've had three seasons Mick – a good run at it," I said to him. "It's gone now. Save yourself the trouble of trying to get it back. Time to go."

He just stared out into space and made a 'hmmm' response. Then our flight was called. I had selfish reasons for pointing him in that direction: my international clock was ticking, I knew his race was run and I could see Jimmy D, ready and waiting.

In 2017 there was a 30-year reunion in Dublin for that Rugby World Cup squad. Nigel didn't travel down because he didn't feel a part of it. I understood perfectly how he felt, and yet I was profoundly sad he gave it a miss. It's a funny thing with sportsmen, a feeling that if you're not getting your head wet you're not one of the lads.

Even if you've been a part of the group for every minute on the training field and you're a regular on the team, you miss a couple of games and suddenly you feel a bit detached. I am proud that I was a part of Ireland's first Rugby World Cup, sorry that we didn't make more of it, and sad that Nigel didn't get to have that experience. His career was over. In 2021 he was awarded an MBE on the Queen's Birthday Honours List. How well deserved for such an accomplished man.

8

Conflict

I UNDERSTOOD EARLY THAT RUGBY WAS different to most sports in the way it accommodated violence. There were rules – or laws as rugby calls them – but they were loose enough when it came to the physical stuff. Everything was a battle. Whether I was playing second row or back row there was always conflict. Always a war to be won.

Two brutal challenges in my career stand out. The first – would you believe it – was against the French. Few people are aware we even toured there, but we did. And the second was against the All Blacks where you need to man up before the game even starts. I'll come back to that one.

By the time I went to Parc des Princes for the first time I was a veteran of five Tests. Jeepers, that place was something else. It's in the 16th Arrondisement, a nice, leafy suburb in the south west of Paris. I don't know enough about art or architecture to tell you if the stadium design is something special. To me it looks like some piece of industrial machinery designed for crushing things. In the circumstances it was perfectly fit for purpose. In the history of Irish rugby I don't think there was another stadium in the world where so many suffered so much for so little.

What did Ireland versus France mean to me? I became a running joke alongside my opposite number, Jean Condom, in my first game against them. 'Our Willie is Bigger than your Condom' said the banner in Lansdowne Road in March 1985.

Many years later I read reports linking French teams with the use of amphetamines and I have to say it added up. When you played them in Paris some of them were wired coming onto the field.

McKinney was the first man to wise me up about France. His Ireland debut had been in Paris. Over time that trip was to be a career killer for backrowers making their debut, but not that man. Being a first timer, he got the usual treatment from the local forwards. Their flanker, Victor Boffelli, had to be carried off after his shin connected with Stewie's head. I remember reading years later that Boffelli was "not a fighter" in the grand tradition of French psychopathic forwards, but he could have taken McKinney's head off that day. So the Dungannon man was concussed and ignored, with a lump on his head, while the TV commentator was ladling on the sympathy for Boffelli, who was getting carted off on a stretcher with a broken shin.

By the time my turn came around for Paris, the first game of the Championship in 1986, I thought I was ready. We were beaten out the gate. They scored three tries – which doesn't sound like a landslide – but we scored none. It was just another chapter in the story of France and Ireland in Paris, a place you went to get beaten, and beaten up. In the summer of 1988 I was determined that wouldn't happen on our wee four-match trip.

It wasn't supposed to be an exercise in development because the IRFU hadn't gotten around to that concept yet. But the rate senior players went missing changed the picture. Hugo MacNeill had just retired. The go-to backline at the time would have had Trevor Ringland, Brendan Mullin, Mick Kiernan and Keith Crossan across the middle, with Paul Dean and Michael Bradley at halfback. All of those lads were either injured or resting – or working. It was an amateur game. Up front there was no Donal Lenihan – our captain – Phil Matthews, or Des Fitzgerald. Of the starting pack from the France game in the Five Nations only Mike Gibson, Don Whittle and myself were available for the tour.

It would have been handy to have Davy Irwin around but he was injured, so it really was an adventure for greenhorns. At least I would get to be captain for the first time. Jimmy D didn't need to explain how hard it might be. It didn't matter. This was massive, and he knew I'd go through a wall for him. All I saw was a chance to make a positive impression on guys around me.

I knew enough about captaincy to understand that having someone ploughing his own furrow was a disaster. We had to be tight. Jimmy had real concerns about trying to gel such a diverse group in a short space of time. We were in the Westbury Hotel for the final session before flying out. I got everyone together in a meeting room and spoke to Jimmy in the corridor.

"Right, you get the waiters to bring in 25 pints every half hour, for the next four hours," I said to him.

We all sat around a table and played drinking games. Some guys started to sing. Others would take a turn telling jokes.

Some guys took to dancing. Some went quiet, others got stroppy. After a few hours they were in flying form, songs all sorted for the tour, and we all knew a wee bit more about each other. There was a group keen to go on up to Leeson Street. With Jimmy McCoy and John McDonald in the room – both RUC men – we had to have a few Garda minders. They offered to provide the transport. So we got one player into the front of the Ford Granada with them, maybe four or five in the back seat, and another two in the boot. Then we went up to Strings till about 4am. Massive craic.

I was determined that fellas would feel a part of it, that they would give everything to the cause and then see where they stood with their careers. I thought about what each player would want from the experience, and what I could do to make that positive. Craic was central to that.

As we had seen with the Rugby World Cup, touring in those days was a logistical challenge. The last person considered was the player. So for this trip we left Dublin on a Monday morning, 9th May, and came back on Sunday 22nd. France doesn't sound too far away, but we managed four flights and six ball-breaking coach journeys in that time. We lost count of the hours spent looking out the window. We sucked it up without complaint. Especially new lads who were just delighted to be there.

We had a squad of 24 players, led by Ken Reid as manager. We kicked off with a seven-hour journey from Dublin to Biarritz. Fly to London. kill an hour or two; fly to Paris, transfer to the domestic flight; fly to Bordeaux; fill another hour getting our stuff off the plane and on the bus then drive 130 miles to Biarritz. Your image of Biarritz in summer is probably the same as mine: beaches with big waves, sunshine, beer and pizza. It was like opening the door to a monsoon in a town that had shut up shop. Our first training session was an exercise in staying afloat. The itinerary didn't look like a minefield. Cote Basque to begin with in Biarritz, then a combined Armagnac Bigorre selection – whoever they were, in Auch – followed by a France XV in Lorient, and then the French Barbarians to finish in La Rochelle. Then home to a summer of fun.

We lost the first game 33-23 but we had played some decent rugby. I was mindful of being positive, so told the lads not to go on the piss because we had the Armagnac-Bigorre crowd a couple of days later. Then I changed course at the post-match and ordered them to get stuck into Benghazis. For the uninitiated this is a hurry-up where you have to drink whatever's in front of you in one go. All of it. It's route one to obliteration, and would have been common enough back in the day.

The French alickadoos were looking at us like we were on day release from *One Flew Over the Cuckoo's Nest*. We kept going into the early hours. Then I got a tap on my shoulder and a whisper in my ear.

"Excuse the interruption but we're playing an important match in two days," says Jimmy D.

The next morning I gathered the players and apologised for having led us all on the pish. I asked for everyone to switch on and be prepared to give it everything. It's a bizarre situation if you think about it, but I'll never forget that moment. It was like flicking a switch. We climbed on board the bus for the three hours haul to Auch, the home town of France coach and former scrumhalf Jacques Fouroux. Some called him Le Petit Caporal. Others Le Petit General. Either way, for a wee man of 5ft 4ins he carried a lot of weight.

CONFLICT

We should have worked out they'd throw a curveball at us given his family and friends would all be on hand. Sure enough, the second we got sight of the Armagnac Bigorre selection poor Ken Reid nearly keeled over. It was France, thinly disguised. They had eight of the guys we had faced in Paris three months earlier. All but one of the side that started against us would be heading on their tour of Argentina a few weeks later. The odd man out was scrumhalf Rodolphe Modin, who had been capped in the Rugby World Cup the previous year. They were full metal jacket compared to our shorts and t-shirt.

In the changing room I was in a lather of sweat. The theme of my rant was fairly simple: it was all about victory.

"OK guys, what I want to tell you is that there's only one thing I want today. And that's a win!"

Paul Clinch later told me he hadn't a clue what I was on about. He would be facing Serge Blanco, who was playing in the centre. Naturally enough he was fairly nervous. Blanco was a star, a shoo-in to most people's World XV. The previous year in New Zealand he had scored one of rugby's greatest ever tries to beat the Wallabies in the Rugby World Cup semi-final. Clincher was uncapped. And confused.

He was getting more anxious with every passing moment. 'What the fuck is this guy on about?' he was thinking. 'What's a one? One what?' He looked over at Tom Clancy for help, and Tommer just smiled and shrugged his shoulders.

"If there's anyone in this dressing-room who isn't with me then he can get the fuck out," I roared. "You have to believe we will 'one' this game!"

'Aaah,' goes Clincher. 'It's a win he's after. OK.'

It would require violence. That was part and parcel of rugby back then. For example the regular season had finished with a 'friendly' game against England, a month after we played them in the Five Nations. The second game was in Lansdowne Road, to mark the Dublin Millennium. There was nothing at stake, aside from pride – and a score to be settled. On the night of the previous game Mickey Skinner, the England flanker, was deeply disrespectful to the wife of Phil Matthews.

"I'll be seeing you again," Phil said at the time. Skinner was a big, gobby, physical player. Phil was nothing like him, personality-wise, but he definitely had a dark side.

There was no team plan, just a general understanding a price would be paid. The game had barely started when opportunity knocked: Stevie Smith threw the ball long over the back of our first lineout – no better man – and as everyone turned to follow the flight of the ball Phil whacked Skinner hard in the snot. It was a haymaker. By the time the phase of play ended the medics were still cleaning up the mess. In fairness to Skinner he arrived late for the next scrum, looking like he had fallen out of a plane, but didn't utter a word of complaint. Matthews, packing down opposite him on the blind side, was waiting.

"You know what the fuck that was for" he snarled. Lovely!

They swapped shirts after the game; Skinner apologised to Mrs and Mr Matthews; and the two men ended up working together in later years as rugby analysts on BBC. England had a few big hitters in those days, none bigger than my opposite number, Wade Dooley, who could throw a punch with the best of them. He was a sound man though. We got on fine.

I don't remember getting on with any of the French forwards.

If they weren't snatching your bag they were poking you in the eye. So on that 1988 tour I opened up on the 99 call. Lots of teams have copied the Lions use of the 'all-in' signal, from the South Africa tour in 1974, to get their retaliation in first. I knew enough about French rugby to expect the violent worst.

"If I shout 99 then everyone gets stuck in. Tag your opposite number and give the fucker everything you've got. Nobody's to stand back!"

Clincher is busy processing that bit of information. 'Great,' he thinks to himself. 'We're going to go out here against a full-strength French side and we absolutely have to 'win'. And we're certain to get into a fight.'

When it came to the first crossroads in the game I was on my own. We had been defending for a while and at the back of a lineout, Laurent Rodriguez dropped Mike Gibson like a stone. There was a bit of a scuffle. The ref blew his whistle and gave them a penalty for some reason. The crowd were whistling as our boys were trudging back expecting them to take three points. Meanwhile I was still at the scene of the crime. Right.

"Nine nine!"

I waded into Rodriguez and started throwing punches. It wasn't long before I realised I was on my own. I was getting hammered from all sides.

"Ninety Fucking Nine!"

I was like Custer at the Battle of Little Bighorn. I think the Indians took pity on me and eased off on the punishment as the Cavalry arrived. We had a court session among the squad a few days later and I was prosecuted for glory-hunting.

We recovered from that little hiccup and settled into the game, point blank refusing to take a backward step. The setting helped: it wasn't Parc des Princes; it wasn't a Championship game; this was one of those days where if you stood your ground it might be enough to give you a chance. It helped that we had Tony Ward at the top of his game. The outhalves on the trip were Wardy, on his last lap, and Nicky Barry, who was taking a break from his Leaving Cert studies in Limerick. Wardy was fantastic that day, pinning the French down with a stream of accurate kicking.

The man of the match however was Neil Francis. He dominated the lineouts and showed what an athlete he was when he got the ball in open space. He was a revelation. So good in fact he became a marked man.

We came from behind three times that day, thanks to Wardy picking off points and reeling them in. Midway through the second half we were 18-10 down, as Wardy stood over a penalty. If he got it we were making a statement of intent; if he missed they would have kicked on. He nailed it. The whistling of the crowd was music to my ears. The moment that nailed it for me was the impact of Pat O'Hara who came on for Don Whittle. His first tackle knocked Gilles Camberabero, Didier's brother, back about five metres. It was such a surge of adrenaline to the team.

A few minutes later Wardy carved through for a try which he converted himself for 19-18 to us. He even went close with a drop goal attempt before the end. The final whistle was one of the happiest moments of my life on a rugby pitch.

It was mayhem in the changing room afterwards. The handful of travelling pressmen were overcome. For a change they had something good to write about an Irish team in France.

For the record the 16 men who featured that day were: Phil Danaher; Johnny Sexton (no relation), Vincent Cunningham, Paul Clinch, Peter Purcell; Tony Ward, Gus Aherne; Tom

Clancy, Stevie Smith, Jimmy McCoy, myself, Neil Francis, Don Whittle (replaced by Pat O'Hara after 53 minutes), Mike Gibson and Denis McBride.

When the post-match festivities had wrapped up at the ground – they later named it in honour of Jacques Fouroux – I made a point of getting to the bus first, to shake the hand of every man as he climbed aboard.

"Congratulations, you've beaten France," I said.

We had barely settled into our seats when Ken Reid made an emotional address to the squad. The gist of it was we deserved to be capped for what in effect was an international match, and he'd be taking it up big-time with the IRFU when we got back. Jimmy McCoy looked at me with a deadpan expression. "Right, can't wait for that one," he said.

It was a wild night. We had t-shirts made up and berets to go with them, and by the time we set ourselves up in the centre of Auch, a lovely medieval town, the locals knew who we were. It's a proud rugby area but they were happy to celebrate our win with us. The next morning we dragged ourselves up, heads pounding but never happier, to start the crazy trek north to Lorient. We stopped in Nantes to train, and have lunch. Door to door it took over seven hours to get to our hotel. Much to my surprise we were minor celebrities there as well. Walking around the streets of Lorient the locals had us pegged as the team that had put one over on France. Our lads loved it.

The second 'Test' was only four days away, so there wasn't much time to recover. France came fully loaded again, expecting this time to put us away in style. The first part of that plan was to take Frano out at the first opportunity. He was done comprehensively at a lineout, which ended his tour. Nicky

Barry was in at outhalf for Wardy and came over to collect the ball to kick the penalty.

"Forget the posts, put it into the corner cub."

I don't think I had the 99 call out of my mouth but we were wading into them. Frano in that sort of form was a huge loss, but we made it clear we had absolutely fuck all interest in taking a backward step. We maintained that all the way to the finish line where I thought we were about to make it 2-0 in the series. We settled in for a few attacking scrums, trailing 12-7 but were clearly on top. We should have been rewarded with a penalty try only to be called back for a lineout. Nobody knew why. That was the final score. To beat them by out-scrummaging them would have been perfect.

Jacques Fouroux looked very relieved afterwards. At the post-match dinner he spoke about how good it was to see the return of "the fighting Irish". I took that as a reference to the hammering we got in Paris a few months earlier. I'd rather he had been talking about "the victorious Irish". We soldiered on another few days, lost to the French Barbarians in La Rochelle, and packed our bags.

I thought the measure of our tour was in the regret among lads who didn't make the trip, that they had missed out on something special. I'm pretty sure none of them reckoned on that outcome when they were declaring themselves unavailable.

And for those who signed up? I live in hope that one day the IRFU will backtrack and see those two games for what they were: Test matches. God knows how many fellas subsequently got a few minutes here and there playing for Ireland and can declare themselves part of the international club. The boys of '88 deserve better than that.

CONFLICT

In Jimmy D's office in Stranmillis there was a note pinned to the board above his desk. It was from Tom Kiernan on the IRFU committee, telling him his request to assemble a wee bit earlier to prepare for the New Zealand Test in November 1989 had been denied.

At the time the International Board Regulations had a timetable that prevented teams from getting together more than 48 hours out from a game. It was part of the regulations protecting the game from the evil of creeping professionalism. It was insane.

Given Jimmy's personality it was probably equally mad to pin the note where he couldn't miss it. He had one of his own beside it which read:

'It took three approaches, and two appeals, to get one session for the All Blacks match. Only then did they grant permission, but with two stipulations. 1. The Sunday session must finish at midday. 2. There was to be no physical contact. It is f***ing madness!!'

Jimmy's obsession with beating the All Blacks put the tin hat on it. He'd be getting on with his day, putting pieces into the jigsaw, then he'd catch sight of the note and his mood would go dark. It was like being hit by friendly fire. How could we win when we had one hand tied behind our back?

Most All Blacks tours are special events. They always leave behind something worth learning. The tourists of 1989 played breathtaking rugby. The spine of their team read: hooker Sean Fitzpatrick, number eight and captain Buck Shelford, halfbacks Graeme Bachop and Grant Fox, and John Gallagher at fullback. They were 11 wins from 11 games by the time they came to play Ireland in Lansdowne Road. Jimmy had managed to get enough intelligence on them in that period to fill a filing cabinet. He just needed a wee bit more time with the players to get his messages across. Sorry boss, no can do. After running with Phil Matthews as captain for the previous Championship Jimmy gave the captaincy to me. I was mad for action.

Over the previous two weeks New Zealand had played Leinster, Munster and Connacht. In addition to how we were going to stop John Gallagher hitting the line at speed, and from angles we couldn't work out, there was one recurring theme: teams looked beaten before they started. The Haka was a killer. It was like: 'Ye stand there like sheep while we work ourselves into a physical and psychological lather. And then we'll wade in to ye!'

The timing of it was perfect for them. The Haka didn't happen before the anthems, but after. So the second they signed off with the last, blood-curdling roar, it was game-on. We would have loved that leg-up into a contest.

Some teams dealt with it better than others. On the last leg of the Wales section of the tour the All Blacks played Newport in Rodney Parade. One of the proud clubs of South Wales with a colourful history, in 1963 Newport were the only one of 36 teams to get into the ring with the All Blacks, who were on a four months tour, and be standing at the final bell. In 1989 the Newport lads decided the best way to deal with the Haka was to go off into their own 22 and ignore it. Mistake. The All Blacks pursued them. It looked like the Welsh had just seen their home territory invaded.

Newport were huddled tight, trying to pretend they weren't being humiliated.

By the time Shelford had finished the war dance the match was as good as done. New Zealand won 54-9, the biggest total they ran up in the seven games in Wales.

Munster were watching too, and took note. They lined up directly opposite the All Blacks in Musgrave Park the week before we played them. It didn't do much on the scoreboard but at least they retained their self-respect. How we handled it was top of Jimmy's to-do list. It dominated our discussion on the way back from the Munster game.

"We can't let them feel comfortable in any way," he said. "It has to be a confrontation. We have to change the tone, the whole psychology of this. We want the crowd cheering us, not the fucking Haka!"

In the week of the game we got some interesting insight from Andy Leslie, the former New Zealand captain. Jimmy knew him well from Ireland's tour to NZ in 1976. Andy was in town leading a supporters group and we met up for a chat. Off his own bat Andy mentioned how the All Blacks loved it when teams wouldn't meet the challenge of the Haka full-on. Better still if they conceded ground.

"It's like we're taking your territory – that's the mental advantage," he said.

Andy wasn't giving us advice. He had no idea what we planned, but the moment the words came out of his mouth I could hear the wheels spinning in Jimmy's brain. Many years later Ireland would beat the All Blacks in Chicago. I watched that at home on television and was struck by the composure of our guys facing the Haka in their figure of 8 formation, commemorating the recently deceased Anthony Foley.

They had practised who was going where. There was no way

Joe Schmidt would have allowed for any ad-libbing. They told the All Blacks in advance what was coming. It was different in 1989. Truth be told, I got a bit ahead of myself.

The plan was to link arms on the halfway line, look them in the eye, and stand our ground. I had Davy Irwin on my left and Phil Matthews on my right – two men you'd be happy to have in the trenches with you in any battle. I was wired. From the moment the All Blacks were getting into their wee shape my focus was locked on Shelford. I started shouting at him: "We're gonna bate ye! We're gonna bate ye!"

Then I started inching my way forward towards him. He had the loose head prop Steve McDowell sharing the leadership role. They were out front with the rest of the team spread out behind them. Shelford was already halfway to 'Kamate Kamate' land with his nostrils flaring and eyes bulging. And I was en route to joining him. The march forward was spur of the moment stuff. It just felt right. They were able to stomp their feet and make all sorts of gestures and we had to stand there and admire them? No, I wasn't having that. But it rattled some of our lads who weren't sure how it was going to end. Davy and Phil managed to find a balance between supporting the cause and not starting World War 3! Not easy in the circumstances.

If everyone had taken my lead it would have been mayhem.

I wasn't thinking about that at the time. It was incredible how quickly the mood escalated. In an instant the crowd were on board and my heart was beating out of my chest. Thankfully we hadn't made contact before Shelford got to the last line, by which point the crowd were going mental. I was nose to nose with him. McDowell was pretty close to Nick Popplewell, a few yards to my left, who was winning his first cap. As it all broke up Sean Fitzpatrick was hovering with a menacing look on his face. We didn't budge as the All Blacks broke up to take up their positions for the kick-off. That wasn't planned either but the wee pause added dramatic effect. Then we broke ranks and I waved my arms to encourage the crowd as we went to receive the kick. The noise was incredible.

Honestly I've never been as pumped in all my life. My adrenaline rating would have been off the charts. But the thing about laying down a challenge to New Zealand is you need the tools to back it up. As we ran over to the East Stand side it felt like that's exactly what we were going to do. I don't think people appreciate that the pre-match toss allowed the advantage to swing back to them. What better way to put manners on us than to wade in from the kick-off?

But it couldn't have gone better. Grant Fox left it a bit short, barely on the 10m line – so while they reclaimed the ball they couldn't control it and it hit the deck. Bingo, the door was open again! Donal Lenihan hacked it ahead. You don't see much of that anymore, and fair play to Shelford he gathered well only to be swallowed whole by the green-eyed monster. A creature with many legs. There was a scramble between us to give him a good shoeing for his trouble. You don't see much of that anymore either.

As Buck was being tended-to the noise from the crowd was off the charts. Lansdowne Road was like a bearpit that day. He was asked afterwards if he'd been scared. Quick as a flash he said: "Yeah, I was scared he was going to kiss me we were so close!"

When the media asked me about it I said New Zealand won

the game and we won the dance. On the day they recovered quickly enough to win well. That's what good teams do, and they were excellent. Jimmy D was proud of the effort but I knew he was hurting that we hadn't got over the tryline.

"You took it to them Willie," he said. "That's what I asked you to do."

Noel Mannion was at number eight that day. He was still relatively new on the scene and his 70m try against Wales in Cardiff was one of the highlights of 1989. Jeepers it was a stunning effort. He didn't see the year ending with a different kind of theatre though.

"Jesus Willie you're some bollocks!" he said to me afterwards. "I was trying to do the sum in my head out there: will the last verse of Haka be over before we arrive into the middle of them?"

I had a smoke and a few beers with Grant Fox in their changing room. They had absolutely no problem with us. I'd say a few of them were glad to be able to tell the story from the winners' perspective.

"I thought 'bloody hell, what's going on here?'" Sean Fitzpatrick said to me years later. "It was terrific. You accepted the challenge."

In a way I was lucky to be on the field at all that afternoon. The day before the Wales game my back was giving me a lot of trouble and I asked Joe Doran, our physio, if he had a painkiller. Joe, a wonderful man who was part of the furniture with Ireland, gave me two distalgesics, which I swallowed without giving it a second thought. After the game I was called out to do a dope test. Again, I didn't have a moment's hesitation. My only problem was getting enough into the wee cup to keep the tester happy. Early the next week I got a call from someone in the IRFU to say I had registered a positive test, but to do nothing. The distalgesics had some ingredient on the banned list, but there was a kind of margin for error in those days, so if the amount of the banned substance was under a certain limit it was a 'no case to answer' job. That was me.

But the story was reported in Wales first, I think, and then picked up locally in Belfast. Poor Heather was blindsided at school. A kid came up to her in the corridor.

"Mrs Anderson is your husband a drug dealer?"

She made a beeline for the Principal's office where they got out a copy of the paper that ran the story. Poor Heather was mortified and went home early. It didn't even merit a line in the IRFU's annual report and I'd say most of the lads on the team didn't even know it happened. I wonder if I'd thrown another few tablets down my neck would the story have turned out differently.

*****

The All Blacks game wasn't long over though when I was getting dirty looks from men in green blazers. Departures from protocol weren't welcome. Marching into the middle of the Haka was a departure from protocol. I get that. I was on a different emotional wavelength at the time. I made another diplomatic blunder in my speech at the dinner that night. A couple of days earlier a good friend of mine, Bob Glover, was blown up a few miles from where I live now. He was 38, a partner in Acheson & Glover who supplied building products to the security forces as well as the general public. That made him an IRA target.

Bob left a wife and three kids, one of whom – Pamela – many years later would marry my son Thomas. His car exploded into a Semtex fireball on the road as he drove home from work.

Because of my close connection to Bob I wasn't told about his death until immediately after the game. That would hardly be possible in the current age of instant news, but it was manageable back then. I was stunned. Bob was later described by the Dungannon priest, Fr Denis Faul, as: "A good man who has given valuable service to the community."

It was not directly related to the game but I wanted to mention him in my speech. "We play rugby as if our lives depend on it, which feels right at the time," I started. "But real life is going on beyond the pitch. Real life for me is the death of my friend Bob Glover, blown up by the IRA a couple of days ago, and I'd like to pay tribute to a good man tonight." I was told flat out that the IRFU was apolitical. Well, apolitical or not I felt entitled to mention it.

A lot of the All Blacks came up to offer condolences, saying they understood what the northern lads on the Ireland team had to contend with. They seemed to have a better understanding of it than the IRFU committee. The only one of the blazers who spoke to me that night was Roy Loughead, a decent man and a wise rugby head. I always appreciated his words of support.

"I understand perfectly where you're coming from Willie," he said. "You have to live in Northern Ireland to understand Northern Ireland."

Ulster played the All Blacks the following week in Ravenhill. The Haka had been all over the news in the meantime. The referee warned us beforehand to keep our distance and we took up a position to make sure there was no nose-rubbing. We were flat as a pancake. The IRB sent out a directive about observing the gap between rugby's most famous dance and the opposition. I could see where they were coming from all right. I was clean mad that day in Lansdowne Road. I don't regret a second of it. And when people ask me would I not rather have a famous moment attached to a win rather than a loss, I tell them life's not like that. At least not mine.

Everyone remembers that game for the Haka and the raw emotion, but another remarkable thing happened: a wee lad barely turned 14 had a direct impact on the final score. Garrett Tubridy had become the team's ball-boy before being a ball-boy was even a thing. He started by getting the bus in from his family home in Blackrock to watch squad sessions in Lansdowne Road, and from there he became a fixture. So when Grant Fox scored what he thought was his first Test try, Garrett was pressed into service.

"Jim Fleming was on the West Stand side with his flag raised because Sean Fitzpatrick had overstepped the line when throwing into a lineout," he says. "Play moved on and Jim stood there with the flag raised. When I asked him why he didn't run after the referee he said: 'I can't – I'm not allowed!'

"In those days there were touchline seats in front of the stands so when Grant Fox scored in the other corner people were hollering at me to run over to the ref, Sandy MacNeill. I had to run on with the sand anyway for the conversion so I went up to Sandy and told him about Jim on the far side. That was the end of the Grant Fox try."

Twenty nine years later I was taking my seat in the stand in the Aviva, along with my brother Ollie, for Ireland against the All Blacks. And who was sitting beside us, with his wife Tatiana? The same Garrett Tubridy. We took it as a good omen. And we were right. He didn't have to run after the ref that day. The All Blacks were the ones being chased. It was a great day out.

9

The Bug

IF YOU HAVE EVER COACHED IN ANY SPORT AT any level it's likely somewhere along the line you'll have felt conflicted. It was probably over selection.

Did you have set rules for picking only players who put in the hours on the training field?

Did you try and serve the hunger for victory by selecting someone who's clearly a better player but is a lazy git, over an ordinary Joe who never misses a session?

For me it was a different sort of conflict. In 1983 I had to drop tools in Grosvenor and jump at the opportunity that came up in The Rainey. The job was head of the PE department. No decision to be made. Except that I was leaving a group of lads who I loved coaching, and who had just won their quarter-final of the Ulster Schools Cup. I had taken them on as first years, when I went into the school. What unfolded as they grew up involved a few tears, a few stand-offs, a lot of laughs, some great rugby and a huge sense of satisfaction that I had been part of their development.

Grosvenor was on the wrong side of Ulster's rugby tracks. I always appreciated principal Ken Reid keeping the door open for me when I had been detained in Argentina, and I understood what he was trying to build in the school. Ken was a big rugby man who believed the game could offer the school benefits across the board.

There were plenty of hard lads there. They would have had a much deeper affection for the Cock and Hens – the local rhyming slang for Glentoran FC, the pride of East Belfast – than Ulster rugby, let alone Irish rugby. That changed because Ken filled the staff room with rugby men, so the kids couldn't get away from it. International referees Stephen Hilditch and Ronnie Gilliland, former Bangor and Ireland full back Ronnie Elliott, plus a couple of future Ulster branch presidents in Chuck Evans and Ian Graham. That's a fair chunk of rugby knowledge. The sporting menu had rugby for main course, followed by a dessert of athletics. That was pretty much it.

It was a hard environment where we harnessed the toughness of the lads with discipline that would stand to them on and off the pitch. We knocked lads around, plain and simple. We also got on very well with them. I remember one athletics championship down in Belfield in Dublin where our boy won the 800m and we all headed over the road to the Montrose for a few pints. The lad was well oiled by the time we got back on the minibus. Teachers and senior pupils having a few pints after sporting events was standard stuff in those days.

When I was packing my bags for Magherafelt, and The Rainey, the schools semi-final draw had not been made. The Rainey were defending champions at the time, a terrific achievement for them. Sure enough they drew Grosvenor in the semis. I found it a challenge to invest myself 100 per cent with my new school having such a fondness for the one I just left. Grosvenor won 9-6, and then went in as long-odds underdogs against the mighty Inst – RBAI – in the final. They won that too. They invited me to join in the celebrations that night, which was a very attractive proposition. The staff room in Grosvenor had been mighty craic. I remember one time being in a gang of about a dozen stuffed into a minibus on a pub crawl around the Ards peninsula. There were a few times in that school when you'd avail of a crash mat in a quiet corner of the gym to catch up on some sleep. Never slow to sign up to a party, the night of the schools cup final was one pish-up I avoided. When you're gone you're gone. I didn't always have that discipline.

*****

By the time I went to work for the IRFU in 1988 I had a solid block of experience between coaching the schools and club game. I had squeezed every last drop out of my playing career. From Omagh Academy through to Dungannon I had been blessed with fantastic experiences. I had no intention of stopping there.

Effectively I had become the coach in my six seasons as captain in Stevenson Park. I had firm ideas on how the game should be played, and what needed to be done to create that environment. The culture in Stranmillis had steered me towards coaching and things were ticking along nicely by the time I became a Union man.

I was a year into my job in Magherafelt High School when the job with the Union came up. They were putting development officers into the four provinces, and I was a racing certainty for the Ulster one if I wanted to saddle up. I did. Everything from mini rugby up to elite senior players was in my parish, across the nine counties of Ulster. I was given a desk in the office of Sport Northern Ireland, near Queen's, in Upper Malone. At first I thought they were stuck for space in the Ulster Branch office in Ravenhill, but I think it was all part of Syd Millar's plan to expose me to broader influences. Syd was chairman of the Northern Ireland Sports Council. As ever, he was an influencer.

So I was sharing office space with Stephen Martin, the Ireland and Great Britain hockey international. It was a great place to work because you were mixing with people across a range of sports, all involved in developing and promoting their codes one way or another. Stephen was great company and gave me loads of useful info. At the time hockey had a very high profile in Northern Ireland, getting good exposure on UTV and BBC NI. He was dipping into so many aspects of that sport from promotion to commercial, as well as being a world class player and an Olympian.

Soon enough I was putting up 60,000 miles a year chasing my tail across the country. It was tough on Heather. Jonathan, our first boy, was four when I started the job, and Thomas was a year old by then. It would be another few years before Chloe came along to complete our family, but one thing that never changed was my absence. I was either training or playing or coaching, or socialising around one of those three – but never where I was needed: at home.

THE BUG

The job could take you from a small, rural outpost working with guys who were really up against it to the big set-pieces, if you like, at Greenmount Agricultural College in Antrim, or Clongowes Wood College in Co Kildare, where we ran residential courses for coaches and players at all levels. I was busy writing content and delivering sessions and thinking about rugby most of every day.

I was well settled into the role when in 1992 I took off for a few weeks to Australia on a fact-finding mission for the IRFU. Through George Spotswood they had come to realise the development side of the house needed more structure and manpower. Australia were well ahead of us on every front. Rugby there had hooked up with the Australian Institute for Sport in Canberra. We didn't have one of those on the island of Ireland. So off I went to see what I could learn. That's where I met Matt Williams, and our paths would cross again soon enough.

I did a lot of travelling across Queensland, New South Wales and Canberra in the three weeks, met a lot of very sound rugby men and had heaps of stuff to bring back and put in my report. The thing that stood out most was the way they were aligned. Australia had won the Rugby World Cup, beating England in the final, the previous year. It was explained to me how it all started with the mission statement that they wanted to win it. Then they figured out what had to be done and who would do it. Every box was ticked, everybody was on the same page feeding into the same script. Picking the squad would have been the easiest bit. On the long journey home I started writing. Every so often I'd stop and wonder: 'Jeepers is there any chance of us catching up with these guys?'

Working for the IRFU was like being in a time warp where

some people were trying to get up to speed and others wanted to stay exactly where they were. Stephen Aboud – like me, an employee – was very much in the first group. He was my equivalent in Leinster, with Declan O'Leary in Munster and Eddie O'Sullivan in Connacht. We were the infantry. The generals were out of sight somewhere in the background. Because we were employees we were supposed to avoid contact with players over 18. Sounds odd, but there you go. Coaching adult players, as a paid employee, would have contravened International Board Regulations on amateurism.

This stuff all came from committee level. A lot of the committee men I came across were not arsed about Irish rugby being competitive on a world stage. The majority of them were elected, and therefore honorary and unpaid. The committee men made the decisions. The employees followed the orders that came out of the committee room. Status quo was everything.

Steve Aboud and I got on straight away. I have a mad streak that's not hard to spot from 20 paces. He could see it coming from twice that distance and was able to cope with it. As an outgoing, highly social animal, I could see he was my opposite: introverted and studious. He has a serious intellect which he decided to apply to rugby. He was always too far ahead of the committee men on the rugby stuff but the politics of the place used to frustrate the fuck out of him. And me.

We both reported to George Spotswood, the IRFU's first technical director. The impetus to set up the IRFU Foundation, in 1993, came from him. The basis of it was the information I brought back from Australia, which Steve used, along with our own input, to write the programme. The provincial Academies we have today are based on what Steve did in 1993.

THE BUG

George is a Dungannon man. I liked and respected him. He knew the game backwards and was mixing with like-minded souls across the other unions in the Five Nations. Still, we managed to clash over a fair few issues over the years. For example at first I put in a lot of time on the minis front, an area of the game just taking off in Ireland. We had a huge opportunity to get stuff right from the start and George was very much onside – he saw the crazy stuff going on in rugby schools where it was 15-a-side for kids aged eight. Madness.

"It's honeypot rugby," he said to me one day. "They all gather round the ball."

I wanted George to make it a law of the minis game that kids carried the ball in two hands. So if a wee boy or girl forgets and tucks the ball in their armpit it's turned over to the other side. Think of the positive effect of getting this right from the age of seven, eight or nine? Jeepers the grief you'd save yourself trying to get teenagers to break a bad habit. I had a big hand in putting together Leprechaun Rugby, which was the IRFU introduction to the game, and it was popular and effective.

George would regularly be giving Steve and myself papers to read from rugby's big thinkers across Europe. Pierre Villepreux in France for example was always innovating. Danie Craven in South Africa. Dick Greenwood in England the same. It was a good time for coach innovation. We were always learning and George was always encouraging us to learn.

He could see we had the coaching bug.

So in late 1992 I was working away when out of the blue Noel Murphy, manager of the Ireland team, called me up to work with the squad. He said I'd be helping on a technical front with the forwards. Noisy, as Noel was known to everybody, was talking in riddles when explaining the situation to me. What it boiled down to was this: Ciaran Fitzgerald was stepping down as Ireland coach after the heavy defeat by Australia in November 1992. His assistant for the previous season, Gerry Murphy, would become head coach. They needed to fill in some gaps around Gerry but because I was already a paid employee of the Irish Rugby Football Union I could not be listed as an official coach of the Ireland side – that would have contravened the game's regulations on amateurism. So officially I was to be a technical advisor – unofficially I was to be the forwards' coach. It was bullshit, but it was an opportunity to work in the international game so I was ready for action. Like peas in a pod, Steve Aboud would be beside me – him working with the backs under the same cover of being an advisor rather than an official member of the coaching staff. That grey area would cause me problems later.

I don't know what sort of arrangement they had with Gerry Murphy but they magicked up some deal that didn't ring the alarm bells on amateurism, and didn't leave him out of pocket at the same time. So off we went, the three of us, into the 1993 Five Nations Championship. We lost the first two games, to Scotland and France, before doing the unthinkable. With 11 defeats in a row clocked up, going back to Scotland in the 1991 Rugby World Cup, we beat Wales in Cardiff. It was a massive relief all round. Eric Elwood had made a successful debut at outhalf behind a pack of forwards I knew could deliver something special. There was the standard craic post-match. I had a few drinks with the players at the dinner that night, and then called for a few Benghazis. On the Wednesday or Thursday of the next week I got a phone call asking me to come and meet some of the past presidents of the IRFU. It sounded a bit odd, but I motored on, thinking about the England game coming up. I rang Steve to tell him.

"Maybe they want to clap you on the back for the win in Cardiff," he said.

The meeting was set for the morning of the England game, which obviously suited the past presidents who would be all together for that, having had dinner in the hotel the night before. The meeting was more a kick in the arse than a clap on the back. Basically it was a bollocking for having got stuck into a few drinks with the players after the Wales game. If I had been an unpaid coach rather than an under the radar hired hand it would have been fine. I had to compose myself before going back to the squad, who were playing a few hours later. We beat England that afternoon. I gave the players a wide berth afterwards.

Our next meeting with England was the following season in Twickenham, February 1994. We had lost to France and Wales in the first two rounds. If we beat them it would be our first back-to-back wins in that fixture since the five in a row run from 1972-76. Nobody gave us a snowball's chance in hell. The night before the game I had a few pints with Gerald Seymour, the best-selling novelist, and his son Nick, in a quiet wee hotel bar in Richmond.

I had met Gerald a couple of years earlier in Dungannon when he was researching his novel, The Journeyman Tailor, set here during the Troubles. Gerald reported from Northern Ireland as a news journalist with ITN during the early days of the conflict. He's a lovely man, a big rugby fan, and we stayed in touch. Sometime after the 1993 win over England in

Lansdowne Road he came across one of the English forwards at a dinner.

"At what stage of that game did you realise you were going to lose?" Gerald asked the player.

"About 15 minutes before we went on the pitch," was the reply.

Gerald was recounting that to Nick and myself as we were having our few pints, describing it as a moment of truth in sport.

"Your lot haven't a chance tomorrow, have they?" he asked me.

"Throw a few bob on Ireland to win," I said. "I'm telling you: we're more ready for this than we were last year."

Kyran Bracken was selected at scrumhalf for England. He'd made his debut for them the previous November in a famous win over the All Blacks. He was a cocky, handsome wee lad was Kyran. He's from Skerries, in north County Dublin. I knew precious little about how Kyran's family had moved to England but presented him anyway as a cross between Judas Iscariot and the Devil Incarnate. Our lads were happy to buy into that.

There was no lifting in the lineouts in those days, so getting clean ball from that phase was tricky. We looked to spoil on their throw, hammer through on Bracken, and kick seven shades out of him. The knock-on effect would limit the supply going to Rob Andrew at outhalf, and in turn to the flying Underwood brothers, Rory and Tony, on the wings. Even if Bracken got the ball away cleanly the instruction was to run over the top of him. Continuity was my thing, and technically we were making progress. But when you married it with some violence it was a potent mix. Simon Geoghegan scored a lovely set-piece try to clinch a great win, 13-12. It was a touch of class on a day when we had been hard-arsed in our approach.

A few months later we toured Australia: five provincial games, an Australian XV and two Tests. It was like any Irish tour abroad, except with a bit more excess. In my case, a lot of excess. My reliance on drink was really developing by that stage. That spin has become known as the last of the great drinking tours. As the Aussies say, it was full-on in that regard, starting in Perth with an almighty pish-up to ease our way out of the jet lag. It didn't let up much after that. In keeping with Irish tradition however we trained hard. That was my first time away with a senior representative side in a 'coaching' capacity so I had to play both sides of the park. I enjoyed the craic no end, but I always led the charge at training the next morning. That was part of my rationale with myself at the time, on the odd occasion I thought about my intake: if I'm getting up in the morning and getting the job done then it's not out of control.

If you weren't physically fit going out on tour then no matter how much you drank you'd be fitter coming home, simply because of the training and playing load. That tells you something about how unfit our top players were at the time. It was an ongoing issue, a direct consequence I thought of being obsessed with amateurism. After winning handy in our opener against Western Australia we had 55 points stuck on us by New South Wales in Sydney. It was one of those days when you want the ground to open up and swallow you. I was embarrassed looking at their coach Matt Williams in the eye after that. But we got better. We ran Queensland to three points the following week and looked good against Australia in the Second Test, having been blown out of the water in the First. That Second

Test, in Sydney, was our eighth and last game. We were fit and the lads had gone through many sessions where I had the rucking nets out to get them lower. I had a fixation about body height at the ruck. I'd whack lads on the arse with a flagpole as they were coming under the nets if their rear ends were too high. Of course then we went home and there was no follow up to take advantage of the work.

The lowlight of that tour though, the darkest moment by a distance, was in a town I had never heard of before I went there, and have never had cause to look up since: Mount Isa. It's worth checking it out on the map. Google it and you need about four goes at increasing the size of the map before you come across another town. It's up in northern Queensland, a long, long way from anywhere. The venue suited the Aussies on a couple of fronts: they were subjecting us to somewhere with all the positivity of death row and just getting there and back would tire us out.

The game stands out in my career for the feeling of utter helplessness. If I had been embarrassed by the hammering we took from New South Wales then this was just a whole new level of shellacking. It was an Australian XV, but in the way that the French XV in Auch in '88 was not exactly a bunch of random lads. Stacked against what was mostly our midweek selection, you could sense danger at hand. We had to throw Ken O'Connell into the back row, and him barely off the long haul flight from home, coming out to replace the injured Paul Hogan.

Ken had been heroic in Sunday's Well's Munster Cup final win over favourites Young Munster the previous weekend. It had been a brilliant season for them: promoted to the First Division of the AIL, and then success in the Munster Senior Cup. Ken had been on the lash solidly since receiving the trophy. It was a lot to ask of any man, to go out that night against that level of opposition, and expect a happy ending.

At various stages of a high-speed demonstration of skill and aggression, their forward pack featured Richard Harry, Dan Crowley, Owen Finegan, Willie Ofahengaue and Brett Robinson. A young Ryan Constable started on the wing for them. He was about to win his first cap that week.

We had to take four players off injured. The First Test was a few days away. It was like having a wet sack over your head and getting whacked from all angles.

At one stage, with us trailing 52-9, I could hear the opening bars of a well-known song striking up among the hardy band of Irish supporters in the stand. Monty Python's *Always Look on The Bright Side of Life* caught the mood. It was black, gallows humour. I wanted to die. In the changing room afterwards I looked at Ken, shattered in the corner.

"Jesus Willie," he said. "I sidestepped Willie O maybe three times out there. Unfortunately he had the ball at the time!"

We flew down to Brisbane the next morning, relieved that no TV highlights would follow us. The floodlights at the ground were, like us, not up to the required standard.

I wasn't long home from the tour when I had a major decision to make.

Here was a fork in the road ahead for me: one route pointing towards Dublin and sticking with the IRFU job, which I had been doing for six years, the other towards Dungannon and taking up a new role as the club's first Director of Rugby. The club was attractive for a few reasons: the AIL may not have been Jimmy D's ideal model to serve Irish rugby but it was still a shot in the arm for clubs. We were getting good crowds at games and there was a buzz about the place. It was good for club life.

I had learned a fair bit over my years in the IRFU job and was keen to put it into action in an environment where I was on solid ground. That was Dungannon. And it was close to home. Life there had already changed in a way that shook me to my core.

10

The Tragedy

IT WAS 2ND DECEMBER 1992.

To this day I'm not sure why I waited to wave him off, but I did. And to this day I regret with every part of me that I didn't just drop him at the gate, wish him all the best, and head back home. Maybe it's because it was Andy Leslie, former All Blacks captain, and a good man. He had been a guest at my house. I wanted to look after him, if you like.

Andy was considered a friend of Irish rugby. He had been captain when New Zealand beat Ireland in Wellington in 1976, an Irish side that contained a few heads who would go on to have prominent careers in the IRFU: Ian McIlwrath, Tom Grace and Pa Whelan among them. A bond was forged in those days.

Soon after the All Ireland League got started Andy was brought over by the IRFU to take a look at the game here and make some recommendations. He would come back a few years later to coach Garryowen to their second AIL title, in 1994. As part of his IRFU report he consulted far and wide, including a few meetings with me. Given my exposure to the game from grass roots up to international level I had plenty of ideas. So I invited him up to The Loup, the wee village in Co Derry where we still live, to chew the fat. To be honest I was honoured to have him. He's a knowledgeable, humble man, and very good company. We got on famously.

We had a great chat about lots of things. The next day after lunch I dropped him back to Portadown Railway Station to connect with the train from Belfast to Dublin. We were in good time. We agreed to talk again soon, and off he went. I stayed until he was on board and the train was actually pulling away.

I headed back home along the normal route. It's about a 40 minute drive.

It was getting on for 4.20pm when I was driving through The Loup. From my right hand side, coming from behind a school bus, a wee lad ran out, straight across my path. There was a tractor parked behind the bus. He ran through the gap between the bus and the tractor.

I slammed on the brakes but the collision was unavoidable. It felt like a dull, heavy, horrible thump. I have an image of his school-tie on the windscreen. I couldn't move a muscle when the car stopped. The driver of the tractor rushed over as people were already gathering around. He helped me out of the car. I ran into a shop and called for an ambulance. I don't know if I called the police as well but it took them a long time to get there. It was suggested to me later they wouldn't have been rushing to The Loup, a Catholic village, for fear of being set-up for attack.

My next phone-call was to Heather, who was at home with our wee girl Chloe. Heather swept her up, put her in the baby seat, and drove straight to the village. I was in bits when she arrived. I don't how long we were there but I knew how serious it was, that it wasn't going away. Why couldn't I just rewind to the point where I was at Portadown Station and start all over again?

The feeling of having no control over what was happening was overwhelming. And it felt never-ending. Then a fresh panic set in. Heather went to check on Chloe in the back of her car and let out a scream. Chloe, who was a couple of months off her second birthday at the time, had slipped down halfway out of her baby seat but got caught on one of the straps. It was choking her. She was literally blue in the face when Heather realised what was happening. We hadn't heard a sound. It was like an internal alarm went off with Heather to go check on our wee girl. Christ, we didn't know where to turn next.

The lad's name was Glen McLernon.

Heather came with me when I went in to the Mid Ulster Hospital in Magherafelt that night to see him. I knew I had to do it but I had no idea what would happen when I got there, what shape Glen would be in and what way his parents would react to me being there. I was petrified it would be hostile. I was prepared for the worst but it passed in a blur. Glen was on life support. His mum and dad were in that limbo zone where things were happening around them. They acknowledged my presence but could hardly speak.

My brother Ollie and our parents were at our house when we got back. There are a few points in my life when Ollie got an emergency call to come over and lend support. None as traumatic as this. We had a few people calling to the house, offering support. I couldn't sit still. I was walking from room to room, playing it all over in my head. Two scenes kept popping up on my screen: instead of waiting for Andy to board the train I would beep and wave and drive off; the other was the moment of impact, and Glen's school tie.

Sometime that evening a sturdy looking car pulled up outside. The sort of car fortified against attack. It was like a tank. This was 1992, before any Good Friday Agreement. Two minders got out. One stood there with a hand inside his jacket as if it was resting on something important while the other opened the back door. At first I thought they were RUC detectives. Then I realised it was a different sort of visit. The Rev Willie McCrea, minister of the Free Presbyterian church of Northern Ireland and a DUP member of Magherafelt District Council, got out and walked up to our front door. What was this? We let him in. I don't know why, other than I was still in shock and Heather was busy trying to keep me together. His visit was probably well intentioned but basically he gave us a party political broadcast on life and the evils of drink. I just didn't have the room in my head to process a scene like that.

Glen died the next day. He was 11. Everyone in the village attended the funeral, walking behind the hearse. I literally struggled to put one foot in front of the other. Heather is not a tall woman but she had to cope with me leaning on her from start to finish. In the days that followed I visited the McLernon house. Glen's dad Will showed me his son's room. There was a rugby ball sitting in the corner.

It was one I had signed for him on a Leprechaun Rugby course I had given at The Rainey, where he was in first year.

THE TRAGEDY

He was a bright, sporty young lad with a keen interest in the game, enjoying all the excitement and craic that goes with meeting new kids and making new friends in secondary school. I took that away from him. There is hardly a day where I don't pass the graveyard, half a mile from our house, where Glen is buried. His parents continued to live in the locality for a fair while afterwards. We would pass each other on the road occasionally. Every time I saw them it felt like I was wounding them all over again. The guilt was crushing.

At some point over the next day or two after the accident the local parish priest from St Patrick's, Fr O'Byrne, came to see me. I knew him to say hello to in the village. What a sound man. He visited a few times after that, and listened, and never made any judgements. In writing this book I contacted Will, to ask his permission to use Glen's name. The family had moved to the UK. We spoke for a while and he was incredibly gracious. I also contacted Fr O'Byrne to thank him for his support at the time, and to ask him why he had crossed the line to help a Presbyterian who had no contact with the Catholic Church. He downplayed it.

"I was just giving you a bit of support to help with the terrible pain you were going through," he said. "Like so many other things in life, until you go through them yourself you don't realise what people suffer, both the victim and the family as well as the person concerned."

For weeks after the accident when I tried to talk about it I would break down. Andy Leslie was very supportive. He would ring on the pretext of some rugby detail and then let me share with him what I was feeling. Years later Steve Aboud said when he checked in with me over that period it was like talking to a shell of a man. I don't remember taking time off work from the IRFU. I don't remember anyone there asking what state I was in, or if counselling would be a good idea. I don't know if counselling was even 'a thing' in the early '90s, but I was a candidate, surely. Every time I engaged with someone in the IRFU office I was waiting for a kind word, an offer to go for a coffee or whatever. It was like the accident never happened. As time went on I struggled to understand why there was so little understanding from my employer. I was told the first question asked when they heard of the accident was if I'd been drinking.

No, I hadn't.

But I did a lot of it after that.

*****

The inquest followed a couple of months later in Cookstown. The testimony of the man driving the tractor was crucial. He had seen Glen run out blind between the tractor and the bus and into my path. I hadn't been speeding. There was no attempt to lay blame at my door. I suppose that should have been a relief, but when you're in that situation you will accept any punishment because all you can feel is guilt. If you get punished then there's a measure of atonement.

That inquest took place a couple of days before we played England in the Five Nations in Lansdowne Road in 1993. So I arrived a bit late to the gathering in Dublin. The players knew something was up but the Ulster lads – Paddy Johns, Brian Robinson and Denis McBride – were very protective of my situation and managed it very well in the squad. Mick Galwey is the sort of man who can convey more than the average man with the wink of an eye, which is what he did when I got down to Dublin. No words were exchanged but it meant the world at the time. Going back into that group was like being wrapped up and protected. Again, there was no official recognition from the IRFU of what was going on. We beat England. Gaillimh – to give Mick Galwey his Irish nickname – crashed over the line to kill the game off, and then he was swallowed up by supporters coming in off the touchline seats. It was a huge win, followed by a huge session that started with waiters serving us champagne in the Berkeley Court Hotel. I drank that night to celebrate, and to forget.

Up until that point I drank the way most Irishmen drank. Whatever the occasion, happy or sad, you would gather in a pub or club or private house and drink would be common to all occasions. Baptisms, engagement parties, weddings, funerals. Whatever. As a sportsman I'd have been exposed to more sessions than those outside that wee bubble. Drinking in a team setting is pretty much all destructive. It's never a few pints and home – it's always a heap of pints and where are we going next? If it's a particularly big event then there's the follow-on the next day. Lots of folks would knock more craic out of the follow-on than the night itself because the night itself would throw up a few more stories. I was always leading the charge.

After the accident I took to drinking at home. Whiskey mostly. That's when I was at home. There was no let-up in the travel with the IRFU job. I was still putting in massive mileage every week, and huge time preparing sessions and delivering them. I was constantly on edge, living a pretty unhealthy lifestyle and thinking mostly about myself as I was doing it.

This continued right through 1994.

The tour to Australia that summer was something I had mixed feelings about: great to get away and work with the players which I really enjoyed, not so great if there would be a lot of spare time on my own. Time on my own was time for self-loathing.

Gerry Murphy, the head coach, did a lot of after-dinner speaking on that trip and was off meeting a lot of people. I was drinking with the players. Then I'd have a nightcap of a few glasses of red when I got back to the room. When we were staying in the Travelodge in Brisbane it was right next door to the Brisbane Transit Centre on Roma Street. There was a bottle shop, as the Aussies call an off-licence, in the station. I gave it a fair bit of business. Whiskey, wine, if I didn't have a stash in the room for whenever I got back I didn't feel fully dressed going out.

We had a lovely local bagman on that trip, Anton Toia, who worked with a lot of incoming tours. Anton was a Maori, with a granny from Fermanagh. He took me off to a few interesting bars and I really enjoyed his company. He was a great listener and I valued his friendship. I opened up to him about the accident in a way I struggled to do with people I knew better.

Seven years later, when he was doing bagman for the Lions on their tour of Australia, Anton suffered a massive heart attack and died. He was missed by so many rugby men lucky enough to know him.

In those team settings I was desperate not to be spending too much time on my own. It's funny, years later Gerald Seymour expressed amazement and appreciation that I was prepared to meet himself and his son Nick for those few pints the night before the England game in Twickenham, earlier in 1994.

Except it wasn't a few pints – at least not for me. Gerald couldn't believe his eyes that I could horse through a gallon of porter and a packet of fags and be up the next morning, ready to work flat out at a Test match. It was he who was doing me the favour by giving me a reason to get out of my room.

To add to the pressure, in late 1994 I had taken on coaching Dungannon. So I still had the IRFU job, which included coaching the Ireland forwards, and then this avenue back to Stevenson Park to guide the club that was a big part of my life since leaving Stranmillis.

I rounded off as a player there in one of those storybook endings: after captaining the club for six seasons in a row, my sign-off in the blue and white hooped jersey was against a star-studded Five Nations XV in Stevenson Park in April 1993. The crowd on the grassy bank thought they were watching the Harlem Globe Trotters. It was a massive night, and of course it wasn't quite the end of my playing career. I kept popping up here and there when required, until finally calling a halt against Bective Rangers in January 1995, a few months short of my 40th birthday. Paddy Johns and Jeremy Davidson were the cubs who had outgrown the pack leader. Was there ever a better club second row pairing than those boys?

It was always on my to-do list to coach the club, especially with all the stuff I had learned through my time on the IRFU job. The All Ireland League was going full throttle at the time and we had worked hard to play our way into it, after being on the outside looking in when it kicked off in 1990/91. It was the golden era for the club game in Ireland and this was something I desperately wanted to do well in, partly because I felt I had the tools but also because I owed the club. They had stood by me when I was stuck in Argentina in 1980 and needed help.

I'm not sure how many other clubs in Ireland had a paid Director of Rugby in place in 1994 but I know Dungannon went about it the right way. Anything Victor Scarlett did he did right. A legend in the club, he served as player and coach and chairman of rugby. He suggested the role for me and he sorted the resources when I wanted to do it full-time. My role didn't stop at the senior team. They wanted to get the structure right the whole way through the club, and they had the backing to do it.

Even though Dungannon is only a half hour down the road, that didn't mean I would be spending more time at home. I had swapped playing for coaching where the commitment was roughly double. I put a lot of effort getting all the relevant people in Stevenson Park on the same page. Whatever you were doing and whatever team you were doing it with I wanted everyone aligned, working towards the goal of being the best club in Ireland. Meanwhile back at the ranch Heather was holding down her teaching job in Magherafelt High School, running a home and rearing three kids: Jonathan was 10, Thomas was seven and Chloe was three. One Sunday morning after a big Dungannon win I shuffled, bleary eyed, into the kitchen to get some water, and Jonathan was already there setting the table for breakfast.

"It's Sunday morning son, go you back to bed and have a lie-in!" I said to him, in that way we have up here of getting our verbs back to front.

"Don't tell me what to do," he fired back. "You're never around."

THE TRAGEDY

Hungover as I was, that stopped me in my tracks. Jonathan continued what he was doing and I was the one who went back to bed. I won't claim it was a game-changer for me but for sure it was a slap in the face. Still, the season ahead with Ireland was going to be a big one, leading to the Rugby World Cup in South Africa in summer 1995. There were six games on the schedule leading to that tournament, starting with a November international against USA in Lansdowne Road.

In the run-up we had a squad session in Merrion Road, and to my surprise Pa Whelan was on hand as well as me, with a whistle. I had lots of experience of Pa from Ulster versus Munster games. He was a fairly ruthless hooker on the field and he took that with him into his coaching career. Suddenly team manager Noisy Murphy had produced Pa, who was an Ireland selector at the time, like a rabbit out of a hat. He was to do scrummaging work with the forwards when I was working with them, at the same time in the same place. As an exercise in undermining a coach it was pretty blunt. I dug in on the night. So did Pa. The players didn't know whether to follow me or him. An absolute fucking shambles.

That was the nudge I needed to re-examine how my job fitted into the rest of my life. I had invested myself 100 per cent in my career. For me it was the dream job. But the physical drain was enormous. And emotionally I was all over the place. In my head I couldn't make the connection between the effort I was putting in and the cold shoulder I got back when tragedy walked into my life. So if I reversed from the IRFU job I'd be getting some balance back. And I wouldn't have to put up with the kind of shite Noisy and Pa had pulled on the coaching field that night in Merrion Road.

It would mean giving up coaching the Ireland forwards, which was a huge wrench, but it was a price worth paying to save my family life. I was in constant touch with Steve Aboud anyway and he was acutely aware of my dilemma. When I told him about the sudden appearance of Pa with his whistle he just groaned.

"I'll ring Noisy to give him some warning and then send in a letter of resignation," I said to Steve.

"And what do you think will happen when you ring him?" he asked. "He'll talk you out of it! He'll still want you on board and doing the RDO job. If you want to make a change in your life then post the letter first. You can ring whoever you want after that. Your life Willie, your call."

I posted the letter, and immediately felt a sense of relief. Sure enough Noisy rang anyway, managing to sound hurt that I was putting myself and my family ahead of the IRFU. I served out my notice before going full-time with Dungannon.

I kept up an involvement in the summer camp work for the IRFU but I was no longer their employee, no longer running around the country, no longer at the beck and call of an organisation that had left me in the lurch at the most stressful time of my life.

I visit Glen's grave every year on the anniversary of his death.

And I still yearn to turn back the clock.

11

The Exiles

ON A LOVELY EVENING IN LATE SUMMER 1996 Dungannon took on London Irish at Stevenson Park. They had just been promoted back into England's Courage League Division 1, and were on a pre-season tour in Ireland. They were fully loaded. As a First Division club in the All Ireland League we were a decent outfit with ambitions, but on paper there was a fair gap between us. Yet we played them off the park. We were accurate and quick and low and kept the ball moving out of the tackle. It was great rugby to watch. I was absolutely buzzing.

Mark McCall was incredible that night. We drilled them up front with Gary Leslie and Hugh McGaughey – Dungannon men through and through – taking the game to them. Meantime Mark was making breaks and scoring tries and offloading for the craic. We had a huge crowd, a great atmosphere and the sort of post-match bar business and socialising that keeps clubs turning over. Once the head fog cleared the next morning it was back to local business for me. Games like this confirmed I was doing something right as Director of Rugby. I had learned a bit more about myself and my weaknesses and how best to manage them. When I say a bit I mean a bit. It would be a long, painful climb but I was up for it. I accepted that as coaches we weren't coaching rugby, we were coaching people to play rugby. So the more you could understand about those people the more you'd know what they'd be like under pressure. That started with knowing about yourself.

The whole process of self-awareness and your impact on people around you was introduced to me by a man called Eamon Kelly, a communications consultant who did some work with Roly Meates when Roly was coaching Trinity and Leinster. Roly introduced Eamon to Steve Aboud because Steve devoured anything related to sports psychology and he thought the pair of them would be a good fit. That led Eamon to me.

He worked with business leaders on strategy and crisis management – the kind of stuff that's all the rage nowadays but was hardly being addressed in the mid 1990s. With any industry in its early days it can be rough around the edges. Eamon's approach with us – Steve and me anyway, I'm not sure about Roly – was brutal. It was warts and all: ask those closest to you for complete honesty about your weaknesses and what had to change. I found it harrowing but made up my mind to stick with it, knowing I had a lot of demons to deal with. Because I had a fairly high profile it appealed to Eamon to work with me. Between Steve, still in the IRFU, and me well up the coaching ladder, we could probably open a few doors to more business for Eamon. When London Irish came looking for my services my profile went up again.

The initial approach from Sunbury was to assist the head coach Clive Woodward. He had brought them back to the First Division after they had been relegated under Hika Reid, the former All Black hooker. This was before Clive was knighted, but he was a hero in Sunbury the way they raced back into the top flight scoring tries left, right and centre.

The first thing Clive had done when he met the players for training was to take the meeting out of a dark, dingy bar on the ground floor of the clubhouse and out the door onto the pitch. It was like 'Open' was to be his policy. I liked that when I heard it. Inside two seasons he had built up the squad and a stream of Ireland's best talent were on their way across the water thanks to another transformation: rugby going professional. So season 1996/97 would be the first full-on season for rugby as a pro sport. The IRFU weren't keen to get on board with it but a load of their best players were mad for action.

If that wasn't enough there would be another turn in the road before I arrived. The London Irish AGM in summer 1996 turned into a clusterfuck. Having gone along on the night expecting to be carried shoulder high from the room, instead Clive ended up walking out in disgust. Some of the older brigade were accusing him of trying to change the club into little England. And he in turn was accusing them of racism over their rules and regulations. If you've ever been part of a club you'll appreciate the AGM can either put you to sleep or set you on the path to war. Gary Halpin had to run out after Clive to try and drag him back into the meeting. He wasn't for turning. At least not in the carpark.

When everyone calmed down Clive withdrew his resignation and agreed to continue, but it never looked like lasting. When he rang me originally he explained that he was already running a successful business and couldn't afford the extra time that professionalism would demand. So I would be there to fill in the gap. As far as I was concerned my teaching career was in the past. So was the IRFU job. I was two years into the gig with Dungannon and had seen both sides of the coin: we were relegated in year one; promoted in year two. I wanted a crack at professional rugby.

My home life had settled down a fair bit after the crazy schedule with the IRFU job. Dungannon was demanding, but it was local. Heather was happy teaching in Magherafelt High School, a few minutes out the road, and we were busy with the three kids. When the call came from London she could see I had to take the opportunity. There was no question of us moving lock, stock and barrel. I'd commute between London and home, and Heather would come over the odd time as well. I don't remember thinking at the time 'there's no way this is going to work.' But there wasn't.

Ultimately that decision would cost me, and in those days before budget airfares the money was only the half of it. The sheer scale of the transition from an amateur club to a professional club needed a full-time team of people on the ground. We weren't even close. Clive was unhappy with the way it ended for him at Sunbury. But he's an intelligent man and I'd be surprised if he didn't figure what was behind the door he opened by bringing me in. His head was already half turned by his business commitments. I arrived, hungry for a crack at a very attractive opportunity, and pretty soon the club were showing him the door. It happened quickly and brutally. He arrived for training in Sunbury one night and the club CEO

Duncan Leopold met him in the corridor to the changing room. Duncan looked like a man dancing on hot coals as he waited for Clive to arrive. After a very short conversation Clive was gone. When the club had asked me would I be interested in taking over from him I didn't suggest we could tweak a few things here and there but continue under the current boss. I said yes, immediately, I'll fill the gap. Clive was a big picture guy who had no idea how to fill in the background. When I spoke to him about rugby detail, about planning and getting everyone aligned, about how we would actually play the game, he just zoned out. No interest. That took me by surprise. When there was no sign of it changing I realised we were on different paths.

Years later, when I looked at the England set-up for the Rugby World Cup in 2003, you could see how he prospered in a high-powered environment with so many experienced players. In fairness to him he put that operation together and managed it well. That was his strength. But as a technical rugby coach he was clueless.

The exodus of Irish players had started in 1996 when it was clear the IRFU had no interest in contracting players. Of the 1994 Ireland squad I had toured with in Australia, six had gone to Sunbury to play professionally: backs Conor O'Shea and Niall Woods, and forwards Gabriel Fulcher, Jeremy Davidson, Victor Costello and Ken O'Connell. Gary Halpin and David Humphreys were there already. So were Rob Henderson and Justin Bishop who had come through the IRFU's Exiles programme. Mal O'Kelly, Justin Fitzpatrick, Mark McCall, Niall Hogan and Kieron Dawson completed the crew who were either already capped or on their way to play for Ireland. Over my two seasons it was a great collection of Irish talent but a squad always short of a couple of big hitters. I thought I could put in place a framework that would do the players justice. I had a rapport with them, and I valued that. I really enjoyed working with those guys. In truth though if they weren't ready for the demands of pro sport then neither was I. In his book *Winning,* published the year after England won the Rugby World Cup, Clive Woodward wrote: *'Even though we had only just been promoted back into the First Division, I knew we could have won the Premiership that year if we hadn't become lost in ludicrous distractions.'*

I'm not 100 per cent sure what the ludicrous distractions were but fairly quickly my target was to survive in the top flight. Winning only three of 12 games in the first half of the season opened my eyes to the scale of the task. Week after week it was one dogfight after another. It was like coming up for air and getting dunked under the water again. We never had the kind of front row power required to dominate consistently.

I needed to be on site 24/7 to manage it. Instead I was flitting between home and work. Mostly I'd fly home after home games on the Saturday and then come back over on the Monday night or on a red eye Tuesday morning. That left the lads to their own devices. So Saturday and Sunday night on the pish with no recovery other than sleeping it all off. We would train on Tuesday night to accommodate the lads who were still working. We had put a strength and conditioning programme in place but I'd be lying if I said it was closely monitored.

We worked very hard in training. Some maybe thought it was too hard. Part of my approach was to balance the wild craic they would get up to every weekend with brutal stuff on the field. It wasn't beasting for the sake of it. Because of my obsession with technically strong forward play it was all game related, but there were no prisoners taken. It was always hard. I needed coaching support but for one reason or another it never happened.

Mike Gibson, who I had played alongside for Ireland – the number eight, not the legendary centre – was on the board of the club and suggested a few names to me, but I managed to reject every one. I didn't trust people easily who I didn't rate, and couldn't get past that. It meant that the players didn't have enough variety in coaching input. Basically I had Conor O'Shea and David Humphreys running the backs and I'd look after the pack and our overall approach. For a guy with no coaching experience Conor did a good job.

For the times Heather came over for the weekend it was like a wee glimpse of what our lives could be like if that was the permanent set-up. With no commute there was more time for everything. When I stayed over after games I would be on the pish with the players. This wasn't in the coaching manual but it was in my DNA. Self-awareness is not an achievement – it's a constant experience. It's like log rolling: just because you jump on and stay upright doesn't mean the next time you're going to get the same result. With me it was a very slow process, complicated by my reliance on drink. So when we had a warts-and-all team meeting one day and Jeremy Davidson piped up that maybe it would be a good idea if I stopped drinking with the players I immediately got his point. These sessions were open and honest and you needed a thick skin. We all enjoyed each other's company after games but even Jeremy could see a gap was needed between coach and players.

"I'll not be on the pish with you boys again," I assured them.

It was late in the season and we were scrapping for survival.

But we had found some form with a run of three wins from four games, between league and cup, when trips to Sale and West Hartlepool popped up next on the fixture list. We lost to Sale. On the way back from that game all I could think of was the long trip home from the north east the following weekend if we didn't get a win. It's the guts of five hours from Hartlepool back to Sunbury. Seven days away and my stomach was already in a knot. On the day itself I was struggling to stay calm, but we went 30-3 up after 28 minutes playing great rugby. We let them back in towards the end but, for a change, it was comfortable. It was also our fifth game in 14 days and we were running on fumes. The result put us above Bristol in the battle for survival. I was incredibly relieved. So as the players climbed on board for the marathon journey home I announced we were going on the monumental pish. There was a roar from the back of the bus and off we went. The commitment to Jeremy was quietly parked. My nature was to overstep the mark. I had some distance to travel on that road towards change.

That result gave us a bit of breathing space but you were never far from the horrible tension of relegation. Some genius decided that out of 12 First Division clubs two would go down automatically – fair enough – and the two above them would then play off against the third and fourth placed teams in Division Two. So you could have a third of the teams disappearing through the trapdoor at the end of the campaign, and this when they were trying to get to grips with professionalism? Jeepers why make it so hard?

Orrell and West Hartlepool were the two clubs who went down automatically. Bristol and ourselves were the pair caught in the crossfire. We had two matches against Coventry to decide our fate, the first leg away in Coundon Road on a Wednesday night in May, where we lost 16-14. For the second leg in our place we were at fever pitch. Jeremy and Gabriel Fulcher were an awesome combination that day. Niall Hogan and David Humphreys were in complete control at halfback. We won comfortably. You can imagine the night that followed. It was all about how the next season would be different. We'd strengthen the squad and beef up on the coaching front as well. We wouldn't be sweating buckets at the end of 1997/98 trying to stay in the top flight. But of course it didn't work out that way. Again we were scrapping from early in the season, and losing Jeremy in October with a ruptured knee was a hammer blow. Having been a star with the Lions in South Africa a few months earlier his season was over just after it started.

By that stage I'd gotten to know the players very well, and they knew me. So they weren't too surprised when an early season European game in Romania was heavy duty stuff. I knew what to expect in Romania from my Ulster days. Things had improved off the pitch but it was still dog rough on it. We were up against Farul Constanta, down on the Black Sea. We won well and climbed into the drink, with no regard for the early start the next morning. In fairness to team manager Kieran McCarthy, he had organised for packed lunches from the hotel for everyone to take with them as we were leaving to get the bus, to the train, to the plane, to get back home. I'm not sure how there were Bacardis and Coke in the bags, along with a sandwich and a biscuit, but there were.

There had been a scene to sort out in reception first, after a couple of lads had a row on the way home with a taximan, but we got clear of that and onto the bus. Sandwich bags open, the lads were delighted with the contents, and started to wade in. Still drunk from the previous night, I marched down the aisle roaring that there would be no more drinking, confiscating the alcohol and then went back to my seat at the front. It wasn't long before I helped myself to a few drinks. There was consternation. It was funny, and it wasn't funny. You don't pick up where you left off the night before unless you've got a problem.

Back on the field the lads really wanted to play for each other and loved the style of rugby we were trying to play. The addition of Isaac Fe'aunati in the back row and Brendan Venter at centre made a huge difference. I liked Brendan from the word go. I'll always remember the pair of us walking around the pitch in Sunbury before he'd even signed, discussing all sorts of ideas and thinking: 'Why the hell couldn't we have met a year ago?' He was signed as a player but you knew you'd get the leadership and coaching input as part of the package. I had barely got to know Brendan when the curtain came down for me. I felt we were turning a corner on the field when the clubs decided the Premiership would be expanded by two for the following season. Great! The bottom club would still go down and there would be a play-off for second last but it reduced the danger a wee bit.

We were due to play Bristol at home in February, with both of us hovering over the trapdoor. Early in that week I noticed a few people looking uncomfortable when I was talking to them. Not a good sign. Especially with Kieran McCarthy. Macca has been a part of the furniture at the club for most of his adult life, mostly as the rugby chairman. He knows where the bodies are buried. He also knows all the sites considered before burial. I would often pick him up on the way in at 7am and drop him off on the way home, 12 hours later. We got on like a house on fire.

Macca wasn't making much eye contact on the Wednesday and had gone early when I left that night.

When I showed up at Sunbury on the Thursday morning for training I was called aside and given my cards by a man called Chuck Nelson, who had a short spell as CEO at the club. I had an hour to get my stuff, leave the car, and get out. Jeepers! I was devastated. Jeremy took me off somewhere to talk, and the rest of the squad joined us in a local pub that night. There was a bit of fighting talk among the players which was good for the soul but never going to amount to anything. Then my replacement, Dick Best, rang and ordered them all back to the club. Business was business. I had my supporters on the London Irish board but they were taken by surprise with the speed of it all as much as me.

The printers of the club programme were caught out as well. My column was there on the Saturday, urging the London Irish faithful to get behind us in the battles ahead. By the time the teams ran out on the field, Best was already in my parking spot. And I was back home in The Loup.

If you speak to the guys now, 'carnage' is a word they use quite a bit to describe that time. Not on the field, but off it. As I write this we're more than 25 years on from rugby going professional. In Ireland's case they didn't have any interest in it. But if you were a player reared in a game where money was considered dirty, then suddenly you were offered pots of it to do something you loved – and you would be doing it as a young man living in London with your mates – then you can imagine the scene. As Jeremy Davidson put it: "Professional rugby was just a dream come true. I had three out of four years done on my European Business degree, and I was away, playing rugby with quality

Irish guys who had plenty of potential. We all loved it, getting this cheque that you looked at every time you got it because you couldn't believe it. And you're thinking: 'Is that really for me?' You were doing barely more than you did already!"

Jeremy was one of a gang of four living in a house, rented by London Irish, on The Avenue, a long, leafy road literally around the corner from the club. Ken O'Connell, Gabriel Fulcher and Niall Woods were the other housemates. Their teammates were all nearby, but that place was party central. In the madness of the time all the players were given cars: dark green Rovers. I got one too when I arrived. The car registrations were all in sequence. The four guys would be trying to squeeze the cars into a driveway designed for two. When they were having some of the other lads over to watch a match on tv there would be a squadron of green Rovers all over the road.

On any given night when they wanted to unwind they might head in a bit closer to town for a few pints. Volts Nightclub in Kingston was a favourite for them. They'd drink for Ireland, jump about the place and try and hook up with some blades. Most often they'd end up across the road in Chickoland for a chicken burger on the way home. I think it became a ritual. Then they'd try to train the next morning.

This routine was pretty much set in stone by the time I got there. From the start the training I put them through was much tougher, and they struggled. I didn't come down hard on them because I was a product of the same culture. My only rule was not to let the craic the night before stop you turning up for work the morning after. They were all young men who considered themselves bullet proof, living the dream. They would put up with a lot of punishment from me to keep it going. Looking back I should have come down a lot harder on it, but I was feeling my way around the pro game a bit as well as dealing with my own issues with excess. I remember the first training session after Christmas 1996 hadn't even started when we were off on the wrong foot. It was a clear, frosty morning, and as we were warming up Jeremy and Ken come over to the fence.

"Willie, we have some not very good news," was how Jeremy phrased it. "Mal had a bit of an accident the other night. He's dislocated his ankle. He'll be out for a while."

I think the story for public consumption at the time was the same Malcolm O'Kelly had fallen down the stairs at home. It might be closer to the truth that the players' Christmas party had involved a few of them getting physical around the kitchen table and Mal going over on his ankle, suffering a break and a dislocation. The way I heard it they tried to fix the damage with a packet of peas out of the freezer. Maybe the freezer was a few degrees off the pace because the peas finished up all over the floor with Mal screaming in agony and the rest of them falling about the place laughing. To make matters worse the ambulance men were on the downward slope of their careers and struggled to keep Mal on the stretcher. When he got to the hospital the young doctor looking after him was a novice. He was using all sorts to try and get the ankle back into place. Mal was in bits. A seriously talented player, we really could have done with him fit.

After I was fired, in February 1998, Ken O'Connell would really struggle with Dick Best. It got so bad that when Ken broke his hand one day he finished up in A&E pointing the fracture out on the x-ray to the doctor – not standard behaviour for a player who loved his rugby. He was just so relieved to be away from Best for a while.

I remember Ken and his girlfriend moved in with Mal to a wee barge on the water at Teddington. There were swans and ducks and it was all very laid back – a bit of an escape from the madness of the house on The Avenue. It was quite the bohemian scene there. Then they invested in a house in Vicarage Road near Richmond Park. It had a roof garden, a regular spot for barbecues. I'd bring Heather and the kids there some Sundays when they were over from home. Ken was such a solid guy and great company. It was a lovely time and I treasure those memories. I was already too close to the whole scene, but that was typical of me. By the next season Ken's relationship with Best hadn't improved but Mal was flying. There was a lot of interest in him from other clubs. Castres were leading the charge and were ringing the house trying to lure him over. It was always Ken who was answering the phone. What unfolded illustrates the sheer madness of the time.

'Mal, there's a fella on the phone for you…'

'Ken, tell him you're my agent.'

So the two lads are booked by Castres to fly over to Toulouse on the Saturday evening of a Premiership game. Ken wants to look the part so he goes into a drapers shop in Richmond on the Friday and buys a suit.

"I want to look like an agent," he says to the man in the shop.

On the Saturday night they take off after the game, flying up the front of the plane, and check into a very nice hotel in Toulouse. All bought and paid for. What do they do on arrival? Ditch the bags and get on the monumental pish.

They have a room each but end up sleeping in Mal's. Next

morning Ken wakes up to the phone ringing off the hook. Reception tell him there's a man downstairs waiting to bring them to Castres, about an hour and a half's drive away. They're in bits. No time to shower, they tumble down the stairs, in the horrors: Mal in a pair of tracksuit bottoms sailing well above his ankles, and Ken still in the suit he slept in. The agent's suit.

They are brought to a chateau outside Castres where the boss man in the club, Pierre-Yves Revol, is due to join them by helicopter. It was like a movie, as the chopper sets down on the lawn. I'm not sure what he made of the two boys, but Ken starts negotiating like he's got nothing to lose. Mal was earning £50k at the time in London Irish, an increase from £30k in his first season. He thought £80k would be a nice bump up. Ken had other ideas. Ken was going for it.

He explains to Pierre-Yves that the world and his wife was beating a path to Mal's door. He writes down some crazy figure on a piece of paper and slides it across the table. Plus house. Plus car. As Ken himself put it: "It was crazy – outrageous – but why not like? We were on a weekend away. So he looks at me and he's making faces and he says: 'Tomas Castaignede is not earning that much – how do you think we will pay that?'

"'Tomas Castaignede?' I said. 'I don't even know who the fuck Tomas Castaignede is!'"

Tomas Castaignede was maybe the highest profile star of French rugby at the time. Incredibly the Castres man agreed. He gives Mal a club tie. Straight around his neck, while Ken has to run to the loo to calm himself down. Mal is cool-headed enough to suggest that Ken come as part of the package. He says Ken is a decent player as well as a big-time agent – and they agreed to that too, offering Ken a decent salary after checking with Thierry Lacroix, another French star, who was playing with Harlequins at the time. A good reference from a good source. Ken was sorted.

In the heel of the hunt Mal backed out. London Irish were making things awkward over his contract. He was at the start of a very promising international career and was under pressure from a few quarters to stop messing around with ideas of going to France. That made life very awkward for Ken when he made the jump across the Channel.

"Ou est Malcolm?" was the opening line to most conversations.

It put a bit of a strain on the relationship between Ken and Mal. Castres meanwhile were still short a second row. Despite all the messing around they still trusted Ken. He had another idea. This time he calls up Jeremy, who was recovering from major knee surgery the previous November.

"All right buddy?" says Ken. "I have a proposition for you."

Much to Ken's delight the swap of Jeremy for Mal was as straightforward as he could have hoped. Castres were more than happy with their end of the bargain. It worked out well for Jeremy too. He carved out a fine career for himself in France, and toured with the Lions in Australia in 2001 as a Castres player – he was only the second player ever to tour with the Lions from a French club.

And Ken? He learned the language and the culture, and earned the affection and respect of everyone at Castres. That would be Ken. He wasn't the ideal man when the ball was flying from one side of the field to the other and you wanted a wing forward with the hands of a back. But Jeepers when it got heavy, Ken was your man. One of rugby's great warriors. Like Jeremy, one of rugby's great men. Mal went on to have an incredible career for Ireland and the Lions that probably wouldn't have worked out as well if he'd jumped ship to France. I think all three ended up doing what was best for them. They got great value from their careers, and from each other. I hope they cherish being a part of the maddest time in rugby history. I know I do.

12

The Border

Saturday 26th May, 2001, Lansdowne Road

There is a wave of satisfaction you get as a coach when something you've worked on very hard plays out perfectly in front of your eyes. Depending on lots of factors it might be a once in a career moment, or something you're lucky enough to experience a few times. I was standing on the touchline in front of the West Stand in Lansdowne Road when that wave washed over me from head to toe. It's actually quite emotional. You look at what's unfolding and see your signature on it. It's not a scrawl. It's a flourish. The time to cry is when you're winning, not losing. And when the wave passes you're very thankful for getting it, and hopeful of catching another one sometime soon.

Oddly enough the move that sparked this endorphin rush didn't finish with a try under the posts, but with a drop goal from David Humphreys. That put Dungannon 22-9 ahead against a Cork Con side who knew the game was up with more than half an hour to play. We were about to win our first All Ireland League. Seven Dungannon men got to handle the ball in that sequence of play, but three of them – Tony McWhirter, Michael Haslett and Jonny Bell – produced moments of magic. Three times the move could have died. Three times they used soft hands and good angles of running to keep it alive. That was what I was about. Hours upon hours doing continuity work up and down Stevenson Park – every inch and every drop of sweat was worth it. This was the way I wanted rugby to be played.

We set a number of ambitious targets when I returned to Stevenson Park after London Irish in 1998. The toughest was to win the AIL, which meant getting back into the First Division after the club had just been relegated. By the time season 2000/01 kicked off I had used my profile, and the few bob that was floating around the club game in those days, to attract a hard core of Ulster players to beef up what we already had.

At that stage the provinces were still sharing their players with the clubs, so if you had a backbone of pros who were actually keen on achieving at club level it was ideal. It took a bit of doing but by autumn 2000 we had serious firepower – it was a question of getting them on the field when Ulster didn't need them. The way things worked out we had access to them for a long run-in, made better by the outbreak of Foot and Mouth disease which pushed a few of our games back in the calendar, towards better weather. So, with good players on good ground we took off on a run of eight wins from nine games to make the play-offs. One of those re-fixed games was against Ballymena on a Tuesday night in early May. Our first 40 minutes was as good as anything I'd ever seen in the Irish club game. We were flying.

For example, on our best days we could call on six guys who had never won an AIL Division 1 medal, but had a Heineken Cup one instead! Jonny Bell, Jan Cunningham, David Humphreys, Justin Fitzpatrick, Gary Leslie and Tony McWhirter all featured for Ulster in that win over Colomiers in '99.

In my development as a coach I was getting to where I needed to be. For a start, in Davy Haslett I had an assistant who I respected. He's a Belfast man but he came to love the club and was passionate about it being well run. Davy's son Michael, a chip off the old block, was an integral part of the team. It all felt right. Davy was managing me as much as helping to coach the team. I was an awful man for pressuring players about winning. How bloody stupid was that? I was struggling with the pressure of having to deliver in a results business so I would pass on that pressure lock, stock and barrel to the players. Davy was very good at steering me back to the nuts and bolts and let the prize look after itself.

There was no question we had the players, if we could get them all on the same teamsheet. Bryn Cunningham at full back: Jan Cunningham and Tyrone Howe on the wings with Ryan Constable and Jonny Bell in the centre; Humphreys and Stephen Bell at halfback; a front row of Fitzpatrick, Nigel Brady and Gary Leslie; Aidan Kearney and captain Paddy Johns in the second row; Ali Boyd, McWhirter and Haslett in the back row. Richard Mackey, Allen Clarke, Ralph Mercer, Andy Hughes, Steve Elkinson and Keith Walker all came off the bench.

We won the last seven games on the trot to make the final – the first Ulster side to be there. Cork Con, chasing their third title, were waiting for us. The semi-final win down in Galwegians had been close but we were well worth it. Having got through that we relaxed a bit and played our best rugby in the final to blow Con away. Teams don't often bother doing reviews when it's a final. The last game of the season – why bother? But on a personal level I took a good lesson from it. On the morning of the game I had told Bryn to go out and prove what a talented player he was.

"This will be your game!" I said.

Jeepers I should have kept my mouth shut. Or better still, got him to play for the team. No need to chase headlines Bryn, just play for those around you. Make them look good. There were too many other guys in top form for it to matter, but Bryn took me at my word and tried to shoot the lights out. Lesson learned.

By the time we got off the coach, arriving at Lansdowne Road, I think my old pal Michael Bradley feared the worst. Brads was coaching Con that day and watched as we walked in wearing our number ones – Paddy Johns's idea – complete with white carnations, tinged with blue that I had painted on, in the lapel of the blazer. We looked like we meant business. We had stopped off in Finnstown House in Lucan on the way down. There was a walkaround, a relaxed lunch, and a team meeting rounded off with a video of our best tries of the campaign. Cut into the video were a few wee interviews with stalwart members of the club. That included Berta Patton, a fixture in Stevenson Park for a couple of generations, running the ladies committee and generally being a motherly figure. I looked around the room at that point and settled on Tony McWhirter who had tears in his eyes. It was powerful stuff and I was mindful not to go over the top.

"We'll not be bate today," I said. Then we got our stuff and went out to the coach. It was one of those great days where everything went like clockwork. We won at a canter.

The way the professional game was going I knew we'd struggle to get access to those Ulster players over the next few seasons. I was grateful we had them while the going was good, and I think they appreciated the style of rugby they were asked to play. By then the pro game was already reeling me in again via regular sessions I was doing for Matt Williams down in Leinster. Within a year they'd have an offer on the table for me.

*****

"I'm sure there are some people who aren't very happy with that but that's their problem. I was asked to do a job and not only do I feel it's been fairly successful, it will get better. I've got a great opportunity here. I'm a professional, I come in and do my job, and then I go back and do my job in Dungannon. It's still my ambition to coach Ulster one day. I'm an Ulster man."

That's a quote I gave in a newspaper article in late summer 2001 after Leinster had wiped Ulster on a Friday night in Donnybrook. The few Ulster fans there got full value during the warm-up from me being in a Leinster tracksuit.

"Bout you big man!" one of them was hollering. "That a wee harp on your chest there?"

I'd say he already had a few pints in Kiely's, Leinster's watering hole, a few steps up the road from the ground. I was uncomfortable enough to let it under my skin, but proud that I didn't react. Jeepers it was touch and go though. At one point he spat over the fence in my general direction. Not close enough to be a clear attempt to hit me, but enough to make the point. A few years later, when Trevor Brennan had left Leinster for Toulouse, he climbed the fence in Stade Ernest Wallon to slap an Ulster fan who was abusing him in a European game. I understood his mindset 100 per cent.

I prided myself on giving Leinster everything I had, to develop a style of forward play that would make them very hard to live with. If Ulster had asked, I'd have been doing it in Ravenhill. They didn't.

I offered though – three times over the years. The first was in January 2001 when Harry Williams retired as Ulster coach having made history by bringing the first Heineken Cup to Ireland. I applied to fill the gap, thinking I was well positioned. The European success was phenomenal, with 48,000 people packed into the old Lansdowne Road for the final against Colomiers. You could never before have imagined Ulster featuring in a scene like that.

But when the party stopped it was clear that Ulster had a job to do right across the province in making some capital on the back of that success. I couldn't think of anyone else with the rugby pedigree as well as a reach across to the GAA community, where we needed players. For example, every year the rugby and GAA clubs in Dungannon would play a charity match: one half rugby laws, the other Gaelic football. It was always mighty craic and I loved it. Travel around the country and around the world had broadened my horizons from the simple lad who thought Catholics were alien folk we just didn't mix with. There was a column in the *Irish Times* when Alan Solomons was given the Ulster job to replace Harry Williams. It suggested Ulster was missing the bigger picture going for a South African rather than one of their own. Referring to the annual charity match in Dungannon the journalist, Des Fahy – yes, he's an Omagh man – wrote: *"In the closeted world of Northern sport it is an occasion that shines like a beacon."*

Not in Ravenhill it didn't. So when Matt Williams rang me one day to do regular sessions with his Leinster forwards I was happy to oblige. Matt and I went back a long way, and he was well settled as Leinster coach, having succeeded Mike Ruddock in summer 2000. At the time Eddie Wigglesworth was the IRFU rugby director.

"Matt do you know what you're doing here?" Wigglesworth said to him when he heard of my involvement. "He's told everyone in the IRFU to get fucked at some point."

"He has not!"

"He's told me to get fucked a number of times."

When Matt came back to me at the time with Eddie's response I told him that sounded about right.

"Mate, you can't do that! You can't go round telling people to fuck off!"

The relationship with Leinster started with maybe one session a week in early 2001 before ramping up to a few overnight stays. So a 5.30am alarm call on a Monday; drive to Dublin for morning lineouts and a full session in the afternoon. Stay in the Montrose Hotel that night. Another session on the Tuesday morning and then spin back up home for training with Dungannon that night. I was also coaching the Ireland Under 19 side but that wasn't a huge drag on my time.

By the time the new season kicked off with the first Celtic League in August 2001 I was steadily getting sucked more into the Leinster set up. They had seven rounds out of the way before the AIL even kicked off so I was able to keep the two balls in the air, no problem. By the time it turned into a full-time role, the following May, I was pretty much part of the furniture in Leinster.

We were champions of the new Celtic League by then, and I had done my wee bit well enough. We had an unbeaten run to the final stretching to 13 games between Celtic League and Heineken Cup by the time we faced Munster in the League final. It was just before Christmas and a crowd of 30,000 turned up. Images of a grim holiday period flashed across my mind in the first half when Eric Miller put a boot into Anthony Foley for no good reason, and was sent off. Our coaching team was made up of Matt as head man, with Roly Meates coaching the scrum, Alan Gaffney running the backs with Steve Aboud doing some sessions as well, and me doing the forwards part-time. It wasn't in my job spec but I remember laying it on the line for Matt in the changing room that we absolutely had to run the ball in the second half despite being a man down. We did, and it was an epic win. I remember reviewing things myself over Christmas and thinking the sky was the limit with this group.

I wasn't specifically asked to put more mongrel into the forwards but it was clearly understood. My rugby philosophy was based on players who could keep the ball alive and play with pace, but there had to be a hard edge when the ball broke down. We had to be ruthless, with the technique and the attitude to restart it on our terms. We needed to be more aggressive in contact – not so willing to accept tackles. There was one drill I used over and over that required footwork in the first place and leg-drive in the second. It made a difference. Leinster had a collection of guys who were not short on talent but they definitely needed some more of the dog.

They already had plenty of style. In one stretch of the winning run Leinster had three games in an eight-day period where we scored 137 points. I had never been involved with a team who did that. Next we played Toulouse on a Friday night in Donnybrook and put 40 points on them. It was like that day with Dungannon against Ballymena, except better. A bigger stage, a whole different level of rugby, and our forwards were playing like French teams did in Parc des Princes when they were making fools of men in green. We were 26-3 up at half time. We lost our way a bit in the second half before hitting them twice in injury time. It put an unreal look on the scoreboard.

Our back row that night was Miller at six, Victor Costello at eight and Keith Gleeson at open side. Eric had been a Lion in South Africa in 1997. Trevor Brennan didn't care about that. They were chasing the same spot on the team, and every time they set foot on the training field they were up for a scrap. I facilitated that 100 per cent. I always believed training should be a battle because matchday was war. You had to learn somewhere. In December 2020 Gordon D'Arcy wrote in his *Irish Times* column about his fear of paying a price for the head knocks he got over the years. He mentioned the way we trained in Leinster: '*The brutality of rugby union in the early 2000s was best summed up by a drill Willie Anderson came up with called Murder Ball. There was no end game, no tries, no scoreboard either. Just two fully stacked XVs squeezed into a quarter of the pitch. The intention was to harden us up ahead of the weekend. Murder Ball struck a primal chord. It was about "sorting the men from boys" with the added threat of "you'll get injured if you're not going full bore".'*

I wouldn't dispute that account. Neil Francis in the *Sunday Independent* also wrote about the crazy treatment he got on our tour to France with Ireland in 1988. He had been deliberately poleaxed in the second 'Test', because he had been the man of the match in the first game. He was knocked out and taken to hospital. He was in a bad way but Jimmy D was expecting him to be up and at it the next day. If there wasn't much appreciation of concussion in the early 2000s you can imagine where it came in the pecking order in 1988. The other side of it was that Jimmy thought Frano was talented, but lazy. Frano's a great guy and was a fine player, but he didn't always make it easy. Himself and Jimmy didn't get on because, I think, they didn't have enough time together to work each other out, which was a pity.

As a player I was guilty of inflicting a few concussions myself. Mostly it was in the give and take of trading punches. Some of it was plain crazy. For example on that France tour where Frano got concussed, the last game was against the French Barbarians and I waded into one guy who thought 'Barbarians' meant we'd be throwing the ball around for the craic. He looked at me like I should have been locked up.

But one act I am ashamed of occurred in a Five Nations game against Wales in Cardiff. Des Fitzgerald was struggling at tight head against Jeff Whitefoot and I was scrummaging behind Des. After a few troublesome scrums I was losing patience.

"Des, I'll sort the fucker out," I said. "Leave a gap the next time it goes down."

On the next scrum collapse Des – as he was getting up –

left enough room for me to come through and fill the space. I followed through and buck-rooted Jeff in the head. Somehow he stayed on the field, but Des had an armchair ride after that. The truth is I didn't give it a second thought.

At number eight Victor Costello didn't have any similar competition for his place. His battle was with himself. Between Ireland and London Irish I knew Victor well by the time I hooked up with Leinster. Explosive athletes were rare in the Irish game but Victor was leading the field. If he got the ball in his hands early in the game, and made a good carry, he was on the pig's back. If not he could drift through it as a spectator. I tried hard to take the element of chance out of Victor's game, but I came up short. He was an unfinished project.

Then there was Keith Gleeson. If Matt Williams ever makes a list of his best recruits over a long career in professional rugby I'd say Gleeson is in the top three. Matt did a good job in moving Leinster along the road towards being a professional outfit, a journey Mike Ruddock started. Gleeson was the perfect man to bring into the dressing-room. He was a social guy but I was fascinated by the way he didn't care about challenging the team leaders: Reggie Corrigan, Shane Byrne, Mal O'Kelly; and Matt's star pupils behind the scrum: Brian O'Driscoll, Shane Horgan and Denis Hickie. Gleeson had no problem making teammates uncomfortable about how they prepared.

We were having a team meeting one day where staff and players were opening up about the strengths and weaknesses in the group. Basically you wrote after each name what the guy did well and what he could do better. Matt wanted the comments to remain anonymous. But Gleese put his initials after each comment he made. About Brian O'Driscoll he said something like: "I wonder do you know how good you'd be if you got your act together?"

O'Driscoll was already a British and Irish Lion by then. The try he scored for them in the First Test in Brisbane in 2001 made him a world star, but Gleese was happy to call him out. I remember one morning Dave Fagan, the S&C coach, sending Drico and Shane home because they hadn't sobered up enough from the night before. There was a wee bit of a wild side to Drico that I could spot a mile off, and a warrior core to him that I loved.

Under Matt we played a lot of touch rugby. Drico would get ratty if things were let go and wouldn't be slow to turn a touch into a slap if the mood took him. He was coachable, which you don't always get with star players. He understood that backs had as important a role to play as forwards in the continuity game I was trying to develop. And he was good company too. I spent more time with the forwards than backs, but I remember sitting beside him on a flight to an away game and we got lost talking about Paul Britton's brilliant book, *The Jigsaw Man*, which we had both read, and loved. You could see why he made such a successful captain.

Keith's arrival was a game-changer for Liam Toland, who had been Mike's captain. I first came across Liam as a schools player at a training camp. He was a good prospect – a high achiever-type personality who never quite got as far as he wanted. He had been in on the ground floor of Leinster's journey, but when Gleeson arrived into his spot at open side it robbed him of his reason to be happy. With me, Liam said his position was that he didn't doubt what I was saying, but he wanted to test everything thoroughly. In theory that's fine, but when you can't put a full stop to a sentence because there's a hand raised at the back of the room it becomes painful. At times Liam was like the guy at the club AGM who has a point of order on everything from bar receipts to the bibs and balls. He was a challenge.

By the time we kicked off season 2002/03 Liam was on the periphery. We didn't look remotely like retaining our Celtic League title but Europe was a different story. The back to back games against Montferrand in the middle of the campaign would either make or break us. It was all about standing up in the away leg. We talked about it a lot and Brett Igoe, our analysis man, did a really good job assessing their strengths and weaknesses. Connacht and Munster were the only teams who had won in Europe. Even Ulster had their European Cup in the cabinet in Ravenhill without winning in France. We were going after this one.

In 2002 Montferrand hadn't yet changed their name to Clermont, and hadn't developed their stadium into one of the great venues on the rugby circuit, which it is today. Still, they were a serious outfit who had made the quarter-finals in two of the previous three seasons. And that's how they played: hard; on the edge; sometimes over the edge. I was pretty stressed that day. If we were going to do this then our forwards would need to man-up. If they didn't I'd feel I'd failed. The previous night I'd had a good few drinks. There was a drinking culture in Leinster so I fitted right in. If you think about it there were two bars inside the Donnybrook ground – the Bective and Old Wesley clubhouses – and then you had Long's and Kiely's within 30 metres of the front gate. You didn't have to go too far for a sherry.

The Montferrand game was a few days after the 10th

anniversary of young Glen McLernon's death. Since that day, early December became a dark time for me. My week started with visiting his grave on the Monday morning, when it was barely light, and then driving down to Dublin. Leinster were putting me up in a lovely apartment in Ballsbridge and I had time to stop off there before hooking up with Matt and the others. I needed that wee bit of breathing space to get my head clear.

By the time we flew to France on the Friday I wasn't sure how the guys would approach the challenge. That night I went out for a few drinks with Matt to a local bar in Clermont-Ferrand and it was rammed with Leinster fans. That should have been the signal to go back to the hotel and a have a quiet drink there, but I got stuck in. There were a few journos in the bar as well, including the man who helped me with writing this book. For whatever reason in those days we had a tendency to bounce off each other with the odd comment, and pretty soon we were exchanging unfriendly looks. At one stage he was mouthing something at me and I roared at him: "What do you know about life?"

Matt understood my mood and was getting nervous, fearing I'd take Brendan's head off if I got within swinging distance. Which I would have.

"Look at me big man, look at me!" Matt was imploring.

I can't remember how the night finished up but there was no issue to face the next day. I knew only too well the feeling that hits you the morning after a skinful, when you start piecing the sequence of the previous night together. That one was all clear. My stomach was in a knot, but only about the game.

As it turned out, it was an historic day on Leinster's journey towards becoming a top team. Montferrand had most of the ball, and we only got our noses in front at the end when Denis Hickie scored in the corner. We were delighted, but angry at what had happened to Gordon D'Arcy. He got a bad dunt from his opposite number, David Bory, into the base of his back as Darce slid over to score. It was sly and dangerous. All the talk was about citing Bory but by the time the 50-hour window was closing – the time you had to get your spoke in – we had changed our tune. There was a lot of tit-for-tat citing in those days in Europe. If we cited Bory they would have gone for Drico who had given some shoe to Gerald Merceron, their star player, in a completely separate incident. There was some bullshit line for the public about us not being able to prove intent, so there was no point in pursuing Bory. In truth we didn't want to run the risk of losing Drico, so suck it up Darce! The second leg, on the Friday night in Donnybrook, was hot and heavy. We beat them 12-9. That put us comfortably clear at the top of Pool 4, and with Swansea at home early in January it was all about positioning ourselves for a home draw in the quarter-finals.

Sunday 27th April, 2003, Dawson Street

I probably shouldn't have been there. Well, I definitely shouldn't have been there. Heather had gone away up home after the game and I should have gone with her.

In the changing room afterwards there was the usual scene of devastation with a big loss. And this was a huge one. An open goal missed. Most of the guys were staring at the floor as we reeled off the usual shite to an audience that wasn't listening. There was hardly a sound. No one was blaming anyone else – it was just that no one was speaking. I've been in a few very uncomfortable changing rooms where games that should have been won had been lost, but this was the worst. It was deathly.

Then I was standing to the side, talking with Steve Aboud and Matt. There was a reference to later on that evening where a booking was made for the squad in Café en Seine on Dawson Street.

"No, I'm heading home," Steve said. "Just promise me one thing: you won't go drinking with the players? *Do not go drinking with the players.*"

"Absolutely not," I replied.

I went drinking with the players.

*****

We had just lost a Heineken Cup semi-final that had been all teed up for us. A home run – that was the phrase that was being used in the press. All the pieces were on the table in front of us – they just had to be popped into place. We had our home draw in the quarters easily sorted – we were the only side in the competition to win all our pool games. The draw meant that the winners of that quarter-final, against Biarritz, would be at home in the semis. And ERC, the tournament organisers, had decided well in advance that Lansdowne Road would be hosting the final.

The Biarritz game threw up a few issues: we looked really rusty, not having played since the last pool match, against Bristol. The real worry was our scrum, where Peter Coyle had struggled at tight head. We brought on Niall Treston at the end of the first half and he did very well. So, would he replace

Coyler on the bench for the semi-final? If he did then it meant Coyler dropping out of the squad, because our captain Reggie Corrigan would be fit to face Perpignan.

Reggie had resurrected his international career through consistently good performances for Leinster. Then he broke his arm against Italy in the Six Nations, which left him without a game until the Heineken semi-final more than two months later. Perpignan were no world beaters but I knew they'd be tough, awkward hoors who would come after us if they saw a chance.

We started mulling over the Reggie situation. There was no question he would come straight back into the team but I didn't think he should automatically pick up the captaincy as well. Roly and Steve felt the same. We weren't short of leaders: Byrne, O'Kelly and Gleeson up front; Horgan, O'Driscoll and Hickie behind. Drico was already filling in for the injured Keith Wood as captain of Ireland. I was no great fan of Eddie O'Sullivan, going back to our time working as development officers for the IRFU. I didn't like his rugby-by-numbers philosophy and wasn't wild about his personality either. He felt the same way about me. But even Eddie could see the value of O'Driscoll having the armband for his country.

But Matt wanted to stick with Reggie. He had played a part in re-floating Reggie's Ireland career, so the natural thing was to stick with that relationship. The greatest threat to us preparing for Perpignan was complacency. I felt we could cope with the lack of match practice but we needed to shake things up a bit and get some edge to cope with what was coming. Going back to Reggie was just too comfortable.

The captain's run ahead of the Perpignan game was shite.

I was guilty sometimes of keeping lads out too long on the training field but that day we needed to run through a few more lineouts to get back in the flow. Reggie called it early and that was that. On the way out Steve came across Gleese who was throwing his gear in the boot of the car, clearly pissed off with the way it had gone. I didn't like the sound of that.

I didn't like what I was seeing the next day either. Early in the game we had a penalty that needed to be put in the corner for two reasons: our goal-kicker Brian O'Meara didn't need the pressure of a kick on his wrong side in a tricky wind; also we needed to put Perpignan into the corner and go after them. Reggie pointed to the sticks and Brian missed.

Perpignan were messers in the best sense of the word. They fucked around at the set-scrum and everywhere else as well. They weren't highly rated and got full value from that insult. Jeepers if ever you wanted a sergeant-major for a referee it was that day. I think the Perpignan guys reckoned Nigel Williams could be pushed a long way, so they did. He binned two of them but he could have gone to town on them. Free kicks were no punishment, and no use. We needed our scrum to give us a platform for launch plays but it was a shambles. We also needed a kicking game but Matt had long since opted for Christian Warner ahead of Nathan Spooner at 10. Warner was a good rugby player but not a good kicker of the ball. He just wasn't a flyhalf. Spooner was a flyhalf by trade but he had fallen out of favour with Matt, and I had no problem with that selection.

The sight of Drico going off early with hamstring trouble reinforced for Matt that he had made the right call on the captaincy. We didn't fall out about it. But I was utterly depressed and maddened by what had happened. Munster lost their semi-final the previous day in Toulouse. That scrapped ERC's dream of an all-Irish final in Dublin. I wasn't remotely interested in Munster – I just wanted Leinster there. We took our eyes off the prize and ended up with nothing.

There was a reception of some sort around the corner in the Berkeley Court. The mood was grim, but Paul Wallace chose that moment to analyse for Matt and myself where it all went wrong.

"You know what happened there?" he asked. I wasn't sure what was coming or if I wanted to hear it.

"No hunger! Munster would never have lost that game."

I wanted to throttle him. Paul was still on contract but there was no way he could play again because of injury – and this was his parting shot when we're already on our knees? Cheers pal.

That line went straight to the dark side of my brain. It was still playing over and over when we moved on from the Berkeley Court to Café en Seine. A public bar on the night of a crushing defeat is not the place for a match review, but that wasn't stopping me. Years later Liam Toland reckoned the defeat triggered "a deep loss" in me, that it cut me to the core. He was right. But what really angered me was that an Ulsterman should be feeling the loss more than some of the Leinster men, and that it had all been so avoidable. Alcohol in a situation like that is just fuel on the fire. I started having a go at Liam, and the next thing Andy Dunne intervened.

Andy was a talented wee outhalf who had every reason to be pissed off having missed most of the season through injury. He stuck up for Liam, telling me I was out of line. He was perfectly entitled to do that. I shoved him physically out of the way to focus on Liam. Andy didn't exactly go flying across the bar, like a scene from a Wild West saloon, but it was enough for everyone to notice. The place was packed. Christ, what have I done now?

My night ended soon after that. A couple of days later I was sitting in the office of Mick Dawson, the Leinster CEO, explaining myself. There had already been a squad meeting where Denis Hickie called me out for my behaviour on the night of the game. He was dead on. I had the apology ready.

The meeting with Mick wasn't as bad as it could have been. He's a very easy-going man and wasn't looking for my head on a plate, but he needed to know there wouldn't be a repeat of a Leinster coach manhandling a player in public. It wasn't a lot to ask. And it did nothing for my career prospects. Not long after that Matt got the approach to take over in Scotland. My immediate future was uncertain.

13

The Last Chance

THE DUST HADN'T SETTLED ON THE PERPIGNAN disaster when Matt Williams told us he was in line for the Scotland job. We were there, tying up loose ends on the season, when he came out with it. Jim Telfer, Scotland's Director of Rugby, had rung him. There would be an interview, with Telfer and the SRU boss Bill Watson, but they were keen. So was Matt. So were we!

First things first: he needed to prepare for the interview in Edinburgh. This is where Steve Aboud and myself came in. Steve loves this stuff: assessing who the interviewers are, their personality type, what they'll want to hear and what not to hear. Steve gave him a plan to follow. Matt was very good at that. He'd read the script and practise it and deliver it like it was a performance.

His wife Chrisanne liked to tell the story that the greatest mistake her mother-in-law ever made was to tell her wee boy he looked like Robert Redford. There was no way back from that one. I don't know if the Hollywood star knew anything about rugby but Matt certainly knew a thing or two about performing in front of the camera. When we were going well he'd like to get his hair trimmed on a Friday to look his best for the post-match media gig. I used to slag him that if he was chocolate he'd eat himself. He'd wink at me and laugh: "Mate, you're just jealous."

So Steve and I spent a fair bit of time prepping Matt, in the old Portakabin that passed for the Leinster coaches' office in Anglesea Road. We knocked good entertainment out of it. 'Alignment' was a key word. Scotland had three sides then below the national set up: Edinburgh, Glasgow and Borders. Getting the three of them on the same page would be critical to the success of Scotland. Steve would howl at Matt if he started losing the run of himself with ad libbing. He'd reiterate they didn't need the same gameplans across the three teams – just the same approach to skill development and strength & conditioning. It was vital.

"Stick to the script for Christ's sake!"

By the time Matt went over for the interview he was word perfect. The other thing we told him was to make room for us as well. Any new coach would have to make changes, and it's far better doing that if you have a couple of your own crew on board. Off went Matt, aced the interview, and came back beaming. The job offer followed soon after. He said the SRU hadn't a pot to piss in and weren't interested in him bringing anyone over, aside from our analyst Brett Igoe, who Matt wanted to bring with him. So Matt would inherit Todd Blackadder, who already was assistant coach to Ian McGeechan. The plan was for McGeechan to move upstairs as Director of Rugby after the 2003 Rugby World Cup in Australia, and Matt to take his place, with Blackadder staying where he was. I can't remember if I actually used the words – "Matt, mate, you're doomed" – but that's what I felt.

Matt's successor in Leinster was presented with the same sort of scenario at his interview. Whoever got the job would be inheriting me and Roly Meates, and Steve wanted to see who got the job before committing. I interviewed for the position and deliberately brought the conversation around to the Café en Seine incident to try and put it in perspective. It was pushed aside though. Let's move on. I made a case for Roly, Steve and myself to continue with me as head coach. Defence had been Matt's strongest suit so if we needed help there we could hire it. I didn't get the gig. They wanted a Southern Hemisphere voice for the top job. But they asked me to continue working with the forwards, and I accepted the offer.

That was the trend in Ireland at the time. When the AIL came in first clubs were falling over themselves getting overseas coaches. The provinces followed suit in the professional game. In March of that year I had missed out on replacing Alan Solomons in Ulster – that went to Mark McCall – so I sucked it up and accepted the Leinster offer. I waited to see who would be the new boss.

Gary Ella, come on down! He's the youngest brother in one of the most famous footballing families in world rugby. Gary's first experience of Ireland was with the Australian Schools side who toured here in 1977/78. His brothers Mark and Glen were also on that squad, and Gary was voted player of the tour. I remember it well because of the quality of their rugby. They were miles ahead of everyone then, and brilliant to watch. I don't think Gary's coaching career was in the same ballpark as his playing one. He inherited a wounded Leinster squad with a pretty obvious division in it. There were the stars who were never going to get dropped, and the bag holders who got to stand there and admire them. I think Matt would admit he was very close to the first group.

The second category called themselves the Women's Auxiliary Balloon Corps, inspired by the Blackadder television series. Every squad has its untouchables and its assistants to the untouchables, and it requires careful management to keep folks happy.

I did my level best to treat everyone the same but it was an issue in Leinster. We should have managed it better, but initially the problem was we didn't have enough games to keep lads happy, to give them a chance to impress and progress. For example in 2002/03 we had literally four competitive fixtures after Christmas, all in Europe. If we hadn't qualified from our pool it would have been two!

They changed the structure of the Celtic League for 2003/04, so instead of two pools you had one big division playing home and away. Huge improvement.

At last there was scope to create genuine competition for places, but unfortunately we were already headed into a hole in the road.

The routine under Matt was for coaching staff to be at their desks at 7am. On Gary's first day on the job Brett Igoe and I were there at 6.55am. Half an hour later no sign of Gary. By 9am we were genuinely worried and rang team manager Ken Ging.

"Do you think he's lost?" Brett asked. "Should we go and pick him up?"

Ken said there was no cause for concern. Gary rocked up at 10am for a session that was scheduled for 10.30. That became the norm. I struggled to get my head around that. If you grow up on a farm you're accustomed to having a lump of work done by breakfast. Gary is a grand guy but he needed to grab the bull by the horns, take the opportunity offered by a season with maybe over 30 games in it, and drive us on. Early in the journey he asked Brett if we had a computer. Brett wasn't sure if he was taking the pish. Then Gary gave him a floppy disk that contained the New South Wales Waratahs playbook.

"Mate, can you go through that and everywhere you find a reference to New South Wales or the Waratahs can you change it to Leinster?"

Brett did that. Then he had to park himself by the photocopier and run off maybe 35 copies – each the size of a small telephone book – and distribute them to the squad. I watched this unfold and asked myself why Leinster had given the job to Gary Ella instead of me. Yes, I wasn't the finished article – I had issues that needed constant work – but I was passionate about the job and bringing something to it. I understood what was meant by 'The Leinster Way' and wanted to add to it. I didn't want to copy and paste the Waratah way on Leinster.

The season was a long, slow slide backwards. I followed the same routine as the previous season but with less enthusiasm. Had I been more invested in it I probably would have shouted sooner when it was clear Gary was drifting. The untouchable players didn't take to him and when that happens there needs to be a confrontation to deal with it. Gary wasn't cut out for that. And it wasn't my job to intervene. I was the assistant for a job I clearly was never going to get, so I focused on what was in my job spec.

The season is best remembered for solving the flyhalf issue, and then turning it into something worse. Before Matt left Nathan Spooner had been let go pretty late in the day, which Spooner was very unhappy about. The speed of it all was down to Felipe Contepomi agreeing to move from Bristol to Dublin. It was a massive signing.

Contepomi was a star. More than that he was a warrior, and a great guy to work with. There was some grumbling about the way Spooner had been treated but the Leinster supporters were delighted with landing Contepomi. The same Leinster supporters went ballistic when it emerged a few months later he hadn't been registered in time to play in the Heineken Cup. It was a huge story at the time. He had been signed in May but wouldn't be available until November, after the Rugby World Cup, and a week before the start of Europe.

Felipe had arrived in Dublin and was hot to trot – then the problem emerged. Leinster thought the IRFU were submitting the supporting release papers from Bristol and the English RFU; the IRFU thought Leinster were looking after it. Contepomi got caught in the middle. The only silver lining on the cloud was he'd be eligible for the knock-out stages, when teams were able to make changes to their registered squads. So we had to qualify from a pool containing Biarritz, Cardiff and Sale. Of course we didn't. It all came down to the last pool game, away to Biarritz on a bog of a pitch. Brian O'Driscoll was out injured. We looked like a team with no ideas. Even so we were within a score of getting through. When Keith Gleeson got our third try, with time running out, we could still qualify with two losing bonus points. I was screaming at Gary to get the info onto the pitch. Biarritz restarted and sure enough we kicked the ball away. In my head I was gone. Out the door.

*****

Things were so bad in Leinster I didn't even draw breath to think when Matt rang to tell me there was an opening with Scotland. He had come through his first Six Nations, in 2004, battered and bruised, and was preparing for the summer tour: Samoa followed by two Tests with the Wallabies. He didn't pretend it was an easy gig.

At first he was mostly observing and analysing as the Scots went through their schedule in the 2003 Rugby World Cup in Australia. Once that was over the SRU moved McGeechan upstairs to replace Telfer as Director of Rugby, with Matt succeeding him as coach. I think McGeechan struggled with that role and all the shite that went with it. He was a coach with a good feel for what players needed. But Matt found him unresponsive to his demands. So the notion of having Edinburgh, Glasgow and Borders aligned went out the window early, because it would have involved busting a few balls to make it happen. I got the impression McGeechan didn't have the appetite for that.

They were in desperate trouble for a flyhalf. Matt thought he was on a four-year gig to the Rugby World Cup in France and had the space and time to develop a new number 10, so he told national hero Gregor Townsend it might be a good idea to announce his retirement. Jeepers! There is no such thing as time and space in the Six Nations. Meantime the SRU committee were at war with the SRU board over all sorts, and there was Matt, sitting in the middle, on a short stick.

This was not what he had been used to in Leinster. Every door Matt knocked on in Dublin was opened quickly. There was a decent supply of home-grown talent. The results were good. They loved him and he loved them. None of that was available in Scotland. They were already at a low ebb when he arrived and, unlike the club game, with Test rugby you have to hit the ground running.

As a player I had lined out against Scotland five times between 1985 and 1990: two wins and three losses. In every one of those games I started out thinking we would win. Chris Gray, Derek White and John Beattie were my opposite numbers in those matches. I'd say they were every bit as confident as me. The widest margin across that sequence of games was four points. But the fixture had changed dramatically by the time I went over to their side of the water to coach.

Because of my involvement in setting up the IRFU Foundation I had a good grasp of the connection between activity beneath the water and what happens on the surface. So while the Ireland tour to Australia in 1994 looked like another failed mission I could see the value of the development work put into lads like Jeremy Davidson and Jonny Bell. They were still kids heading out in 1994, our first Academy lads thrown in the deep end. But they could compete, power-wise. That was a first for us.

Years earlier when the IRFU sent me to Australia on the fact-finding mission I felt I'd need an extra bag to take home all the info. Rugby men like Brian O'Shea, Bob Dwyer, Warren

Robilliard – whoever I met I was taking away stuff that showed how far behind we were in Ireland on every level. I remember one day sitting in a high-tech suite in the Australian Institute for Sport in Canberra, looking at a step-by-step breakdown of Michael Lynagh's kicking action. Lynagh was already a Rugby World Cup winner. Unlike us they were all the time trying to get better. They had detailed elite player profiles on all their talent, all aligned, and it didn't stop once they became Wallabies. When I went over to Edinburgh in 2004 those feelings of playing catch-up resurfaced. Scotland were like Ireland used to be – only worse.

My first involvement was on that summer tour in '04. I was appointed as forwards coach just as they left, so I hooked up with them over there. It was a challenging schedule that got off with a win over Samoa. Then came the two Tests in Australia. From the start the atmosphere was plain awkward. Todd Blackadder was being kept on as a technical consultant. He had been involved as a player with Edinburgh all along, so the Edinburgh contingent in the Scotland side weren't wild about me coming in to move their man aside. Todd was a cult figure with the club. He was to Edinburgh what Gary Teichmann, the Springbok captain, had been to Newport in Wales. I didn't feel Scott Murray for example, the experienced second row, had much interest in listening to what I had to say. To be honest I didn't have much interest in trying to mollycoddle a player who didn't want to be coached – at least not by me. And when it came down to it there wasn't that much time for actual coaching. It was mostly about organising for the next game.

Meantime the issue at 10 was never resolved. Chris Paterson was tried, and then Matt introduced Dan Parks from Australia, where he would hardly have been capped had he stayed. Chris had a sackful of caps as a wing or fullback before being given the flyhalf shirt by McGeechan at the 2003 Rugby World Cup. I don't think he was cut out for it, but Matt tried him as well. And Dan was never going to be the answer. That went down badly with the Scotland supporters who probably would have been happy with an import if he was top of the range. Dan was not in that category.

The autumn 2004 schedule was brutal: two Tests against Australia, with Japan thrown in the middle, and South Africa to finish. If we had beaten Japan with a million points instead of the hundred we ran up it wouldn't have made any difference. We were competitive in both games against the Wallabies without looking like winners. South Africa pasted us in Murrayfield to finish. There was a squad meeting after that game where Matt threw every toy he could find out of the pram. It was emotional but it was pointless.

It wasn't a great Christmas for anyone involved. Despite the crap results I felt the team were playing better by the end of the year. Matt had support from the chairman there, David Mackay, but then he got chucked out in a heave. Mackay rang Matt over that Christmas to give him the bad news, and shared with him the number of a good employment lawyer because he reckoned Matt would need one.

France were first up in Paris in the 2005 Six Nations. I remember thinking at the lineout walk-through on the morning of the game that the preparation had gone well – despite the results the mood was good. In a dogfight of a match we defended really well and were leading when Ally Hogg was called back for a foot in touch that could have sealed the game for us. Our pack that day had Gordon Bulloch as hooker and captain and a back row of Hogg, Jason White and Jonny Petrie. They were all good men to work with. Coincidentally Jonny ended up as CEO of Ulster after his playing days. Having gone so close that day I think the defeat killed whatever wind was left in their sails. It was like: if we're not going to win today, will it ever happen?

As an exercise in frustration the whole experience was right up there. Looking back my main gripe is that Matt didn't play hardball with the SRU from the start: get his own coaches in with him and get a guarantee the three club sides would all be on the same plan.

Even then, how well would we have done? I'd say three years of pain, at the end of which we'd have been sacked but the groundwork would have been laid for the next men in. Matt was hammered in the press for talking down the team all the time, but it's hard to be optimistic if you're spending so much time on skills work in the week of a Test match when it should be done by the clubs.

I don't think there was much appreciation in the Scottish press that two tiers had emerged in Europe, and they were in the second one, along with Italy. Maybe there was and they just didn't like it. The first tier was based on a generation of good players being developed in each of the top four nations.

In 2002 France had won a Grand Slam with Bernard Laporte bringing discipline to a talented group.

In 2003 England had won a Grand Slam and then a Rugby World Cup with a team who had been knocking on the door for years.

In 2004 France won another Grand Slam, and Ireland won

their first Triple Crown in 19 years. Ireland added another two in the three years that followed.

In 2005 Wales won their first Grand Slam since 1978.

It wasn't a good time to be off the pace. But Scotland were happier carving each other up in the boardroom and standing still on the field because they hadn't done the work on development.

Matt Williams got a lot wrong, and three wins – Samoa, Japan and Italy – from 17 Tests was a killer. He talked the talk at the start and then had to backtrack when he realised the scale of the climb that was ahead of him. I made mistakes too. Maybe I should have tried a different approach to win lads over when they didn't like me replacing Todd Blackadder. Instead I didn't hold back. But the sad state of Scottish rugby was something they managed all on their own. Matt rang me in April to tell me the inevitable.

"Mate I've just got the chop," he said. "They'll be coming for you next so brace yourself."

Sure enough we were barely out the door when Frank Hadden was appointed, and in his first Six Nations they beat France and England. Jeepers, you couldn't make it up. But for the two seasons after that they were back butting heads with Italy to stay off the bottom of the Six Nations. I don't know if the press piled on Frank the way they piled on Matt, because it's always easier to beat up a foreigner. By then I had lost interest. I was back home and had other stuff to sort out.

Years later, for some reason, Jim Telfer stuck the boot into me with a quote that was defamatory, and ran in a Belfast paper. I don't ever remember talking to Jim Telfer. I'll hardly be starting now.

14

The Reckoning

MY ROUTE TO RAVENHILL FROM HOME WOULD finish off along Cregagh, swinging right into Onslow Parade, and then left at the end – close to the house I once shared with the lads, fresh out of Stranmillis. Then swing in the main gate of Ulster's home. By the time I went to work for the Academy in 2016, Ravenhill had become Kingspan, and the entrance moved around the corner, beside the Free Presbyterian Church on Mount Merrion Avenue. All changed.

It was odd making a fresh start in your 60s, but here I was, beginning again, this time as Elite Player Development Officer with the Ulster Academy. My job spec basically was to prepare Academy lads for the rigours of the pro game. Odder still when it's a place where you experienced so much joy and pain over the guts of 40 years. The great big hole on my CV is where the Ulster head coaching job is supposed to be. My three applications for the post went as follows.

THE RECKONING

The first was in 2001 to replace Harry Williams, European Cup-winning coach. They gave it to Alan Solomons, from South Africa. I always thought of Solomons as a kind of Red Adair of the rugby world. If there was an oil well on fire he'd be called to put a cap on it. Then, when things settled down, he'd move on to the next one. Ulster wasn't exactly ablaze at that point, whereas I reckoned I was well positioned. Not that well as it turned out.

The second application was in 2004, when I was with Leinster, and Solomons was moving on. Mark McCall was in the frame, along with Brian McLaughlin, who had coached in RBAI, Allen Clarke and myself. Mark played on the Ulster side headed for that European triumph with Harry Williams but had to pack it in half way through the campaign because of a neck injury. Straight away he started helping Harry out on the coaching front. When Solomons replaced Harry they decided to keep Mark on board. Now he was in for the top job. Ulster had actually offered it to Munster's Declan Kidney first, but he wasn't keen so it became a contest between us local lads. If I thought I was in a decent place the first time round then by 2004 I was even better qualified. I was actually tutoring two of the other candidates – Mark and Allen – on the IRFU Level 5 coaching course at the time!

The interviews were held in the old Berkeley Court Hotel, where the IRFU was a big client. They often used one of two suites there – Donnelly 1 and Donnelly 2 – near each other on the same floor. I was sitting downstairs in the foyer looking at my watch, thinking whoever was going to come down and fetch me was cutting it fine. When the appointed time for my slot came and went I got a bit panicky and headed upstairs. I couldn't remember which suite the interviews were being held in, so I kind of tip-toed, self-consciously, along the corridor, listening at the doors to see what was what.

One of the doors opened just as I was bending my ear to it, and a startled face stared back at me. To be honest I was as gobsmacked as he was. He stepped out into the corridor and launched into me.

"What do you think you're doing eavesdropping on us?"

I tried to explain myself but he was going from 0-60mph in about three seconds. His killer line has stayed with me forever.

"While I'm alive you'll never coach Ulster."

I then had to go in and do the interview a few minutes later, facing the panel. It didn't go well. I rang Steve Aboud the moment I came down into the foyer, giving him chapter and verse. I hadn't been confident going in, despite being miles ahead of Mark and Allen on experience, but even so I was shocked by the incident in the corridor. Years later I got the following feedback indirectly from Eddie Wigglesworth, who had been representing the IRFU on the interview panel that day.

"There was an underlying feeling that Willie's style of management was too personal, which in the amateur game – bingo – but the professional game was a different kettle of fish," Eddie said.

"From the IRFU perspective if a province was very strong about having somebody that's how it went. You couldn't do it any other way or you'd be divesting them of authority. You couldn't have the coach always running to Dublin. We had to ensure that the province was proper and above board the way they operated but at the end of the day it ultimately boils down to people making decisions."

The third time I applied was in 2007 when Mark had enough. I knew I hadn't much of a chance. They gave it to Matt Williams. It wasn't long before he gave me a shout to do a session with the forwards, which went very well. A few days later Matt was talking to Syd Millar.

"I hear you got Willie in," Syd said.

"Yeah, went really well – great coach."

"Yeah, great coach – such a shame you can never use him."

I had my faults, well documented, about being explosive and struggling with boundaries. But Ulster is a small rugby community, and if some folks take against you they can't see the qualities you'd bring. The rejection hurt. But mostly it angered me. Some of the men I faced on those interview panels didn't know the first thing about coaching in the professional game.

*****

When I arrived back from Scotland in 2005 I needed a job. Plain and simple. I went on the dole. For the first time in my life I was signing on. On the short drive to the social welfare office in Magherafelt I was playing stuff over in my head. Like, what would I say if I bumped into someone I knew? What if a former pupil of mine was behind the counter? I was spared that, but the whole process was demeaning. I had worked hard all my life. Now I had to ask for help in finding work.

"There aren't many teaching jobs at the minute," the lady I was dealing with told me. "Is there anything else you might be able to do?"

I stopped short of saying I could coach rugby. Even that fire wasn't burning very bright. Heather was struck by my lack of ambition. She was bracing herself for me taking off to Wales or France or wherever the next professional gig was coming up. Instead of worrying about me going away she was thinking about how to lift my spirits. And putting food on the table. The SRU hadn't covered themselves in glory on the exit arrangements from Scotland. While I was reflecting on that I got a call from my good friend Jimmy McCoy. He had successfully made it over the line into retirement from the RUC. He wanted to know if I needed a few bob to tide me over. That was Jimmy to a T.

The break, when it came, was like the bounce of a rugby ball: sometimes it just hops your way. I got a call from Mike Rodgers, head of PE in Sullivan Upper School, to say they had a hole that needed filling – urgently. Coincidentally a lad I had coached back in the day, Jonny Davis, was lined for a job there but then got an offer from Ulster for their S&C staff. It was one of those happy coincidences: I was delighted to get the opportunity and Mike was equally glad to have me.

What unfolded over the next 11 years in Holywood, Co Down, a beautiful part of the world, was a very happy period in my life. Sullivan is a fine school. It's a funny thing: I'd cut my teeth in Grosvenor in East Belfast in the late 1970s/early '80s, a tough spot on the map with a fair few edgy kids; and I would finish out my teaching days in a place voted in 2019 as the most desirable place to live in Northern Ireland. The relationships I made, with kids and fellow teachers in both schools, will stay with me forever.

You know you're getting old when one of your former teammate's kids ends up working alongside you in the staff room. Ian 'Bruno' Brown was our drop goal sniper extraordinaire with Jimmy D's Ulster. His daughter Lyn is every bit as sharp, and we had many a laugh together over the years in Sullivan.

Holywood is a fairly affluent part of the world, and the school reflected that. Rugby wasn't their only outlet but they took it seriously. So when it came time to tour it wouldn't be to the west coast of Ireland – more like the south west of Portugal. Browns Sports Resort in Vilamoura was a go-to spot. There were always opportunities for lads to let their hair down and have a few pints, and I was always up for letting them at it. There was one night where a couple of my colleagues were reading the riot act to them lads when they came in hammered from their wee excursion downtown. It was a full-on bollocking. As the lads were shuffling away, quiet as mice, I gave a few of them the nod and they came back to my chalet for a nightcap and a few stories. It was the best of craic and they turned up on time for training the next morning.

I didn't make many allowances on the field for the fact I was dealing with young men in their mid-late teens rather than adult professionals. If Sullivan wanted to compete with the big boys in Ulster schools rugby they needed to behave like big boys. Training was physical and intense, and sometimes boiled over. One day it developed into a full-on scrap between two lads and I could see the issue escalating into something that might end in the headmaster's office. A squad meeting had been arranged by one of my colleagues in the school hall, to sort the trouble out. I arrived in with two pairs of boxing gloves, set up a makeshift ring, and let the two lads sort it out. They shook hands when the contest was done and never looked back.

A bit of hardship was no harm. On another trip to Vilamoura we had a game in Seville, a couple of hours away. Well, more like the outskirts of Seville. Almost on the side of the motorway, in fact. The surface was rock hard. There were more dead birds on it than tufts of grass. There were a fair few anthills as well. Right away the lads started pissing and moaning, looking for a way out. I exploded. I stormed around the field picking up the birds with my bare hands, steam coming out my ears.

"I don't wanna hear another word about dead fucking birds!" I roared at them. "We're here to fucking play and that's what we're going to do!"

We played. We won. We sang all the way home. From my earliest days in rugby, music had a place near the centre. Everybody sang. In the changing room, on the bus, in the bar. Jimmy D was big on it with Dungannon, with Stran, with Ulster. I made it a fundamental with our Sullivan teams. You had to have a song, and everyone had to join in on the chorus. It is an amazingly powerful tool – the glue that binds teams together. The emotion it stirs up is unique.

My special memories with Sullivan include winning the Medallion Shield, for only the second time in the school's history, in 2011, and three years later taking most of that group to the final of the Schools Senior Cup, a first for the school. I was coaching with good guys in Laurence Kelly, David Armstrong, Johnny Quigley and Daniel Allen, and we were a happy wee group. We lost that senior final to Methody, but I'll never forget the reception afterwards at the Culloden Hotel – again, Sullivan didn't do things by halves. My party-piece was the folksong *Will Ye Go, Lassie, Go*. I thought the roof was going to lift when every one of the squad joined in, word perfect. There wasn't a dry eye in the house.

I knew nothing about Coolmine Rugby Club, in west

Dublin, when they contacted me in autumn 2009. They are an ambitious junior club who were keen to get into the All Ireland League, which is no mean feat. They had come off the back of two good seasons with Bernard Jackman coaching them, while he was still playing for Leinster. He would have been sharing a lot of the Leinster stuff with them. I would have taken them back to first principles if you like – so, less structure but a big emphasis on skills and continuity.

The best bit was they were so open to learning. I loved it. I had a great assistant in Donal Crotty, who was making the plays from flyhalf, and Ollie Prunty was our captain on the blind side of the scrum. That scrap for AIL entry was an eye opener for me. Across Leinster junior rugby in those days you had the likes of Enniscorthy, Seapoint, Boyne, Malahide, Dundalk – these were all men on a mission: to get a foot on the AIL ladder. The rugby was hot and heavy, and over time we developed a good mix between the collision stuff and keeping the ball alive.

There was a good buzz about Coolmine. A fair few of their supporters were my vintage so I was happy to chat with them in the bar about the Five Nations in the old days. Heather came down a few times and enjoyed the craic – they have a fine set up there. Thomas had just graduated from the Ulster Academy at the time and I mobilised him for one or two sessions as well.

The first time I brought Heather down to a Coolmine game I was still on crutches after a hip replacement. I was a bit too close to the action when our winger got wiped into touch in front of me. His momentum then wiped me as well, sending me arse over tip with the crutches flying. I was afraid the metalwork was going to pop out of my hip as I lay there, legs in the air with my glasses stretched across the top of my head. The sight of Heather laughing her backside off will stay with me forever.

We were competitive without quite getting over the line. We won Leinster League 1B in my first season and planned on repeating the trick in 1A, but missed out. So ideally I would have stayed with the club for a third season to finish the job. But Ibiza got in the way. We were in love with that place. At the end of the second season with Coolmine we had another family holiday booked there but it coincided with a cup match. For me, and, I think, the players, the league and promotion was the name of the game, but for some of the supporters a cup was a cup. So their attitude was to wade into it. I can understand they were upset I wasn't going to be around for it, and that changed the mood. The club decided to call it a day. A few lads were keen to try and rectify the situation but I'd been around long enough to know when the temperature has changed. I left with nothing but good memories and look forward to the day when Coolmine become an AIL club.

Our kids did a fair bit of growing up in Ibiza. They had an absolute ball there. The island either sucks you in or blows you out, and we were firmly in the first camp. We ended up buying a wee place in Es Canar, on the east side of the island. Hippy country. It played a role in Jonathan's development as a designer because there were so many creative folks there he was inspired by the place. Heather's Dad James was a big influence on him, and on one holiday I remember the two of them spending all their time checking out the markets, car boot sales and boutiques. Jonny developed a love of art and antiques there as well as fashion.

There could be a bit of an edge to Ibiza as well, but in all our years there our only bad experience was the night Thomas needed his head stitched after being hit by an ashtray flying across a bar. The nightclubs were very much part of the experience. One summer we had Labhaoise Glancy with us, daughter of Marie and Ben. Labhaoise and our Chloe were determined to get to Manumission, probably one of the most famous nightclubs in the world. Fair enough we thought, if I drop them and pick them up. I arrived to collect the girls at the appointed time of 5am. They were sitting on the wall outside.

"We've had enough. Let's go home!"

Within a year or two they'd be up for Manumission followed by Space – the all-day club – if they could have gotten away with it. You have to reel yourself in every so often when you're in Ibiza. It's easy to get carried away.

We still get back there whenever we can. Cycling on its quiet country roads and swimming in the Mediterranean would take up a lot of our time. But even on that island you'd catch up with rugby. Larry, one of the lads who works for the bike company we go to, plays for the local team, Ibiza Club de Rugby. When we got chatting I ended up doing a few sessions for them. He's a Romanian lad who made a new life for himself there, married a local girl and became part of the community. They're a great crew.

*****

I consider myself blessed for a few reasons. Most of them come back to family, one way or the other. A day doesn't pass now but I thank God for having my wife and kids close at hand – if not always in person then on the end of a phoneline or a Skype call. It could have been so different.

On 15 August 1998 I was settling in to my second stint as Director of Rugby in Dungannon. The early season was unfolding with our second friendly match, at home against Omagh Accies. We were at my parents in the 'Cross that morning, and as I left to go to the game Heather was rounding up the kids to go into town to buy new school shoes. Town was Omagh, where Dad would have gone to the market every week of his working life, where I had gone to secondary school in the Academy, where I had shopped and socialised and played rugby over the years because it was a 20 minute spin from home.

I had left for Stevenson Park by the time Heather's plan changed. Jonny and Thomas were having a row over something or other so Heather said fine, stay home and squabble among yourselves. She went away out the door, leaving Chloe and the boys with their Pop and Granny. Heather loved every moment driving the brand new Renault Espace we had just bought. It was a machine. It glided along.

She parked in the carpark behind the old Royal Arms Hotel. She popped into a few shops up and down Market Street, passing the parked car where a 500lb bomb filled the boot. After a fair bit of browsing she bought a jacket for herself in a ladies clothes shop. When she came out to head back up towards the carpark she ran into police pointing everyone back down the street, away from the Court House. Heather presumed it was another hoax, so she ducked into Wellworths and out a side door to get back to the carpark. When she came out onto that street it had already been closed by RUC men who were shouting at her to go back the way she came. She ran on into the carpark, and into the sanctuary of the 'crossover MPV' Espace. As she was looking in the rear-view mirror, putting on her lipstick, she felt and heard a dull thud. She drove out, turned right, and away from the town centre, out the Ballygawley Road and back to the 'Cross. Oblivious.

Twenty nine people lost their lives in our town that day. Roughly another three hundred were injured. If Heather had the kids with her the chances are she'd have done as instructed by the police, and headed back towards the point where the bomb was about to go off. All four of them. Of the two of us, Heather is the one who follows orders and abides by the rules.

I remember a man I knew, who worked in the County Hospital, telling me the blood was literally running down the stairwells as the victims were brought in after the bomb. It was absolute carnage.

For a period after that I organised a charity match in Dungannon against All Star teams with the proceeds going to the victims of that day. The Ulster Branch weren't happy with me bypassing the red tape around organising any game that wasn't on the official calendar. I just drove on.

*****

There was one night in summer 2017 when we were at home relaxing, having a drink. Heather had dozed off on the couch. I went upstairs for something and on my way back down I tripped. It was a hardwood stairs with no covering. By the time I got to the bottom I'd opened my head up and was pumping blood. I was also well pished.

Chino, our cocker spaniel, had the nous to rouse Heather

who came out to a grisly scene. She called an ambulance and away I went to Magherafelt Hospital for a good number of stitches in my scalp. That was the last straw because I'd already been diagnosed with a heart condition called AF – Atrial Fibrillation. It can lead to blood clots, stroke or heart failure. I needed a lifestyle change. In fact I needed a profound change. I needed to confront an issue I'd been denying for years.

I needed to look at my drinking.

It's never a great feeling when a colleague confides you smell like a brewery, but that's what Lyn Harte, Bruno's daughter, did one morning at school. Mouthwash and Fishermen's Friends had been companions of mine for a long time. But that was just part of my routine. The jar was just part of my routine too. It wasn't a problem. Things were good at home, I was doing a good job in Sullivan, and then I was down in Dublin coaching Coolmine. It was mad busy but I was keeping the balls in the air. I was on top of things, everything was fine.

The chickens came home to roost after that fall at home. It was too serious to ignore any longer. A lot of people who cared for me had been worried for a long time. I had to face a few facts.

It was a godsend to have Ben Glancy as my doctor. Himself and Marie were a great help when it came to tying the two issues together: I could use the cover of the heart condition to explain to folks why I wasn't drinking anymore. As ever with me, it wasn't straightforward. You don't just turn off a tap that's been running for maybe 45 years and not feel some pain.

I had always been trying to get a buzz. It was a chase. And if I could get away with it the next morning I'd pick it up again. It took poking and prodding from Thomas and Chloe to actually get professional help. One day I was driving Thomas and his wife Pam to the airport and Heather's dad was in the car with us. Thomas was very quiet, tapping away on his phone, writing me this letter:

Dad,

I've spoken to you directly before and it wasn't easy and now to speak to you directly again it's even harder as you haven't taken on board anything I've said. I want this to be you someday driving me and my kids with you. However you'll not make it if you carry on with the way you treat your body. Your heart is a warning sign. Use this warning sign to avoid the emergency. Mum needs you healthy and wants her soulmate with her for life. Chloe, Jonathan and I want to have happy memories with you for decades to come, not the next couple of years. You have the power to ensure you don't alienate yourself, that you look after yourself, that you look after Mum and us all when we need you most.

You brought me up as an honest, committed, hard-working man. I will not stop until you change. I know you can. Over to you now dad. I want you to come back to me and let me know how we can get over this, and how we will be driving with our kids/grandkids in the back and they will also look up to their amazing grandad!

Do not sweep this under the carpet. You taught me to always face up to my problems and fears. I'm sending this with my heart full of love. Please read it and action something different tomorrow – as you know the butterfly effect too well. Call me whenever, wherever. I'm here for you.

We will win.

Thomas.

He did the groundwork for me to sign up to Addiction NI, near Queen's, for counselling. I'll always remember the first day I went in. I was avoiding the issue or dithering or whatever and the counsellor said to me: "Either you want to be here or you don't want to be here. Your choice."

Over time he explained that the buzz I'd been chasing as a teenager when I started drinking turned into an escape hatch to get away from the guilt of taking Glen McLernon's life. Drink was in my blood, but the trauma of that incident changed the picture. There was a popular t-shirt back in the day with the words: 'I don't have a drink problem. I drink, I fall down, no problem!'

I could identify with the dark side of that. When I drank I drank, and it might take passing out for me to stop. There was no element of control in that. It was pain relief. Then it would get to a point where I couldn't feel anything. Eventually I appreciated the unavoidable: when it's hurting the ones you love it has to stop. The silver lining on the cloud was discovering I didn't have to drink gallons to relax. I didn't have to drink to engage with people.

I discovered the sober version of myself was actually better craic. I wasn't slurring my words after a rake of pints. I wasn't slobbering or dominating the conversation or going off on tangents. In the moments when the urge would hit me to have a drink my immediate reaction was to look at what I had to lose.

Between using AF as an excuse, or that I was driving, those explanations took a lot of the pressure coming on from other people to join the round. The only battle then was with myself and my own impulses. That simplified so much for me, and it gave me confidence. So when I decided to stop drinking I stopped drinking.

That hasn't changed.

*****

I'm fit enough at 66 years of age to be coaching still. When Covid grabbed us all by the scruff of the neck I was on the field five afternoons a week in The Rainey, and getting full value from it. My return to Ulster and the Academy in 2016 set me up for a rewarding four years where I tried to make a difference without upsetting the apple cart. A bit like the job in Sullivan Upper, a vacancy came up late in the day and the Academy manager, Kieran Campbell, asked would I be interested. It was appealing because it was going back to something I was still passionate about – coaching young men to be better players and better people. There was also a touch of back to the future about it. Niall Malone, Bryn Cunningham, Jonny Davis, Dan McFarland, Michael Black, James Topping, Bryan Young, Nigel Brady, and Neil Doak – all of them were involved in one way or another on the Ulster management/coaching staff while I was there, and all of them had been either on teams I coached or groups I tutored on IRFU courses. I felt like an auld fella. But an auld fella who had been exposed to sporting life on the other side of the hedge.

That's why I made sure Thomas played GAA in The Loup as well as rugby in The Rainey. Through Ben Glancy when he was team doctor with the Derry footballers I got some insight into their world. Mickey Harte had already opened the door for me in Tyrone. Years after the pair of us were playing the odd game for Omagh Accies as schoolboys we shared a lot of information around high performance. His achievements with Tyrone were just massive and I loved dipping my toe in that water. I did stuff too for Paddy Tally when he was taking St Mary's, Belfast – or Mary I as everyone knows them – to a Sigerson Cup title, and Kieran McGeeney in his days managing Kildare. Those boys were always up for a different take on team-building and motivation. I've always been intrigued by the potential around our sense of place. The GAA never missed a trick on that.

For my money there is still a shortage on that front in Ulster Rugby, where there was a crazy amount of traffic though the head coach's office in my time there. There were conditions attached to me getting the job in 2016. The first was that I was not to try and take over! I had a script to follow. For example I would be a fan of the General Movement style of rugby, as shaped by Steve Aboud back in his IRFU days. GM was the staple on the IRFU coaching courses we ran back in the day. Basically it demanded players to assess situations as they unfolded on the field and then make the best decision, regardless of the number on their back. Over time there was a move away from that, and towards rigid team shapes where everyone knew their position on the field in advance and what their supposed roles were. I was all for the old method, and still am. People also call it 'heads-up rugby'. In fairness you won't see a lot if your head is down.

GM wasn't on the menu at Ulster when I came back so I stuck to what never goes out of fashion: good technique in contact and keeping the ball alive. With everyone gone crazy about defence it struck me as common sense not to let the opposing defensive line get set. So keep changing the point of attack. Simple, but it takes a lot of work.

I topped that up with the human touch. In all the reams of stuff written on nutrition and S&C and attack shapes it's easy to forget you're dealing with people. We all have problems. We all have stuff to deal with when we close the hall door of an evening. I invested a fair bit of time with the Ulster Academy trying to get to know lads as human beings, and offering support where I could.

I've been in a few scrapes in my time. I've had my share of stressful situations. I've also spent a good deal of it having the best craic imaginable. At various points along my journey with Ulster I was able to share bits and pieces with young guys that, I hope, helped.

Nick Timoney for example came to Ulster from Leinster where he had been let go from their Academy. A schools star with Blackrock, that was very hard for him to deal with. I spent some time with Nick, emphasising there were lots of routes we can take to get to the right destination. Life is not a one-size-fits-all. He has incredible athletic ability, and I was delighted to see him capped for Ireland in the summer series in 2021.

Every day I went to work in Ravenhill I passed the Nevin Spence Centre.

I'd say there wasn't a man, woman or child with an interest in Ulster rugby who wasn't shaken to the core by Nevin's death in 2012. And if you grew up on a farm then you'd be familiar with the dangers of working near slurry pits. The accident took the life of his dad Noel and brother Graham as well. Nevin really was an inspirational young man: a high achiever and a terrific rugby player, but very humble with it. Thomas was good pals with himself and Willie Faloon – another solid Ballynahinch man – and they were floored by the news. I'd always gravitate towards lads from a farming background who were trying to make the grade in the pro game. The work ethic is never a problem there and in Nevin's case he had the talent on top. I'd loved to have known him better.

In February 2021 we were all badly shaken by another sudden death. Hearing of Gary Halpin's heart attack stopped me in my tracks. He was one of the most likeable and colourful lads I ever came across in rugby football. I could well understand why he became a teacher. Everyone who came across his path would consider themselves fortunate. Every time I think of London Irish I think of Gary Halpin.

It was energising working with so much talent in Ulster. Robert Baloucoune was hard to miss. I christened him The Cat: he was so laid back he could curl up and have a snooze whenever it suited him. But Jeepers, when he woke up! Already an Ireland player, I think Robert will be a candidate for the Lions tour to Australia in 2025. We had lads from vastly different rugby backgrounds. James Hume came through the front door of Ulster schools with RBAI, and is a fine prospect. Tom O'Toole came to us via Australia and brought lots of potential with him.

Over my desk in the Ulster office I had a chart with four categories: at the top was Warrior, at the bottom was W***er, in the middle were Waverers and Winners. I enjoyed people asking me what box they ticked. I especially enjoyed that the smallest man in the squad, Michael Lowry, was unquestionably at the top of the tree. It's not often you come across someone who can combine modesty with talent and assertiveness, but Michael is that man.

THE RECKONING

When I retired, in June 2020, the staff and players went out of their way to mark the occasion. Stewart Moore, our young centre from Ballymoney, wrote me a lovely letter. It reminded me of my own journey: *'I'm only a prancey back – not hard enough to be in the forwards if you like, but it's an honour not only to have been coached by yourself but been a friend. One of my earliest memories of rugby was Dad showing me you leading the Irish team in front of the Haka, closely followed by the story of you getting up to mischief in Argentina which I captured when I was there last summer (Argie flag emoji and smiling face). Happy retirement. I'll see you soon (maybe even in Ibiza) and have the very happiest of quarantined 65th birthdays. Legend.'*

I wouldn't be putting Stewart in any 'prancey' category. Neither would any of the Australian lads on the wrong end of the stunning try he scored against them for Ireland Under 20s in the Rugby World Cup in 2019. Coincidentally it was in Argentina. I was on my feet in our living room, roaring and punching the air when he beat the last defender to score. That's what it's about. That's what rugby gives you.

*****

On any given Sunday now we go to church in Magherafelt. Over the years I've crossed a few lines. One of them was from the Presbyterian Church to the Church of Ireland. When we'd come out of the Ps of a Sunday I'd look at Heather and wonder why we were tuning into a message that just wasn't us. So we moved to C of I and found kindred spirits in Terry Scott and his wife Alyson. Terry is the Archdeacon of Armagh. Not only have they become great friends but Terry's Sunday sermon on life, and how to negotiate it, has given me fuel for driving players on the rugby field. Discovering your talent and figuring out how best to use it. It's all connected.

I'm invested in the Sunday service now. So I've joined Heather in the choir. I get to wear black robes that make me look like a priest. Every time I lower them over my head I think of the guys who'd be falling about the place laughing at the sight of Fr Willie.

I wore them recently for the wedding of Ben and Marie's daughter Labhaoise. She married a man who previously had been divorced, which ruled them out of a Catholic Church wedding. So after the legal ceremony in the registry office there was a wedding at the Glancys' house where they asked me to be the celebrant. I included the line Labhaoise liked, by John Muir, which we had come across in Jo Burns' anthology, *Circling For Gods*: *'I'd rather be in the mountains thinking of God, than in church thinking about the mountains.'*

For effect I arrived in my robes, which went down beautifully. Then I whipped them off to reveal a tuxedo for the ceremony itself, which I was so honoured to do. It was the start of a great day's craic.

"What's yon Proddy bastard doing in them robes!!"

I still wouldn't class myself as religious but I definitely get something from my involvement in the church. It's such a different experience to when I was a kid in the 'Cross, in between older sister Heather and younger brother Ollie as we trooped in with our parents on a Sunday morning. Jeepers when I think how things have unfolded since then.

Have you ever imagined, as an adult, going back and talking to your childhood self? In my case to reassure the gangly, wild young fella that things would work out OK in the end. But to fasten your seat belt because there was a bumpy ride head.

Dear Willie,
You will struggle in school but come through the far side. You will find a pastime that allows you to express yourself like no other. It will bring you pain and joy, perhaps in equal measure. You will be locked up in a country where human rights count for nothing. You will be responsible for others being locked up with you. Your sanity will be saved by the love and support of a woman who will become your life partner. You will feature in headlines all over the sporting world – sometimes for the right reason, sometimes for the wrong. You will achieve your boyhood dream of representing your country. You will live through an era where many people you know – some close friends, some acquaintances – die violently. You will break out from the religious straitjacket of your upbringing. You will be blessed with three children who will still be talking to you in later life. You will baptise them in the Protestant faith, but will raise them to have as many Catholic friends as Protestant. Or friends with no religion at all. You will lead one of your sons to GAA water and tell him to drink. Some years later he will thank you for the experience. You will consult widely in the same GAA and make many friends there. You will teach for a living, and coach rugby, and sell kitchens. You will fall down drunk and get back up again. You will repeat this many times because you have an all or nothing personality.

You will cause great pain to people you know and people you don't know. You will be a leader of men on the rugby field and a friend to those you coach. You will inspire people and earn their lifelong friendship and respect. You will struggle with boundaries, unable sometimes to keep your distance. You will be asked many times why you don't play the other game – the one where you keep your mouth shut, or open it only to say the right thing, the thing that will get you jobs you want if you play ball. You will struggle to answer that question. Eventually you will say because that's just you. That's who you are. You won't insult their intelligence by saying you have no regrets. You'll have lots of them. But you will also have so much to be grateful for. You will collect a bus pass and be healthy enough to use it. You won't let a day go by without telling your family you love them. You will have a fire inside you to challenge and to explore. That fire will never go out.

Best wishes, Willie, 2021

Index

INDEX

INDEX